A CULTURAL HISTORY OF PEACE

VOLUME 4

A Cultural History of Peace
General Editor: Ronald Edsforth

Volume 1
A Cultural History of Peace in Antiquity
Edited by Sheila L. Ager

Volume 2
A Cultural History of Peace in the Medieval Age
Edited by Walter Simons

Volume 3
A Cultural History of Peace in the Renaissance
Edited by Isabella Lazzarini

Volume 4
A Cultural History of Peace in the Age of Enlightenment
Edited by Stella Ghervas and David Armitage

Volume 5
A Cultural History of Peace in the Age of Empire
Edited by Ingrid Sharp

Volume 6
A Cultural History of Peace in the Modern Age
Edited by Ronald Edsforth

A CULTURAL HISTORY OF PEACE

IN THE AGE OF ENLIGHTENMENT

Edited by Stella Ghervas and David Armitage

BLOOMSBURY ACADEMIC
LONDON • NEW YORK • OXFORD • NEW DELHI • SYDNEY

BLOOMSBURY ACADEMIC
Bloomsbury Publishing Plc
50 Bedford Square, London, WC1B 3DP, UK
1385 Broadway, New York, NY 10018, USA
29 Earlsfort Terrace, Dublin 2, Ireland

BLOOMSBURY, BLOOMSBURY ACADEMIC and the Diana logo are trademarks of
Bloomsbury Publishing Plc

First published in Great Britain 2020
This edition published in Great Britain, 2024

Copyright © Bloomsbury Publishing, 2020

Stella Ghervas and David Armitage have asserted their right under the Copyright,
Designs and Patents Act, 1988, to be identified as Editors of this work.

Cover image © Sarah Campbell Blaffer Foundation, Houston

All rights reserved. No part of this publication may be reproduced or transmitted
in any form or by any means, electronic or mechanical, including photocopying,
recording, or any information storage or retrieval system, without prior permission
in writing from the publishers.

Bloomsbury Publishing Plc does not have any control over, or responsibility for, any
third-party websites referred to or in this book. All internet addresses given in this
book were correct at the time of going to press. The author and publisher regret
any inconvenience caused if addresses have changed or sites have ceased to exist,
but can accept no responsibility for any such changes.

A catalogue record for this book is available from the British Library.

A catalog record for this book is available from the Library of Congress.

ISBN: HB: 978-1-4742-3857-1
      PB: 978-1-3503-8589-4
      Set: 978-1-3503-8603-7

Series: The Cultural Histories Series

Typeset by RefineCatch Limited, Bungay, Suffolk
Printed and bound in Great Britain

To find out more about our authors and books visit www.bloomsbury.com
and sign up for our newsletters.

CONTENTS

LIST OF ILLUSTRATIONS		vi
GENERAL EDITOR'S PREFACE		viii
	Introduction: From Westphalia to Enlightened Peace, 1648–1815 *Stella Ghervas and David Armitage*	1
1	Definitions of Peace *Anthony Pagden*	19
2	Human Nature, Peace, and War *Theodore Christov*	35
3	Peace, War, and Gender *Sylvana Tomaselli*	53
4	Peace, Pacifism, and Religion *Murad Idris*	71
5	Representations of Peace *Jennifer Milam*	87
6	Peace Movements *Stephen Conway*	105
7	Peace, Security, and Deterrence *Doohwan Ahn and Richard Whatmore*	117
8	Peace as Integration *Martti Koskenniemi*	133
NOTES		149
BIBLIOGRAPHY		155
CONTRIBUTORS		175
INDEX		177

ILLUSTRATIONS

INTRODUCTION

0.1	Immanuel Kant (1724–1804).	3
0.2	Theodor van Thulden, *Allegory of Peace and Justice after the Thirty Years' War*.	4
0.3	After Gerard ter Borch, *The Ratification of the Peace of Münster* (1648).	6
0.4	Hugo Grotius (1583–1645), Dutch Jurist and Politician.	9
0.5	Delff, *The Signing of the Treaty of Utrecht on 11th April 1713*.	13
0.6	Jean-Jacques Rousseau (1712–1778).	15
0.7	The Congress of Vienna (1815).	17

CHAPTER 1

1.1	Henry Sumner Maine (1822–1888).	19
1.2	Eirene, Goddess of Peace.	20
1.3	Christian Wolff (1679–1754).	24
1.4	Benjamin Constant (1767–1830).	27

CHAPTER 2

2.1	Frontispiece of Thomas Hobbes' *De Cive* (Paris, 1642).	40

CHAPTER 3

3.1	Pierre Mignard, *Alexander the Great and Thalestris, Queen of the Amazons*.	55
3.2	Margaret Cavendish, Duchess of Newcastle (1624–1674).	58
3.3	John Opie, *Mary Wollstonecraft*.	62

CHAPTER 4

4.1	Thomas Hobbes, 1676.	73
4.2	Jonathan Swift, *The Tale of a Tub* (1721).	75
4.3	George Fox preaching to a crowd in Maryland (1671).	77
4.4	Benjamin West, *William Penn's Treaty with the Indians* (1771–72).	79

4.5	Immanuel Kant (1724–1804).	80
4.6	Meeting of the Society of Friends (the Quakers).	83

CHAPTER 5

5.1	Pompeo Batoni, *Peace and War* (1776).	87
5.2	Elisabeth Louise Vigée Le Brun, *Peace Bringing Back Abundance* (1780).	88
5.3	Gerard ter Borch, *The Ratification of the Treaty of Münster* (1648).	90
5.4	Peter Paul Rubens, *Minerva Protects Pax from Mars* (c. 1629–30).	90
5.5	The Salon of Peace, Versailles.	94
5.6	Charles Le Brun, *The King Governs by Himself, 1661* (1680s).	95
5.7	Stefano Torelli, *Catherine the Great in the Guise of Minerva, Patroness of Art* (1770).	96
5.8	Stefano Torelli, *Allegory on the Victory of Catherine the Great over Turks and Tatars* (1772).	97
5.9	Matvey Fedorovich Kazakov, *Public Celebration that was Held on the Khodynka Field on 19 July 1775* (1775).	98
5.10	Anton von Maron, *Portrait of Empress Maria Theresa as a Widow* (1773).	100
5.11	Benjamin West, *The Treaty of William Penn with the Indians* (1771–72).	102
5.12	Jacques-Louis David, *Intervention of the Sabine Women* (1799).	103
5.13	Antoine Jean Gros, *Napoleon on the Battlefield of Eylau* (1807).	104

GENERAL EDITOR'S PREFACE

RONALD EDSFORTH

When people learn that I study and teach peace history, they often look puzzled and ask me, "Does peace have a history?" *A Cultural History of Peace* is an emphatically positive response to that question. Yes, peace has a history. The original scholarly essays collected in these six volumes clearly show that peace always has been an important human concern. More precisely, these essays demonstrate that what we recognize today as peace thinking and peace imagining, peace seeking and peace making, peace keeping and peace building have long recorded histories that stretch from antiquity to the twenty-first century. All of us who have contributed to *A Cultural History of Peace* believe that present and future generations should have the opportunity to recognize and understand the importance of this peace history.

Very few universities and colleges had faculty who taught and researched peace history before the end of the Cold War. Even today, most professors who do peace history moved into it from other specializations in History or other academic disciplines. Most contributors to *A Cultural History of Peace* are professional historians, but Anthropology, Sociology, Political Science, Journalism, Art History, Religion, and Classical Studies are also represented. These fifty-six contributors work on four continents in thirteen different countries. Their participation in this project tells us that peace history has earned a global recognition in academia that not so long ago was unimaginable. Their essays build upon prior scholarship, but they are also introducing new research and new interpretations. As a whole *A Cultural History of Peace* highlights our humanity, something that has been for too long overshadowed in history by the inhumanity of war and other forms of violent conflict. Pursuing answers to new and seldom asked questions, these collected essays expand our knowledge of when, how, and why people in the past pursued peace within their own societies and peaceable relations with people from other societies.

The South African novelist Nadine Gordimer wisely observes, "The past is valid only in relation to whether the present recognises it." (2007: 7). In other words, what happened in the past is not necessarily history. History is made when scholars produce meaningful answers to the questions they ask about the past. The past cannot change, but history can and does change when scholars ask new questions, and when they use previously undiscovered or ignored evidence to develop new interpretations of the past. Evidence of what people said or did, or said they did, are basic materials out of which scholars shape answers to questions like "Does peace have a history?" Of course, to answer this particular question about the past, we must have in mind some definition of peace. Like most people we probably immediately think of peace as *not war*, a classic definition that describes peace in negative terms, as an absence of the type of violent conflicts that still loom so large popular histories and stories about the past. The American psychologist and peace activist William James succinctly summed up this common way of framing of the past, simply stating, "History is a bath of blood." (1910: 1).

James' description of history still plays well in a world that during the last century experienced the massive casualties and devastation of two world wars, genocides, and numerous civil wars, as well the fears created by transnational terrorism and still-threatening nuclear arsenals. And significantly, a bath of blood framing of continues to shape the priorities of most mainstream reporting of the news from around the world—"if it bleeds it leads"—when, in fact, most people today live in zones of peace where their lives are not threatened by violent political conflict. A human being's chances of dying in war have been historically low in this century, and in striking contrast to the peaks of worldwide violence reached during the global conflicts of the twentieth century. (https://ourworldindata.org/war-and-peace) Yet so accustomed are we with framing history *and* the present as a bath of blood, most of us have difficulty comprehending these facts. Steven Pinker recently noted this problem in the preface to *The Better Angels of Our Nature: Why Violence Has Declined*, saying "Believe it or not—and I know that most people do not—violence has declined over long stretches of time, and today we might be living in the most peaceable era in our species' existence." (2011: xvi). It is not just a coincidence that the rapid growth and globalization of peace studies has happened since the end of the Cold War. Undoubtedly, some of the questions raised in *A Cultural History of Peace* have been influenced by the extraordinary recent decline of inter-state warfare and resolution of many long-standing civil wars.

A Cultural History of Peace demonstrates that for several thousand years peace has been regarded as a highly desirable social condition, perhaps most especially when the violence and cruelty of war have been in the ascendency. Describing this collection of peace history essays as a cultural history—rather than social, political, diplomatic, or international history—is appropriate because throughout history peace has emerged from the cultures of groups, societies, and nations that developed practical ways to peaceably settle serious conflicts. Here I employ the broad environmental definition of culture that psychiatrist and classics scholar Jonathan Shay uses in his brilliant book, *Achilles in Vietnam*: "Our animal nature, our biological nature, is to live in relation to other people. The natural environment of humans is primarily culture, not the 'natural world' narrowly defined as other species, climate, etc." (1995: 207). Surely no human culture is ever truly homogeneous or free from conflicts that arise from serious differences between individuals and groups. Murder and warfare are the bloodiest ways that humans have dealt with those with whom they have serious differences. Bath of blood history foregrounds these activities when we peer in to the past. Peace history does something very different. It reveals the long unfinished task of making human cultures peaceable environments that encourage the expression of our most humane instincts: respect for all others who are human like us, and sympathy for those humans who are fearful and/or suffering.

In a remarkable book, *Humanity: A Moral History of the Twentieth Century*, philosopher Jonathan Glover describes respect and sympathy as "human responses" that although they are "widespread and deep-rooted" are often blocked. Frequently aggressive and cruel instincts find expression in warfare and encouragement in cultures that reserve the highest honors for warriors and their blood sacrifices. Yet clearly respect and sympathy have been absolutely necessary for the survival of our social species. Respect and sympathy are, in Glover's words, "the core of our humanity which contrasts with inhumanity." However, as Glover recognizes "humanity is only partly an empirical claim. It remains also partly an aspiration." (1999: 24–25). *A Cultural History of Peace* presents strong evidence for the empirical claim, as well as the aspiration. It focuses on the many people in the past who worked to establish peace within their own societies and peace with other societies by institutionalizing respect and sympathy; people who are unlikely to be highlighted as heroes in bath of blood histories.

As General Editor of this title in the Bloomsbury Publishers' cultural history series, I have had to follow two major guidelines. The first one required six volumes of essays that follow the same chronological order as other titles in the series. Accordingly, *A Cultural History of Peace* is presented in volumes focused on Antiquity, the Medieval Age, the Renaissance, the Enlightenment, Age of Empire, and the Modern Era since 1920. This chronology order is Western-oriented and something of a barrier to producing a truly global history of peace. Nonetheless, some of the essays in the first five volumes of *A Cultural History of Peace*, and all the essays in Volume Six present peace history in a global perspective. Indeed those essays show that envisioning a more peaceful interconnected world and finding ways of realizing that vision is a crucial component of the complex of historical processes we call today "globalization."

Bloomsbury's other major guideline required the eight topical essays in each volume of *A Cultural History of Peace* to concentrate on identical themes in peace history. My first task as General Editor was developing the eight major themes for these collected essays. Developing the major themes was difficult particularly because I recognized that a kind of "translation" problem arises when applying modern ideas about peace to the study of peace history in earlier eras when those ideas, or at least modern formulations of them, were absent. I only started doing peace history in 1998 after two decades of teaching and writing concentrated almost exclusively on American history. Not surprisingly, I remained focused on the modern era when preparing my first peace history courses and new research projects. That focus on the modern era was reinforced by what I learned in a peace research seminar at the University of Oslo in the summer of 2007. Thus I knew that my initial selection of themes for this collection could be criticized as present-oriented. Many hours of discussion with my colleagues in Dartmouth's History Department convinced me that this "translation" problem was not insuperable, and that after significant revision my original ideas would be viable focal points for *A Cultural History of Peace*.

These six volumes validate this conviction. Each one contains an introductory overview of the historical era written by its editor and eight thematic essays written by specialists. They develop the following themes: Definitions of Peace; Human Nature, Peace, and War; Peace, War, and Gender; Peace, Pacifism, and Religion; Representations of Peace; Peace Movements; Peace, Security, and Deterrence; and Peace as Integration. This structure facilitates long views of key subjects in peace history. Anyone interested, for instance, in putting together a chronologically ordered history of how peace has been defined from antiquity to the modern era can achieve this goal by reading in order each of the first chapters in the six volumes of *A Cultural History of Peace*. When they do so, they will discover the distinction between "negative" and "positive" definitions of peace that are commonly used in peace research today is useful when formulating questions about pre-modern definitions of peace. But they will also see that the modern distinction between negative peace and positive peace is a simple model that may hinder understanding the variety and richness of what people since antiquity actually meant when they spoke and wrote about peace.

How people in different times and places have understood what we usually call "human nature" has deeply influenced what they said and did about making peace and war. Human nature is, of course, a tricky term. Does it even exist? If it does, is it an endowment of fixed characteristics, or malleable and evolving? And if by human nature, we mean "instinctual," does this mean "inevitable," or are instincts better understood as potential behaviors that have been repressed or expressed depending on environmental influences produced by particular cultures at particular times in the past. The essays in this collection that develop the theme "Human Nature, Peace, and War" make clear that prevailing beliefs about human nature, whether faith-based or secular, have always played an essential role in how people understand what kinds of peace are possible in their imperfect material world.

Peace and war are among the most clearly gendered historical categories, as Chapters Three in *A Cultural History of Peace* make abundantly clear. It has been common all over the world for women to be regarded as "life-givers" and men as "life takers." Of course there are deviations from this global historical pattern. The Truong sisters of Vietnam and Joan of Arc are among the most famous transgressors of the male monopoly of military power. However, women like them have been exceptional. More commonly, women have provided material and psychological support to male warriors. And perhaps most significantly, some of them have been peace thinkers and peacemakers. Indeed, the widespread idea that peace is feminine has been a source of political legitimacy for women, not just a barrier to achieving political power.

Although pacifism in Western democracies is now usually understood as a principled and often religiously inspired refusal to engage in violence, in other historical settings people who could justify certain violent actions and some wars were still considered "pacifists" whenever they opposed militarism or an ongoing war. On such occasions the deeply subversive cultural implications of nonviolence—its resistance to the idea that history must be written in blood—have been manifest. The essays herein that develop the theme "Peace, Pacifism, and Religion" enable readers to better understand the ambiguous role of religious faith in peace history. They describe religious traditions that link faith and peace, but also ancient and enduring traditions that link religion to the promotion of war.

Since antiquity countless artists, sculptors, composers, poets, playwrights, and writers have produced representations that reflected, but also shaped, understandings of peace in their cultures. Ancient symbols of peace like the olive branch and the dove that were incorporated into religious iconography have never lost their currency, even when used by secular peace activists. Many other representations of peace created during the last two millennia have also survived. Chapters Five in this collection present a long history of these representations of peace. These representations have often been of peace imagined because their creators could not find real peace in contemporary political cultures. The accumulated representations of peace now form a vast and priceless cultural reservoir, much of it easily accessed via the Internet. Currently, new representations of peace are being deposited in this cultural reservoir everyday, while old ones are revived and reconfigured by peace activists around the world.

Peace and anti-war movements have always produced and deployed representations of peace, but they have not been a constant presence in the past. Chapters Six of *A Cultural History of Peace* describe collective efforts to prevent wars, or to stop them from continuing, as well as organized opposition to militarism. Throughout history peace movements have been condemned as subversive, especially when they resisted ongoing wars authorized by political authorities. And even when they have failed to achieve peace, as they have frequently done in the past, peace movements extended the contemporary cultural bases for challenging militarism and the glorification of warfare. Peace movements have over the long run produced traditions of anti-militarist thinking that in this century are mobilized by peace activists whenever inter-state warfare threatens global peace.

Today, most global peace activists regard the achievement of security via the threat of force as itself a problem, partly because this kind of negative peace has so frequently broken down in the past. The six essays in this collection that explore the theme "Peace, Security, and Deterrence" nonetheless demonstrate the strong and enduring appeal of this approach to peace. Although the perception problem modern political scientists call "the security dilemma" has been recognized since antiquity, the political practicality and immediately recognizable results of deterrence has almost always prevailed in the face of building threats made by military rivals. Enshrined in the modern era as a form of political realism, deterrence policy shaped the nuclear arms that saw rival superpowers each deploy tens of thousands of nuclear weapons that if used would have certainly destroyed civilization. Yet today, most national governments still equate peace with security and produce deterrence policies that create military alliances and threaten adversaries with war.

The last chapters of each volume of *A Cultural History of Peace* address a theme that many people mistakenly identify as a modern phenomenon: peace through integration, as if it must be something resembling the European Union. These chapters show that the social order imposed by expanding empires, kingdoms, and nation-states has long been proclaimed as a form of peace, even when peace was not the reason for the warfare that preceded it. Moreover, its principal beneficiaries often have often identified their empires as an expanding civilization, most famously Pax Romana and more recently Pax Americana. Yet since the medieval age another kind of peace achieved by nonviolent agreements built upon shared characteristics of identity has been imagined, and occasionally implemented.

Christianity's claim to be a universal church that could bring all people together in a brotherhood of Christ opened the door for identifying "humanity," a word first used during the Renaissance. Then science, especially eighteenth-century taxonomy, provided a secular path to a similar end: the recognition that all humans are in very important ways, a single unique species of life. In the modern era, threats to the continued existence of this humanity in the form of global catastrophes such as nuclear warfare and climate change have contributed to an unprecedented "species consciousness" and the claim that all humans have rights that must be respected. Unprecedented communications technologies that today allow us to see and hear people from all over the world in real time have facilitated the expansion of global peace and human rights networks. Although during the five years that *A Cultural History of Peace* has been in the making, politics that divide people into hostile groups have gathered strength in many countries, the long history presented in this collection suggests the cultural foundations for peace, so long in the making, will weather the present storm, and humanity will continue to make itself a global reality.

INTRODUCTION

From Westphalia to Enlightened Peace, 1648–1815

STELLA GHERVAS AND DAVID ARMITAGE

Beati pacifici. Cedant arma togae.

—William Penn, 1693[1]

This quotation placed at the start of William Penn's *Essay towards the Present and Future Peace of Europe* (1693) fused two cultures: the first part ("blessed are the peacemakers") belonged to Jesus' Sermon on the Mount in the New Testament (Matthew 5:9); the second came from Cicero's *On Duties* ("let arms yield to the toga") and referred to the custom of Roman generals removing their armor and wearing a toga before entering the City. Penn amalgamated the sacred and the classical to make a metaphorical appeal for European states to abandon their habit of settling disputes by the force of arms and to replace it by *justice*, by which Penn meant embassies bringing pleas from the wronged party. In other words, it advocated a negotiated settlement of differences. Penn's statement can, indeed, serve as an apt summary of what the cultural idea of peace would become during the European Enlightenment.

It is a commonplace among scholars to take the two dates of 1648 and 1815 as historical milestones, the markers of a "Classical period" of statehood, sovereignty and international relations with global implications well beyond Europe. Though this interpretation has largely lost its dogmatic value, it can still be used with some profit. The year 1648 stands for the Peace of Westphalia, the series of treaties closing the Thirty Years' War (1618–48) that had drenched the Holy Roman Empire in blood, over a rather intricate question: the prerogatives of the Holy Roman Emperor versus the rights of the German states, all set against a backdrop of religious wars between Catholics and Protestants.[2] Similarly, 1815 marks the Final Act of the Congress of Vienna and other treaties signed in that year, as the tail end of a time of troubles that had started with the French Revolutionary Wars, and swiftly proceeded with the conquest of Europe by Emperor Napoleon's armies.[3] In between these two dates, we find a movement known as the Enlightenment, a ferment of intellectual activity that was so intense it came to shape the culture of a time and, in due course, the social and political organization of the European states. Such a chronology is, needless to say, purely schematic and, like all such frames, somewhat artificial. It is grounded, however, in the self-understanding of the period itself, for which peace became a supreme cultural value that informed the Enlightenment, both as a process and as an intellectual movement. The waxing and waning of peace can therefore be taken as a good index for this historical epoch, which is bounded by two peace settlements with profound cultural repercussions in their own times and long afterwards.

WHY A *CULTURAL* HISTORY OF PEACE?

What we understand here by a *cultural* history of peace is distinct from (but tied to) its diplomatic or political history. For the latter, the focus has traditionally been on short-term decisions and events, for example, negotiations and treaties; the main characters have been those individuals or great powers that made or broke peace treaties. In this volume, individuals—philosophers, jurists, theologians, political economists, poets, artists and others—appear on their own, sometimes as original contributors to the intellectual history of Europe; but rarely did they leave the political situation fundamentally changed immediately after their work was published. Cultural influence often takes time to manifest itself: the shared representations of peace (which are the central focus of our cultural history of peace) tend to move slowly. A cultural history, then, studies how these were born and how they permeated European educated societies, eventually to influence them in new directions. It can also show how those originally European ideas went global and hybridized with other traditions of peace, far beyond the Atlantic world of Europe and the Americas that is delimited by the traditional definitions of Enlightenment (see Conrad 2012).

By taking such a cultural approach, the volume diverges from one traditional approach to international relations, which has sought to identify seemingly permanent, abstract scientific objects that transcend time and culture. We will consider here peace as a human product, an intellectual or cultural construct with all its connotations and representations, not as some immortal object of political science floating across time like a mythical Nicolas Flamel or Count Saint Germain. As scholars from Sir Henry Sumner Maine in the nineteenth century to Sir Michael Howard at the end of the twentieth noted, peace was not a discovery but an invention, and hence a human achievement (Maine 1888; Howard 2000). The ideal of peace evolved and aged with human communities, naturally influenced by the course of events; and it frequently perished miserably in war, only to be reborn in new forms. It is only the inbred and tenacious impulse of many human cultures toward a sense of "brotherhood" among human beings (perceived, for example, as *ubuntu* among the peoples of southern Africa), despite all the apparent reasons to believe in the supremacy of brute force, which compels us to acknowledge that some natural law is at play in humanity. Immanuel Kant famously wrote in 1795 that:

> Since the narrower or wider community of the peoples of the earth has developed so far that a violation of rights in one place is felt throughout the world, the idea of a law of world citizenship is no high-flown or exaggerated notion.
> —Kant [1795] 2006: 84–85

Whereas there might seem to be a universal aspiration of humans toward peace, what forms and procedures peace takes definitely owes much to the culture of a time and place. Indeed, Europe in the seventeenth and eighteenth centuries evolved a very elaborate protocol around the conclusion of peace after war: called *l'art de la paix* (the Art of Peace), that was complete with embassies, congresses, and treaties (Bély 2007). And while each new avatar of peace after war may have been recognizable as belonging to the same species *pax*—it is definitely not the same individual. Peace, during that epoch, was part of the great canvas of shared mental representations: not only as the counterpart to war but also as the ideal condition of a state; and it generally invited a sense of ordering reason, safety of rights and prosperity (see Spinoza [1677] 2000, ch. V). Peace among states was thus not merely an intellectual construct: it was also a yearning, represented in visual arts

FIGURE 0.1: Johann Gottlieb Becker, *Immanuel Kant* (1724–1804). Schiller-Nationalmuseum, Marbach am Neckar, Germany. Bridgeman Images.

from architecture to painting, either as the portraits of peacemakers orderly assembled in a fashion evoking concord, or as allegories such as Peace and Justice kissing each other, often complete with a dove and olive branch[4]—as well as in music where it was traditionally associated, as in G. F. Handel's *Te Deum* and *Jubilate* for the peace of Utrecht (1713), with the emotions of pomp, joy, and gratitude. Peace, in that cultural sense, was first and foremost a perpetual quest for a safer and quieter state of affairs for human society (Milam in this volume).

As will be readily seen in each of the various contributions to this book, the time frame of a cultural narrative is thus necessarily larger than a political one—it spans decades, even centuries. While the Peace of Westphalia could be said to have heralded the collapse of cultural foundations that had framed Latin Christianity—notably the ideal of an imperial unity, both political and religious—it is during the Enlightenment that we witness the birth of innovative reflections that would shape the cultural representations of peace in following eras. Political events formed, of course, the background and the counterpoint of this evolution, and they provide us helpful signposts to understand the context; but what matters here is the slow percolation of conceptions of peace and of the European "order," from the educated elites of the continent to political leaders, to societies at large and even to other continents. In fact, we might venture to say that it is during the Enlightenment that peace first became definitively and irreversibly a cultural force in

FIGURE 0.2: Theodor van Thulden, *Allegory of Peace and Justice after the Thirty Years' War*. Deutsches Historiches Museum, Berlin, Germany (DHM). Bridgeman Images.

itself: that is, a central value with its own representations, institutions and norms, and with a constructed history as well as a constructive future. This slow movement of transformation between Westphalia and Vienna, which identified a whole culture with peace and rendered peace a cultural goal in its own right, led to forms of peace and peace-making that are recognizable up to our own time (Ghervas 2014b).

BEYOND PRECONCEPTIONS: TOWARD A NEW HISTORY OF PEACE

And yet the reader should be warned that our attempt to rediscover past cultural conceptions of the political order of Europe, particularly of "peace," also needs to be a process of "unlearning": it might require us to relinquish some of our own cultural conceptions, at least momentarily. This difficulty manifests itself in two ways. The first is that approaching the written sources of the mid-seventeenth and eighteenth centuries is doubly treacherous, even compared to earlier ones. First, the European languages had already developed to be deceptively close to those of our times, but they are definitely not identical. It is too easy for us to fool ourselves by misinterpreting the terms used by authors; texts of the eighteenth century are strewn with many "false friends" that can cause us to trip by unwittingly projecting our definitions and thereby missing their point. Even sources written in Latin—such as the treaties of Westphalia—do not save us from that hazard, since most of us rely on translations into modern languages. We will thus have to forget, for a moment, the canonical terms of political science that we all learnt at school ("state," "sovereignty," etc.) to dive instead into a bygone era of absolute monarchies, aristocratic republics and a Holy Roman Empire. And where we use modern terminology, we should at least make sure that it will not interfere with our understanding of the primary sources.

The second issue is that even if vocabulary was crystal clear, our own cultural (pre-)conceptions of the early twenty-first century could still get in the way. Anglophone societies, among others, are still somewhat influenced by popular narratives relying on a "historical teleology," i.e. the belief that the succession of events of human history is going toward some "manifest destiny." This is understandable, as it is a side-effect of the meteoric rise of European states during the Enlightenment and the Industrial Revolution, which led historians to view Western culture as somehow exceptional or superior to others. We have all been exposed to various beliefs, such as the "triumph of science," the "unstoppable machine of progress," not to mention the nineteenth century's "civilizing mission to the world," Marx's "struggle of the classes," all the way to Francis Fukuyama's premature "end of history" as the victory of American liberal democracy (Fukuyama 1992); and perhaps even Steven Pinker's over-optimistic account of the triumph of the "better angels of our nature" (Pinker 2011). By contrast, many recent historians would dismiss these hypothetical grand designs (which they consider as the reflection of long cherished but now obsolete societal conceptions) as self-centered fallacies. By the same token, no self-respecting historian would today endorse the idea that the history of the European great powers of the seventeenth century represents the totality of human history; European history telling is thus "provincializing" itself in its own estimation (Hobson 2009). As a result, we would encourage the reader not to read any cosmic significance into this broadened "Enlightenment era of peace" framed by the dates of 1648 and 1815. It was merely a practical way of dividing eras of the history of Europe, among other possible ones, within the constraints of a multi-volume collection covering the cultural history of peace over more than two millennia.

Our warning about the hazards of teleology applies in particular to the Peace of Westphalia. After the Second World War, its importance grew so much in Western culture, to the point that it was reinvented as the origin point of all states in existence today—the "Westphalian states," with sovereignty supposedly the *ne plus ultra* of political evolution and the ultimate impulse inherent to any modern state. That "sovereignty" is, however, a modern character, whose birth can even be traced to a precise year: 1948 on the third centenary of the Peace of Westphalia, in the context of the military and ideological contest of the US against Stalin's USSR during the Cold War. This event takes place in the first years of the United Nations (in reality, a club of states, not nations) and the promulgation of the Universal Declaration of Human Rights (Gross 1948). By contrast, the real historical character of 1648, the Latin *superioritas*, was not a gift from the Platonic realm of ideas; it was rather a catchall phrase that synthesized the particular claims of a myriad of German states toward the Holy Roman Empire. In their capacity of members of that political formation, those states were obviously not "sovereign" as we would understand that notion today.

We can, furthermore, notice two additional logical issues with the "cultural" belief that modern sovereignty was born in Westphalia. The first is that the signatories of the treaties had never hoped for or even conceived of such a glorious remote posterity, three full centuries after the events. Indeed, the political and geographical scope of that peace agreement was limited to the Holy Roman Empire (a geographical area spanning from the North Sea to Northern Italy), and it was designed to put an end to political and institutional disputes that were specific to a time and place: "Discords and Civil Divisions being stir'd up in the Roman Empire, which increas'd to such a degree, that not only all Germany, but

FIGURE 0.3: Gerard ter Borch, *The Ratification of the Treaty of Münster* (1648). Reproduced with the kind permission of the National Gallery, London, UK.

also the neighbouring Kingdoms, and France particularly, have been involv'd in the Disorders of a long and cruel War" ("Treaty of Münster" 1648, Preamble and Art. 1). One could perhaps be deceived by the stated aim of the agreement to establish a "Christian and universal peace, and a perpetual, true and sincere amity," but that was a standard rhetorical device used in most treaties of the time (ibid.). But what historical sovereignty may lose in mythical prestige, it gains in authenticity, detail, and interest.

The second issue is that the motivations for keeping alive the myth of the "Peace of Westphalia" may no longer exist in the early twenty-first century.[5] The doctrine of "absolute sovereignty" (a core tenet of the post-war realist school of International Relations associated in the post-War period with Hans Morgenthau and others) has been put into question as a long-term survival strategy. Indeed, several of the largest and most powerful political formations on Earth today are federations, notably the United States of America; and most of the European powers of old seem to have gone this way since 1950, and are now part of a European Union. It is, also, particularly ironic that "sovereignty," in the post-Second World War era, had been of such little succor to the German states that had benefited from the Peace of Westphalia: their number had already been whittled down by Napoleon's "mediatization" in 1812–14, then progressively reduced to only two after warlike Prussia rose to prominence and a Second German Reich was formed in 1871; then summarily fused into one, when the Third German Reich militarily annexed Austria with the Anschluss of 1939. After the Second World War, it was set to naught as the occupied Third Reich ceased to exist as a sovereign state. If there had indeed been a Grand Designer of a "principle of sovereignty," it stands to reason that they would have been kinder to the many German states that had been the first to gather and follow it. In that order of things, a Principality of Münster would have been sitting as a member of the United Nations Assembly in 1948; instead, the constitution of Germany evolved once again toward a federal state. We will thus ask the reader to bear with the authors and consider the cultural manifestations of peace from 1648 to 1815, in themselves and as themselves, *not necessarily as the prelude to our modern political order*.

With such historical myths and absolutes out of the way and with due regard to the cultural context, there is something to be said about important peace treaties or territorial settlements as temporal signposts in a *longue durée* history of peace: they brought a formal end to the periods of violent organized fighting between states, known as wars. Such has long been, after all, a most basic and legal meaning of the term *peace* in European culture: as a treaty, a document putting an end to the state of war, and the resulting political state. "Peace," in that restricted sense, was a condition beneficial to commerce and prosperity. It was alas transient, even though peace treaties were labeled as "perpetual" or "eternal," seemingly as a countercharm. In the period under consideration, *peace treaties* thus appeared to the eyes of contemporaries as welcome pauses to disorders. For today's historians, they serve as useful milestones for a meaningful chronology of peace (Arcidiacono 2011; Ghervas 2020a).

1648: THE END OF A CONVENTIONAL ORDER OF LATIN CHRISTIANITY?

Let us now turn briefly to this "historical" Peace of Westphalia: it came as the result of a victory for German states in general and setbacks for the Austrian Habsburg dynasty in particular. It also brought relative stability to Germany and, by extension, to the lands west of it. The name of Westphalia derives from the name of the German state that hosted the negotiations and is a generalization, because the "peace" is really a series of treaties signed in 1648: Münster (30 January) between Spain and the Dutch Republics, and more importantly, Münster (24 October) between the Holy Roman Empire and France and allies, and Osnabrück (24 October) between the Holy Roman Empire and Sweden. To capture its essence, we can turn to Voltaire a century later:

> This Peace of Westphalia, finally signed in Münster and Osnabrück on 14 October 1648, was agreed, granted and received *as a fundamental and perpetual law*: these are the very terms of the treaty. It must serve as the basis for imperial capitulations [commitments made by a newly elected emperor]. It is also received law, as sacred until now as the Golden Bull [of 1356], and far superior to it by the detail of all the diverse interests that this treaty covers, by all the rights it ensures and by the changes introduced into civil status and religion.
>
> —Voltaire 1827: 319

By settling the relations of the German states with the Holy Roman Empire—as well as Austria—and by severing the link of the Dutch Republic and Switzerland from it, the peace of Westphalia created a regional order that was less monolithic, generally more disposed to compromise and therefore to peace, and in consequence less susceptible to attract foreign powers in search of territorial acquisitions.[6]

From an intellectual or cultural perspective, the stipulations appear however less as a beginning than an end: they mark a break from the top-down dogma of the *alliance of the throne and the altar* (namely the Emperor and the Pope) that had dominated Western

Europe, the land of Latin Christianity, during the late Middle Ages. After the fall of the Western Roman Empire at the end of the Fifth Century, Western Europe had been an anarchy of states. This fact had, paradoxically, allowed the Patriarchate of Rome to emerge as a unifying factor, both religiously and politically. When, in the year 799, Pope Leo III crowned the Frankish King Charlemagne as *Emperor of the Romans* mostly to create a counterweight to the Roman Empire of Constantinople, a particular politico-religious configuration was inaugurated in Western Europe whereby the Pope became the spiritual suzerain of all monarchs. The cultural paradigm was that a benevolent Augustus would impose peace and unity once again for the benefit of humankind, as in the Ancient Roman Empire, but this time he would do so with the caution and blessing of the highest religious figure of Christianity.

There was a wide stretch, of course, from the ideal to practice. For the Holy Roman Empire (which was—in the famous words of Voltaire—neither holy, Roman nor an empire), the alleged "alliance of the altar and the throne" was actually a contrived and glorified confederation, where coexistence was not straightforward and was even a cause of occasional wars. Furthermore, kingdoms such as France, Spain, England, and Poland were not part of it and did not recognize its supremacy. Yet, for all its awkward mismatch with reality, the Holy Roman Empire provided a solid mental and legal framework that held together the lands between Germany and Northern Italy for eight centuries (Stollberg-Rilinger 2013). The figure of the Pope even rose during the Middle Ages to become the arbiter of the affairs of Europe. The inextricable interconnection between the spiritual and the secular, with the spiritual constantly seeking to gain or maintain the upper hand, was undoubtedly a dominant trait of Latin Christianity.

This balance changed at the the turn of the sixteenth century, when European powers started to influence Africa, Asia and the Americas, in what came to be known (at least in Europe), as the "Great Discoveries." On the continent itself, a powerful German–Spanish Empire rose in Western Europe under Charles V. At the very moment when it seemed that Latin Christianity would be finally united politically in an explosion of grandeur, its structure started to crack apart because of the Protestant Reformation and its aftermath. With its rejection of the clerical intermediation with God and its distrust of Church hierarchies, Protestantism had also strong implications for the social and political order: by rejecting the divine right of monarchs and by ultimately supporting the prerogatives of parliaments, Protestantism led to the birth of a new form of secular state, quite different from the top-down paradigm of Catholic inspiration. It is not coincidental that seminal philosophers of European political thought, such as the English Thomas Hobbes (1588–1679) (on whom see Christov in this volume) and the Dutch Hugo Grotius (1583–1645), hailed from countries that had adopted the Protestant strain of Reformation. They would be later canonized as "theorists of sovereignty" alongside the Frenchman Jean Bodin (1530–1596), a figure from the other side of the confessional divide, but who shared their critique of papal power.

Change tends, however, to break the peace if it is resisted too hard against, or fought too fervently for. The "Religious Wars" of the sixteenth and seventeenth century in Europe were less about theology than about two radically opposed conceptions of society and the role of the individual in it. The incumbent Catholic powers, Spain and Austria, considered the reformed states of the Holy Roman Empire (first of which were the Dutch Republic and Prussia), as existential threats to their way of life, and assigned themselves a mission to restore what they considered as the natural order. Conversely, Protestant states were willing to defend, to the last breath, both their existence and their own conception of a natural

FIGURE 0.4: Delff, Hugo Grotius (1583–1645), Dutch Jurist and Politician. Interfoto. Alamy Stock Photo.

society where individuals would have a direct relationship with God and their political rulers. This opposition of two sides which both considered that far more was at stake than interests of power, money, or influence, were conducive to a conflict of the worst kind: a war of mutual annihilation (which is the proper meaning of *internecine* war) (Armitage 2017: 93–120). The shocking cruelty and the human cost of the wars of religion in Germany—some five million deaths in the name of the love of Christ—can only be explained as the instinctive reaction of two mutually incompatible factions that both contemplated oblivion. The political war between states thus doubled as a *civil war* among the states of Latin Christianity, not to mention the frequent occurrence of acts of civil war (in a proper sense) between communities of the two confessions, outside of any public control (Armitage 2017). Barbarism was thus the consequence of the states' angst of an impending collapse of their social order, or the result of the actual collapse of said social order. The literature of the time, seeking signs of God's anger in natural phenomena, turned as a precedent to Jeremiah's lamentations for the destruction of Jerusalem by the Persians in the sixth century BCE (Theibault 1994). Those prophecies of doom were, alas, self-fulfilling.

"Peace" in 1648, after the Thirty Years' War, was thus not a mere termination of "war," which Grotius might have described as a public duel between states: it was first and foremost the relinquishment of deep-rooted hatreds, a lesson in mutual tolerance, the mending of political and societal rifts that had threatened to rip the fabric of Western

Europe (Lesaffer 2002; Asch 2004). This explains the painstaking detail (the second treaty of Münster has 128 articles) with which the peace stipulations sought to settle each jurisdictional and territorial dispute from the North Sea to the Adriatic, without referring to dogmatic notions. It was a diplomatic triumph, not of lofty principles but of the common sense of negotiators seeking to address each and every particular situation in itself and by itself. Of course, posterity can discern a few general principles that implicitly emerged from this catalogue: notably the affirmation of the *superioritas* of each state of the Holy Empire, with its prerogatives and duties; and, most importantly, the exclusion of religious beliefs as a legitimate motive for waging war (Te Brake 2017: 44–90). The fundamental association between religious toleration—the mutual accommodation of confessional difference—with peace both internal (*concordia*) and external (*pax*) would define the self-image of Enlightenment. There is thus a case to be made, at least in the cultural sphere, for tracing one basic strain of Enlightenment back to 1648—to the beginnings of what might even perhaps be called a "Westphalian Enlightenment."

Let us note, however, that those stipulations aimed at leveling the playing field, by enforcing *negative* rights for the German states: in other words, they made peace possible by prohibiting encroachments from the Holy Roman Empire and foreign powers. That was undoubtedly removing a thorny issue, but they did not set either positive principles or any rules for how European states should treat each other in the future, in order to *maintain the peace*. Nor did they provide guidelines for how monarchs should deal with religious dissent within their own borders. The Peace of Westphalia, "the last Christian peace" as it has been called, signaled the end of a feudal epoch based on imperial-religious suzerainty (Croxton 2013). It was however "Christian" only in an abstract, ecumenical sense. Significantly, Pope Innocent X's bull "Zelo Domus Dei" (1650), condemned those articles of the 1648 peace treaties detrimental to the Catholic religion, but this fell on deaf ears and he had to accept the new German order as a *fait accompli*. The Papacy's role in the Holy Roman Empire would henceforth be theoretical—and in practice minimal, since episcopal states did not answer to the Pope for their internal affairs; and furthermore, the last papal coronation of an emperor had been that of Charles V in 1530.

For all this, it was not yet the start of a putatively "modern" world: states were still a highly patrimonial affair, with territories shifting from one dynasty to another according to marriages, inheritances, purchases, or barter. This time-honored tradition, descended from the Middle Ages, had long been a guarantee of safe and orderly transition of political power in Europe, but it was now becoming unsustainable because it was an ever-increasing source of territorial contentions: dynastic wars periodically broke the peace in the Three Kingdoms of Britain and Ireland and on the European Continent. There had to be better ways to ensure both orderly succession and a peaceful coexistence of states. The effort to find such means would consume much intellectual and institutional energy over the following two centuries.

THE "ENGLISH TURN" TO THE BALANCE OF POWER

For European states in the latter half of the seventeenth century, learning new ways of dealing with other states—preferably without recourse to military force—would thus be a next big challenge. It was especially true with a Western power dangerously on the rise: a resurgent France under Louis XIV *le Roi Soleil* (the Sun King). Louis XIV's House of Bourbon had been the historical enemy of the House of Habsburg; but this was of little relief to the states of the Holy Roman Empire on the west bank of the Rhine, as well as to the Dutch Republic, which were now the next targets for his appetite for self-aggrandizement. It was, in fact, fortunate that Spain was firmly holding on to its Flanders dominions (roughly today's Belgium), and thus served as a bulwark against the French threat of invasion. Indeed, the Protestant Dutch Republic and Catholic Spain were forced into a rapprochement during the Dutch Wars (1672–78). This war saw enemies of yesteryear now united against Louis XIV, who nevertheless won the day.

Upon this European war fought for territorial reasons, a second, colonial one was superposed, which opposed England and the Netherlands for control over the seas. Protestant England and Catholic France thus became allied in a war of opportunity. Yet another war was being fought on the East, between a Danish–German coalition and the Kingdom of Sweden on the defensive. All in all, the intricate game of political interests and diplomacy had it so that the complex pattern of European states was drifting into a configuration of two coalitions: France, Sweden, and England on one hand, and Spain, Austria, and the rest of Europe on the other. Or, to simplify it further, the French House of Bourbon and the Spanish/Austrian House of Habsburg became the main components of two opposed military blocs. At this stage, the fates of armies and navies in battle, not diplomats, were still the arbiters of Europe.

The final great upheaval of the old feudal order of Europe occurred when the last Habsburg king of Spain, Charles II, died in 1700 without an heir, bequeathing his kingdom to a Bourbon prince, Philip of Anjou, who happened to be none other than the grandson of Louis XIV. While the prospect of a reunion of the French and Spanish colonial empires was frightening enough for the English, the bulwark of Spanish Flanders, now in French hands, was suddenly turned into a rear guard for military offensives into the heart of Germany: this spelled disaster for the Dutch Republic as well as the minor states on the western bank of the Rhine.

It is, paradoxically, in that very moment that European powers took a turn toward recognizably "modern" cultural conceptions of peace. The impulse came from the one state that was not looking for territorial aggrandizement on the continent but exclusively at the development of her commerce and the conquest of overseas dominions: England. The Stuart King Charles II, while a Catholic at heart, had restored peace in his kingdoms around a sound tolerance policy that acknowledged the country's preference for Anglicanism, and he gained much popular appreciation for it. When his openly Catholic heir James II was deposed in the Glorious Revolution (1688–89), sheer necessity demanded that the government set aside both religious disputes and strict adherence to dynastic principles, to follow a sensible course of action.

England turned toward an unorthodox candidate, but a not unsurprising one in view of the rise of France: a scion of the one family that had given many leaders to the Dutch Republic, the house of Orange. For the English political class, commercial competition from Dutch maritime power had long been a serious but manageable nuisance, even better if an accommodation could be found. By contrast, the prospect of England facing alone the French Sun King commandeering the three combined fleets of France, Spain and the Netherlands would have been infinitely worse. It logically followed that once Spain had switched sides over to the Bourbon faction in 1700, England had to turn around and join forces with the Netherlands to defend their existence as Protestant, trade nations; and that both had to ally without remorse with the Catholic Habsburg of Austria.

From these quite particular circumstances, higher interpretations had to emerge. In England, this was the rise of the *balance of power* as a governing principle of foreign policy: it stipulated that in order to preserve its freedom and peace, the kingdom should side militarily, in any situation, with the less powerful European alliance so as to re-establish an equilibrium. In this sense, "balance" was to be understood literally, as the scales used to weigh merchandise at the market (Ghervas 2017: 407–08). The assumption here was that the European states would always divide into two opposed military alliances; and as long as those alliances would be matched in strength, the continent would not fall prey to a universal monarchy—or a pan-continental empire, in modern terms (Bosbach 1988). And, indeed, France under Louis XIV was edging dangerously close to such a universal monarchy, as contemporary British observers noted with alarm. In this vein, Charles Davenant, a writer and member of Parliament classically wrote in 1701 that "the post of England is to hold the balance of power" (Davenant [1701] 1771: 302–05). This is, after all, exactly what it did in the following year, by declaring war on both France and Spain and starting the War of Spanish Succession. By 1710, the Balance of Power had become a household concept in the political parlance of London and it would have a long and influential afterlife (see Ghervas 2017).

PEACE IN THE ENLIGHTENMENT: BOLD THEORIES, STABLE PRACTICES

After over a decade of indecisive conflict without winners or losers, the European powers decided to come to an agreement, with the Treaty of Utrecht (1713). What England "proposed and insisted upon" on that occasion, quite unsurprisingly, was a solemn relinquishing by the Bourbon Kings of France and Spain of any future claims on each other's throne. The novelty lay in the motivation of "securing for ever the universal good and quiet of Europe, by an equal weight of power, so that many being united in one, the balance of the equality desired, might not turn to the advantage of one, and the danger and hazard of the rest" (Treaty of Utrecht 1713, Art. II). On the continent, the construct of the Balance of Power started to seep into political vocabulary: witness the fact French and German writers later used it quite confidently, while acknowledging the role of England in its development (Sheehan 1996: 97–120; Dhondt 2015). They understood it as a prescription for how to maintain the peace by the preservation of the *status quo ante*: according to which, the patrimonial rights of the ruling families had to give way to the collective interest of a continental community of states. The political configuration of Europe was indeed a bipolar one: two perpetually opposed military alliances, organized around the Austrian House of Habsburg on one hand and the French House of Bourbon on the other (Ahn and Whatmore in this volume). While peace was a desirable object, wars would still be frequent, because preserving the balance of power was more important as a safeguard against universal monarchy.

While Latin Christianity was falling into the background as the dominant cultural reference for peace, a secular "European Republic of States" was emerging, complete with its own Law of Nations and a cultural identity increasingly defined by enlightened values of internal and external peace: indeed, this has been called with justice by J. G. A. Pocock the "Utrecht Enlightenment" (Pocock 1999: 7–9). By mid-century, the Law of Nations was formalized by authors such as the hugely influential Swiss jurist Emer de Vattel (1714–1767), who understood it as a way to better integrate this republic of states according to the prescriptions of natural law and human reason (Vattel 2008). The conclusion of peace, with its armistices or capitulations, as well as its treaties, obeys rituals that may be seem self-evident today, but they are the product of a long evolution,

FIGURE 0.5: Delff, *The Signing of the Treaty of Utrecht on 11th April 1713*. Private Collection. Bridgeman Images.

as well as codification. Conversely, it may seem counter-intuitive that war, by nature a chaotic activity where nothing is certain beyond the fact that it has been declared, would become such a ritualized duel between states. War and peace, under the inspiration of philosophers and lawyers, thus became legal constructs with their *modus operandi*, regulations and norms, which were generally respected by belligerents (Koskenniemi in this volume). In the end, the only purpose of the law of nations was to bring more order in the interrelations of states on the continent and, as such, it was a factor contributing to peace on the continent—or at least to attempt to make wars less cruel.

To paraphrase Immanuel Kant, "the age of Enlightenment was not an enlightened age," and that applies also to political history (Kant [1784] 2006).[7] While established churches did their best to contain and channel the torrent of new ideas—especially those ideas that could call the social order into question—the eighteenth century had its plentiful supply of conflicts. Military deterrence, with Europe divided into two alliances, continued to be the foundation of the European "system." When mixed with dynastic rights and the legal cavils of succession, the logic of the balance of power actually made for new conflagrations, such as the War of Polish Succession (1733–38) and the War of Austrian Succession (1740–48). Nonetheless, the periods of peace were occasions for considerable development of commerce by sea (with the increase of colonial shipping) and by land (with the generalized improvement of roads on the continent).

By contrast, the new economic demands made it desirable for wars to be as short as possible, as well as less destructive, so as to cause minimal disruption to the flows of colonial imports and manufactured goods. This led the rise of the intellectual construct that Montesquieu called *doux commerce* ("sweet commerce"), as an alternative to war between states (Montesquieu 1989: IV, XX, 1 and 2; Terjanian 2013; Kapossy, Nakhimovsky, and Whatmore, eds. 2017). Replacing military conflicts by trade competition was certainly an improvement—yet attaching the adjective "sweet" to commerce may sound, from our horizon of experience, as an oxymoron for a period marked by brutal colonial conquests, the slave trade, and commerce-raiding under letters of marque. At least, the absence of religious fanaticism reduced European wars of the Age of Enlightenment to public duels for settling disputes between monarchies. Conflicts became less cruel to the point of being called *la guerre en dentelles* ("lace wars" or "soft war") at the time of the French Revolutionary Wars (Bély 2007: 581–602).[8] This catchy metaphor is misleading, however, since only officers—that is a fraction of the combatants—could afford to wear lace; and, furthermore, this adornment might have provided relief to aristocratic egos, never to the wounds caused by bullets, cannon shot, or bayonets.

It would be incorrect, however, to assume that Christianity disappeared from intellectual reflections or from the cultural representations of peace. The relative reconciliation between the Catholic and Protestant factions allowed the perception to re-emerge of a community of civilization founded on a common heritage of Europe (Idris in this volume). With the entry of Russia in the European political arena from the reign of Peter the Great, Eastern Christianity and the heritage of Constantinople also had to be taken into consideration. While organized peace movements are really a feature of the nineteenth century, and the word "pacifism" is only attached to the early twentieth, grass-roots movements aimed at preventing or banning war did exist in the period we are considering, with dissenting Protestant denominations at the forefront of criticism against war. Quakers left a particularly strong imprint on the European peace tradition; among them was William Penn who, with his *Essay toward Present and Future Peace of Europe* (1693), was possibly the first to have conceived a Grand Design for uniting the states of the continent under a single banner (Conway in this volume).

Most importantly, the Enlightenment was a moment when new conceptions of European unification saw the light, starting with the *Projet pour rendre la paix perpétuelle en Europe* ("Plan for making peace perpetual in Europe") by the French Abbé de Saint-Pierre ([1713] 1986), which may indeed have drawn upon Penn. This idea was later republished and re-proposed as an *Extrait* ("*Excerpt*") by Jean-Jacques Rousseau (1761) and finally conceptualized and transcended by Immanuel Kant in *Toward Perpetual Peace* (1795) (Pagden in this volume; Rousseau 2008a). Whereas Saint-Pierre proposed an ecumenical European Union, which initially included the Ottoman Empire as well, Rousseau held that Christianity was the civilizational bond of Europe, and argued that the common cultural heritage would be a key asset for reaching peace (Spector 2008: 230–32; Ghervas 2014a: 55–57).

Nevertheless, philosophers of the eighteenth century (among them Rousseau himself) were always skeptical of those plans for European unification, for the simple reason that there was no incentive for monarchs to adopt them: whereas the political system of enlightened Europe born at Utrecht was failing at making peace perpetual, it was at least sufficiently dynamic to take its own changes in stride. In particular, England's policy of counteracting the movements of the balance of power by switching sides did have a dampening effect in practice; and other powers took the cue from England. Indeed, the

FIGURE 0.6: Allan Ramsay, *Jean-Jacques Rousseau* (1712–78). Chateau de Coppet, Paris, France. Bridgeman Images.

spectacular reversal of alliances of the War of Austrian Succession (where the French Bourbons and Austrian Habsburg houses allied for the first time) as well as the rise of Prussia as major power in the Seven Years' War (1756–63) introduced changes to the European balance of power, though neither fundamentally put its validity into question. With economies on the rise, and sciences in full development, there is little doubt the future must have seemed bright for the European cultured elites, for a common civilization on the path to Enlightenment and therefore to peace.

It should not be forgotten, however, that war and peace were mostly made by *men* and that most philosophers we have quoted (foremost among them Rousseau and Kant) held rather disparaging views on the ability of women to assume political roles (Tomaselli in this volume). Conversely, women like the English writer Mary Wollstonecraft (1759–1797) did express their views on an increased role of women in society. They were the exception in political offices, yet in the period we are considering, female rulers paradoxically became a staple of European monarchies. It was, however, only the accidental product of the logic of succession, which preferred women to hold the power than relinquishing it out of the family. In England, Mary II (reigned 1688–1694) and Anne (1702–1714), and in Austria the Empress Maria Theresa (1740–1780) successfully wrestled her throne in the War of Austrian Succession; for Russia, Catherine I (1724–1727), Anna Ivanovna (1730–1740), Elizabeth (1741–1762) and finally Catherine II

(1762–1796) are still remembered as among the most prestigious rulers in Russian history. Royalty was, however, a circle apart from the rest of society, where another set of conventions and morals applied. Nevertheless, the fact that a few of these female rulers actually shined in their political role may have started to introduce some rebuttal to the European cultural prejudice against women in public life.

THE FRENCH REVOLUTION AND THE COLLAPSE OF SHARED BELIEFS ON PEACE

Unfortunately, the well-oiled political balance of Europe started to creak and jam with the French Revolution. This major political experiment had two faces: a positive and peaceful one, applauded by most enlightened elites of Europe, as a welcome liberalization of the kingdom of France and generally a modernization of its institutions. Indeed, the country turned momentarily its back to colonial wars, and the Constituent Assembly passed, on 22 May 1790, a "Decree of Peace Declaration to the World," which was really an attempt to prevent France from entering wars by subjecting declarations of war to parliament, in a context of colonial disputes between Spain and Britain.[9] The second, uglier face of the Revolution progressively came to light in the second half of 1791, after the emperor of the Holy Roman Empire and the King of Prussia jointly declared that they considered the internal affairs of France as a matter of their own concern: this encroachment on sovereignty ("The Declaration of Pillnitz" 1791) prodigiously angered the parliament of that country and put the French royal family under suspicion of being traitors to the nation. The darker side then came into full view when France declared war against Austria in April 1792, paving the way to the fall of the monarchy and the decapitation of King Louis XVI; and the invention of the systematic repression policy known as Terror, led by merciless men such as Jean-Paul Marat or Maximilien de Robespierre (Kolla 2017).

Warfare—at least on the French side—was set back to the Wars of Religion, as the republican armies fought with desperate energy for the survival of their societal conceptions. With ideology, fear and hatred added into the equation, the same causes led to the same effects, with the increase of wanton violence and casualties. This deleterious effect was compounded by demographic increase, which made for armies much larger than a few decades earlier. It seemed that peace between the two mutually incompatible conceptions of the social order in Europe would be impossible once again, unless one side won militarily over the others. Surprisingly, the ragtag columns of the French Republic started not only winning defensive battles against the monarchies, but they proceeded to bring war over into the lands of Prussia and Austria. After Napoleon Bonaparte, crowned Emperor in 1802, gave discipline, first-rate equipment and brilliant generalship to the French popular army, it became the instrument of a new conquering Empire; it soon forced most states of continental Europe into subjection, including the old Habsburg imperial dynasty of Austria; and arguably it inaugurated the earliest instance of "total war" (Bell 2007).

The balance of power, completely jammed, had failed this time to prevent the rise of a universal monarchy; this terrifying fact shook the societal certainties of the European aristocratic classes, even more than the decapitation of Louis XVI. By contrast, the sudden but enforced unification of the continent later gave birth to the myth of a *Pax Napoleonica*, in a Europe coalesced under a single regime and the cancellation of custom barriers (Ghervas 2015, 2019: 99–102). Unfortunately, the United Kingdom and Russia refused to be part of it and the British Navy kept a painful blockade; and with Napoleon's unquenched lust for conquest, peace was at best a lure. A whole generation, from 1792 onwards, was raised in conditions of perpetual war: treaties signed by the French Empire such as Amiens with Britain (1802) or Tilsit with Russia (1807) were only armed truces. At worst, for the occupied populations of Germany and Spain, this imperial peace was a sham that motivated insurrection and the rise of a national identity.

CONCLUSION: ENLIGHTENED PEACE AT LAST?

It is thus that Europe went full circle, from the Peace of Westphalia that closed the religious wars to the Napoleonic wars, from one set of brutal wars to another; and from the Habsburg imperial threat to state "sovereignty" to the Napoleonic one. The Peace of Westphalia (1648) had brought—in practice though not in theory—an end to the political supremacy of the elected Emperor of the Holy Roman Empire, who also happened often to be a Habsburg. The prohibitions it created for the Holy Roman Empire (and the corresponding negative rights for the German states) generally leveled the playing field in Europe; but it did not provide yet any positive prescriptions on how the European states should deal with each other. It would take another half a century before the doctrine of the balance of power emerged in England, and then it was reinterpreted and adopted on the continent with the peace of Utrecht (1713) as a device for preventing the establishment of universal monarchy. It was arguably a limited and imperfect system and not a "system of peace" but a "system of war," as Abbé de Saint-Pierre almost immediately argued; yet it worked sufficiently well for the needs of the time (Ghervas 2017: 411–12). After the

FIGURE 0.7: *The Congress of Vienna* (1815). PRISMA ARCHIVO. Alamy Stock Photo.

Revolutionary Wars, the crushing supremacy of the French Empire was the last blow that jammed the balance of power, discrediting it as the cure-all that would preserve peace. Between Utrecht (1713) and the start of the Revolutionary Wars (1792), the parenthesis of Enlightenment thus stands not as a period of peace, but as one of dynamic equilibrium where wars were contained within acceptable limits.

How European peace had to be completely reinvented at the Congress of Vienna after the Napoleonic Empire met with disaster in the Russian campaign of 1812, and the defeats of 1813–14 is another story (Ghervas 2020b: 24–25). Obviously, the next iteration of peace would heavily draw from the argumentation and proposals generated by the critics of the now disesteemed balance of power. Indeed, both the Russian tsar Alexander I and the Austrian Chancellor Klemens von Metternich came to the negotiation table having read the argumentation of writers on perpetual peace. Furthermore, the four victorious powers—namely Britain, Russia, Austria and Prussia—decided to meet regularly to discuss important matters of Europe, inaugurating the "Congress System" (1815–1823), the ancestor of our modern system of international conferences. While this was definitely not the European federation imagined by Saint-Pierre, it did aim at replacing "the principle of equilibrium, or more accurately of counterweights formed by separate alliances which . . . had too often troubled and bloodied Europe [by] a principle of general union" (Gentz [1818] 1876: 354–55). And it did so to the accompaniment of a profusion of celebratory cultural forms, from balls and fireworks to paintings and works by composers from Beethoven to Rossini (Cavazzocca Mazzanti 1923; Fuchs 2002; Even and Nathan 2015). The Vienna order saw the culmination of idiomatically Enlightened debates on peace, as well as their fusion with artistic expressions of peace as both ideal and practice. It is here that we really find the cultural origins of the modern conceptions of peace.

CHAPTER ONE

Definitions of Peace

ANTHONY PAGDEN

"War," declared the liberal jurist, sociologist, and anthropologist, Henry Sumner Maine in 1888 on looking back over two centuries of international law and seventeen of peace within Europe, "appears to be as old as mankind, but peace is a modern invention" (Maine 1888: 7). Maine was perhaps being unduly pessimistic. Peace may indeed have been rare in the ancient world; but it was certainly not unknown, nor were its virtues unrecognized. The ancient Greek goddess *Eirene*, who stood together with her sisters "Observance of the Laws" and "Justice," for the regulated, orderly resolution of human conflict, was peace personified. The Roman god *Pax*, although rarely heard of before the reign of the emperor Augustus, symbolized all that the Roman Empire claimed to bring to the world. But what Maine understood by "peace," although it certainly involved both justice and the observance of laws, was not the interludes of tranquility experienced by ancient societies, neither was it the unstable harmony created and sustained by the Roman legions. Eirene was also the goddess of spring, and in the ancient world late spring was the campaigning season. Peace and war were therefore symbolically inseparable. Even the celebrated *Pax deorum*, the harmonious relationships between gods and men, was only transitorily preserved by elaborate sacrifices whose outcome was always at best uncertain. Similarly, the famous, and elusive, *Pax romana* was not so much a peace as an absence of war sustained by the ever-present threat of war; and it was only ever understood as synonymous with the Roman Empire. When that disintegrated it vanished altogether. For centuries what had gone under the name of "peace" remarked Gottfried Wilhelm Leibniz in 1693, "is nothing else than the breathing-space of two gladiators" (*Codex iuris gentium* in Leibniz 1988: 166).

FIGURE 1.1: Henry Sumner Maine (1822–1888). Hulton Archive, Stringer. Getty Images.

Throughout the Middle Ages, the petty kingdoms of Western Europe fought incessant wars with each other (and with the encroaching forces of Islam). These could be devastating but they were rarely more than local. The Reformation, and the Wars of Religion that it unleashed across the whole of Europe from the mid-sixteenth to the mid-seventeenth century, changed all that into a virtually incessant, almost global, conflagration. The most devastating of these conflicts, now known as the Thirty Years' War, from 1618 until 1648, raged across the whole of central and eastern Europe drawing into its maw, at one time or another, all the major states of the continent from Spain to Sweden. The huge armies that it created left behind them vast tracts of the continent in smoldering ruins. The death toll has been calculated at 5.75 million, which, expressed as a percentage of the world's population, is considerably greater than that of the First World War (Pinker 2011: 142). Millions more perished from famine and disease. When it was finally over, a third of the population of central Europe was dead. "Is it the history of snakes and tigers which I have just written?" asked Voltaire in astonishment on rereading his own description of all this butchery: "No, it is that of men. Tigers and snakes do not treat their own kind in that manner" (quoted in Hazard 1963: 395).

In 1648 an agreement between the various representatives of over two hundred political entities of one kind or another, was finally reached in the north-eastern German province of Westphalia. This did not result in a single agreement, but in two separate multilateral treaties (that of Münster signed in January 30 and Osnabrück in October 24); nor did it bring an immediate end to the war (the fighting in Germany alone dragged on

FIGURE 1.2: Eirene, Goddess of Peace. PHAS, Contributor. Getty Images.

for another nine years). But the "Peace of Westphalia," as it has come to be known, marked a new beginning in inter-state relations in Europe. It was the first truly international gathering of European states. It was the first formally to recognize the existence of two new states: the United Netherlands which had, in effect, established its independence from Spain forty years earlier, and the Swiss Confederation, which now became a sovereign republic, independent of the Habsburg Empire; it also banished religion as a cause for any future conflict. Henceforth the sovereigns of Europe would decide how their subjects worshipped and no longer would European nations go to war because they disagreed over their understanding of God's intentions for mankind. Most importantly, Westphalia was the first agreement between sovereign nations that aimed to create not another "breathing space of two gladiators" but, in the terms used by both treaties, to secure "a Christian universal, perpetual peace and friendship" between both Catholics and the various kinds of Protestant, for the "glory of God and the security of Christendom." The key term here was "perpetual," and in the attempt to create the necessary conditions for perpetual peace, Westphalia was responsible for raising the possibility (if nothing more) of what in 1802, Friedrich von Gentz, Prussian litterateur, Burke's translator, former pupil of Kant and colleague of the Austrian statesman Prince Klemens von Metternich, called variously the "federal constitution of Europe," the "general union," and the "European League" (Gentz 1802: 11–15).[1] Gentz recognized that, even if Westphalia had not resulted in any "solid foundation for a public law of Europe," it had given to the word "peace" a new meaning. No longer would it be thought of in terms of the end of one particular conflict, but as the end of all conflict.

To make this a reality, however, it would not be sufficient simply to re-order the balance of powers within Europe, as Westphalia had in effect done. It would not even be sufficient to establish, as Gentz had claimed it had, a new and regulated system of diplomatic relationships, governed, at least in theory, by a new system of "international law." True, it could be argued that these had prevented a recurrence, at least before the outbreak of the Napoleonic Wars in 1799, of the kind of wholesale conflagration the Thirty Years' War had been. But Westphalia had certainly not eliminated war as such. A true—which could only mean a perpetual—peace could not be achieved solely through treaties, or even by means of the minimally successful "balance of powers," both of which assumed that sooner or later war would begin again. As the Swiss eighteenth-century diplomat Emer de Vattel pointed out, most states, even in the commercially orientated world of the late eighteenth century, had a very restricted sense of what "peace," and in particular "perpetual peace," was intended to mean. In most peace treaties, he commented wryly

> ... the contracting parties reciprocally engage to preserve *perpetual peace:* which is not to be understood as if they promised never to make war on each other for any cause whatever. The peace in question relates to the war which it terminates: and it is in reality perpetual, inasmuch as it does not allow them to revive the same war by taking up arms again for the same subject which had originally given birth to it.
> —Vattel 2008: 438

A truly perpetual peace, one that aimed at putting an end not to a war but to warfare as such, could only be brought about through a lasting legal and political association between the various states of Europe, and subsequently, for the most ambitious and hopeful (such as Kant), the entire world (Ghervas 2017: 410–12). If "peace" in the Enlightenment had any meaning it could not be extricated, and it could be argued has not been extricated since, from the idea of some kind of European, and subsequently global, union.

This, however, supposed that a condition of perpetual peace was indeed a realizable human goal. That belief derived from an assumption, which had been a commonplace since at least Aristotle, that for humans, unlike other animals, peace was a final cause, and that warfare could only ever be an extreme measure to repair a disruption of the natural, and for the Christian, God-directed order. "War," protested the Dutch humanist Desiderius Erasmus in 1517, "was not a necessary part of the natural or divine order." It was merely a means, in an as yet humanly imperfect, but perfectible world, to an end. Indeed, he wrote, "Nature taught mankind to seek peace, and ensure it. She invites them to it by various allurements, she draws them to it by gentle violence, she compels them to it by the strong arm of necessity." (Erasmus [1517] 1917: 8). One of the consequences, however, of the religious struggles that swept through Europe during the sixteenth and seventeenth centuries, was that many had come to the dismal conclusion that this could only ever be, at best, a pious illusion. Conflict for humans, as for most other animals, was the norm, peace merely a hard-won interlude between hostilities. The most powerful and influential proponent of this view was, of course, Thomas Hobbes. The natural state of man for Hobbes was famously one of "that condition which is called war, and such a war as is of every man against every man" (Hobbes [1651] 1996: 82). Peace was highly desirable, which is why men were prepared to surrender their right to governing themselves exactly as they wished, so as "to live peaceably among themselves"; but it remained always an artificial condition brought about by a collective act of will. And of course, could it be dissolved at any time.

In the relative calm that followed the end of the Thirty Years' War, however, the Hobbesian view of the condition of humanity as locked in a condition of perpetual conflict, restrained only by formal covenant, which had itself to be enforced by the sword, came to seem unduly bleak. Most of the prominent natural-law theorists of the late seventeenth and eighteenth centuries were overwhelmingly concerned with the urgent need to find a remedy for what they generally saw as the unnatural condition of incessant human conflict. The only way to achieve this, they believed, was through a new and theoretically robust account of the "law of nations." And to do this they had to offer a re-invigorated account of human sociability that Hobbes had largely dismissed as a fantasy of the despised "Schoolmen." Samuel Pufendorf, Christian Wolff, and Emer de Vattel, while fully accepting Hobbes' basic view of sociability as a response to human needs, rather than an innate desire, also rejected the supposition that it had arisen exclusively as a means of controlling the perpetual war "of all against all." Most would have agreed, on this at least, with Jean-Jacques Rousseau that "man is naturally peaceful and fearful, faced with the slightest danger his first instinct is to flee." ("Que l'état de guerre nait de l'état social" [1760], Rousseau 1964: 601). Only when flight was no longer an option did humans resort to violence. Certainly bellicosity, irascibility, and conflict between individuals were as natural to the human as they were to any other animal. But this was always a private matter. True warfare was of a different order. It was public. It was organized, involved multiple agents, fueled collective as well as individual passions and was invariably sustained even when the initial cause had passed. Only "the disposition reduced to action" as Rousseau phrased it, to destroy the enemy state "or at least to weaken it by every means possible" was "warfare properly speaking." ("Que l'état de guerre nait de l'état social" [1760], in Rousseau 1964: 607). And this was clearly an unnatural condition. "If by the "natural state of man," wrote Vattel, in repudiation of Hobbes, "we understand (as reason requires that we should) that state to which he is destined and called by his nature, peace should... be termed his natural state" (Vattel 2008: 651). For Vattel as for Rousseau, warfare, public warfare, was not an expression of human nature. It was rather a consequence of mankind's decision to abandon his natural condition of lawlessness and to create another: the state. For Hobbes, of course, it followed that the relationship between states mirrored, if not precisely then in most significant respects, that which had once existed between individuals in the state of nature.[2] For the natural-law theorists of the eighteenth century this, too, offered an unacceptably irredeemable image of the human condition. If man had been truly, if admittedly only minimally, sociable in the state of nature, then surely that quality—which Pufendorf had dubbed *socialitas*—as a property of his being could not be erased when he entered civil society.

One of the most influential proponents of this view, was Christian Wolff (1679–1754), professor of mathematics and "natural philosophy" at the University of Halle, in the German state of Brandenburg-Prussia, known to his contemporaries as "our German Newton." For Wolff it was inconceivable, without the presence of an effective pre-civil bond between persons—what in the eighteenth century went under the name of "sympathy" and we would call "empathy"—that individuals in the state of nature would have been able to create societies in the first place. In politics, as in ethics, we must all, he insisted, look upon others "as if they were one person with us" if for no other reason than that our very survival depends upon it.[3] In Wolff's view, Hobbes' account of the origins of society was so absurdly limited as to resemble a satire on the human condition. The creation of nations, although in itself purely an act of human volition (on this at least Hobbes was right), must have been dictated by some kind of natural instinct—there being nothing else on which it could have been based. The relationship between nations, therefore, could only be the outcome of the same affective bonds, the same moral obligations—the same level of benevolence—as had once existed between individuals. If every individual treated all others "as if they were one person with us," then it was clear that "every nation owes to every other nation that which it owes to itself." From this Wolff argued that "society, which nature has established among individuals, still exists among nations, and consequently, after states have been established in accordance with the law of nature, and nations have arisen thereby, nature herself also must be said to have established society among all nations and bound them to preserve society." And if this were true, then it could only be an absurdity to suppose that the emergence of mankind from the state of nature and the creation of "particular societies" had done away with "that great society which nature has established among men." For "just as in the human body individual organs do not cease to be organs of the whole human body, because certain ones taken together constitute one organ; so likewise individual men do not cease to be members of that great society which is made up of the whole human race, because several have formed together a certain particular society" (Wolff [1749] 1934: II, 11).[4]

Now, if we assume this analogy to hold true, then it must follow that, just as individual communities are able to constitute themselves as states, so humanity as a whole must also possess the ability to constitute itself as something that at least resembles a state. This is, in part, a continuation of the Stoic ideal of what Cicero had called the "republic of all the world"—a shadowy congregation of persons, united only by reason and a shared humanity. Wolff, however, grafted onto this a far more ambitious project for what he called the *civitas maxima*, or "Supreme State": a society or commonwealth based upon the consent of all persons everywhere, "as if they had signed a contract." What exact constitutional shape this mega-state would take Wolff does not say, although he does equip it with a ruler—or "rector"—whose task is to impose "what nations ought to consider as law amongst themselves." For all that it was, as Wolff freely admitted, a "legal fiction," he insisted that

FIGURE 1.3: Christian Wolff (1679–1754). Deutsches Historiches Museum, Berlin, Germany (DHM). Bridgeman Images.

the *possibility* of such a *civitas maxima* was the only possible guarantor of a perpetual peace among all the nations of mankind.[5] Like all legal fictions, it acted as a model towards which all the future would-be architects of world peace could work.

Vattel had begun work on his *The Law of Nations or Principles of the Law of Nature, applied to the Conduct and Affairs of Nations and Sovereigns* (1758), which was to become the most widely used work on the subject during the eighteenth century, by attempting to synthesize Wolff's findings on the natural law. But he soon found both Wolff's style ("in the manner and even the formal method of geometrical works") and many of his conclusions unpalatable. He particularly disliked "the idea of a great republic instituted by nature herself," whose hypothetical laws would constitute the "voluntary laws of nature." The origins of any such *civitas maxima*, he argued, could not possibly be found in a rule of nature, since human societies were, it was now universally accepted, purely artificial creations. And although "nature has indeed established a general society between man . . . yet she has not imposed on them any particular obligation to unite in civil society so called" (Vattel 2008: 14). But if the *civitas maxima* did not exist in nature, and could not plausibly exist even as the kind of heuristic legal fiction Wolff claimed for it, nature had certainly equipped men with the necessary inclinations to create something analogous, if on far lesser scale, for themselves. The closest, however, it had come to this in practice was Europe, which now

> ... forms a political system, an integral body, closely connected by the relations and different interests of the nations inhabiting this part of the world. It is not, as formerly, a confused heap of detached pieces, each of which thought herself very little concerned in the fate of the others, and seldom regarded things which did not immediately concern her. The continual attention of sovereigns to every occurrence, the constant residence of ministers, and the perpetual negotiations, make of modern Europe a kind of republic, of which the members—each independent, but all linked together by the ties of common interest—unite for the maintenance of order and liberty.
>
> —Vattel 2008: 311–12

The problem with Vattel's irenic vision, however, was that Europe had singularly failed to maintain "order and liberty" and that it was in fact very far from being a "kind of republic," if for no other reason that it had no constitution or laws as such. All that restrained the rulers of the individual states of which it was composed from going to war with one another was the always precarious "balance of power."

Ever since the fifteenth century there had been numerous projects for overcoming this problem, by transforming Europe if not quite into a kind of republic, then at least into some kind of union of states capable of bringing perpetual peace to the continent. (The most significant, and most often cited, was the so-called *Grand Design* written sometime between 1610 and 1641, by the duc de Sully who had been Henri IV of France's minister of finance—with possibly some input from the king himself—for a "High Christian Republic.") Such projects varied from the minimally practicable—alliances of existing states against the common enemy, the Ottoman Empire—to the outlandishly utopian. Throughout the eighteenth and nineteenth centuries they became a veritable and enduring literary genre coming, perhaps, to somewhat ignominious end in H. G. Wells' *The Shape of Things to Come* (1933).[6] The most lastingly influential of these was *A Project for Establishing a Perpetual Everlasting Peace in Europe*, published in 1713, by Charles-Irénée Castel, Abbé de Saint-Pierre, a diplomat who had been a negotiator of the Treaty of Utrecht in 1712–13 and the author of plans for a graded tax system—virtually unthinkable in the early eighteenth century—and for free education for all, both men and women (Ghervas 2014a, 2017). The *Project* attracted a wide, if not always sympathetic readership. Voltaire dismissed it as "a chimera which could no more exist among princes than it could among elephants and rhinoceroses, or wolves and dogs" (Voltaire 1770: 2). Leibniz, ironical as ever, remarked that it reminded him of a "device in a cemetery with the words: *Pax perpetua* [perpetual peace]; for the dead do not fight any longer: but the living are of another humour; and the most powerful do not respect tribunals at all." ("On the Works of the Abbé de St. Pierre," Leibniz 1988: 183). But for all the sarcasm heaped upon it, it is a measure of its influence, and its widespread diffusion, that the likes of Voltaire, Leibniz, Rousseau—and as we shall shortly see, Kant—took so much trouble over it. Most of the other such projects came and went with hardly a mention (Ghervas 2014a: 57–62; Mori 2004: 23–25).

As they were currently constituted, the sovereign powers of Europe, were, Saint-Pierre had acidly observed, no different from "the little kings of Africa, the unhappy Caciques, or the little sovereigns of America." And so they would remain, as long there existed among them nothing that could be described as a "sufficiently powerful and permanent society" (Saint-Pierre [1713] 1986: 22–24). The closest they had come to this was the Swiss Federation or the States of the Netherlands; but neither of these had had sufficient reach to ensure any kind of lasting peace. The "Permanent state" would have to include all of

Europe. Any attempt, however, to subsume Europe under one single power (as many previous peace projects had, in effect, suggested) would be both tyrannical in theory and impossible to achieve in practice. The *Project* envisaged instead a superstate composed of the existing European nations combining modern notions of state sovereignty with the kind of federative structure that already existed in the German territories and in the republics of Switzerland and the Netherlands. Together they would be ruled not by a single sovereign but by a council, or diet, on which the princes of every member state would sit (a kind of precursor to the European Council). This, Saint-Pierre believed, would eliminate warfare from the continent forever, bring the greatest happiness to the greatest number and finally demonstrate to princes that their true interests lay not in conflict but in what he called *bienfaisance*, or "beneficence" (a word he seems to have coined, and which Rousseau eagerly adopted).

There are, of course, serious problems with the *Project*, as its detractors were quick to point out. Like all previous proposals it hoped to be able to bring about a radical transformation of the political landscape of Europe without changing, to any significant degree, the constitution of the individual states of which Saint-Pierre's "Permanent society" was to be composed. As Leibniz phrased it, in a world "which would conform to his project, complaints against the sovereign would not be allowed" ("On the Works of the Abbé de St. Pierre," in Leibniz 1988: 181); or, as the pioneer socialist Henri de Saint-Simon was to say later in the early nineteenth century, and rather more emphatically, Saint-Pierre's "Permanent society" would simply have perpetuated the existing political system in Europe as it currently existed. "The remnants of the feudal order which still survived would have become indestructible," he complained, and the people would therefore have been deprived "of every resource against tyranny" (Saint-Simon [1814] 1925, 24–25). In short it, too, would end up by becoming some kind of empire.

Jean-Jacques Rousseau, who in 1760 wrote a brief "Judgment" on the works of Saint-Pierre, came to the conclusion that the "high opinion" which the Abbé had had of "modern understanding, had led him to adopt the false principle of perfectible reason." The kind of federation of states Saint-Pierre had devised would require a situation in which "the sum of particular interests did not overpower the common interest and that each one sees in the good of all, the greatest good which he could hope for himself." But he doubted that a federation would, in fact, have this effect. Historically, as he pointed out, most had been created not for the purposes of war not peace ("Jugement sur le projet de paix perpétuelle," in Rousseau 1964: 594–95). He also questioned whether in fact such a radical re-organization of the existing state system could possibly be achieved through harmonious agreement, as Saint-Pierre had supposed. In his view, the only possible way to bring it about would be "by means that would be violent and dreadful for humanity" which meant in effect, by a revolution. And if that were the case, then, "who among us would dare to say whether the European League were more to be feared than desired?" ("Jugement sur le projet de paix perpétuelle," in Rousseau 1964: 600).

It was hard to escape the force of Rousseau's objection. Most of Saint-Pierre's contemporaries, however placed their hopes as many have done since, not on revolution, but on the supposedly beneficial consequences of that eighteenth-century panacea for all political ills: international commerce. In the eighteenth century, the term "commerce" still retained its original sense of exchange and reciprocity. "Commerce" explained the economist, Victor Riquetti, marquis de Mirabeau in 1758 was "the relationship (*rapport*), useful and necessary between all sociable beings with their own kind" (Mirabeau 1756: I, 5).

The act of exchange, it was supposed, inevitably brought human beings into contact with one another, and in so doing erased, or at least softened, the prejudices and misunderstandings that were so often the initial cause for war. Commerce, Montesquieu had argued in 1748, in what was to become the most often-repeated tribute to the potential of the new trading networks growing up in the eighteenth century, not only enriched all who participated in it; it also possessed the power to cure "destructive prejudices; and it is almost a general rule, that wherever the customs are gentle [*douce*] there is commerce; and wherever there is commerce, customs are gentle" (Montesquieu 1989: XX, 1).[7]

Looking back in 1813 over a Europe laid waste by the Napoleonic Wars, which commerce had, in fact, done little to ameliorate, the Swiss politician, liberal political theorist, novelist, and man of letters, Benjamin Constant (1767–1830), observed that the modern subject, unlike his ancient counterpart, lived in societies that were large and complex, and relatively secure. The peoples of modern Europe (at least) who now had no lingering fear of barbarian hordes massed on their borders, were now, he believed, despite Napoleon, "sufficiently civilized to find war a burden." For this reason, and despite the fact that a truly *perpetual* peace might yet be some way off, the "uniform tendency is towards peace" ("The Liberty of the Ancients compared with that of the Moderns" [1819]: Constant 1988: 312). The "sole aim of modern nations," was therefore, he believed, "repose and with repose, comfort and as the source of comfort, industry." War, he added with nice irony, "Has lost its charm as well as its utility. Man is no longer driven to it either by interest or by passion."

FIGURE 1.4: Benjamin Constant (1767–1830). Musée Carnavalet, Paris, France. Bridgeman Images.

What for Constant divided the ancient from the modern world was, as it had been for Montesquieu, commerce. In Constant's view, however, commerce had replaced warfare not because it was benign or because it could "make men gentle." Like Thomas Hobbes, another survivor from a bitter civil conflict, Constant did not believe that human nature could be improved. It could only be reasoned with and manipulated. Commerce and warfare, he believed, "are only two different means to achieve the same end, that of possessing what is desired." Commerce had not transformed the customs of peoples; it had instead altered the *means* by which humans now calculated their interests. "Commerce," Constant wrote,

> is simply a tribute paid to the strength of the possessor by the aspirant to possession. It is an attempt to obtain by mutual agreement what one can no longer hope to obtain through violence. . . . War, then, comes before commerce. The former is all savage impulse, the latter civilized calculation. It is clear that the more the commercial spirit (*tendance*) dominates the weaker the martial spirit becomes.
> —"The Liberty of the Ancients compared with that of the Moderns" [1819]: Constant, 1988: 54

This modern world, large, diverse, and plural, but also united in its interests and in its recognition of what is of real value to the individual, could simply have no further interest in pursuing its objectives by any other means than managed reciprocity. And for that to be possible the world had to be at peace. Commerce, he went on, "has modified the very nature of war. In the past commercial nations were always defeated by their bellicose enemies. Today they can successfully resist them. They find support even among their enemies." Had the war between Rome, the warrior nation, and Carthage, the polite commercial nation, been fought at the beginning of the nineteenth century instead of in the second and third centuries BCE, it would, he argued, have been Carthage who would have won: "Carthage would have the hopes of the entire world on her side; the customs of today and the spirit of the times would be her allies" ("The Liberty of the Ancients compared with that of the Moderns" [1819]: Constant, 1988: 54).

The modern transition from warfare to commerce, by altering the ways in which goods were acquired, had also inevitably changed the very nature of the goods themselves. In antiquity men had sought glory and despised luxury. Now the positions were reversed. "Our century," wrote Constant, "which values everything according to its utility, and, as soon as one attempts to move out of this sphere opposes its irony to every real or feigned enthusiasm, could not content itself with a sterile glory, which we are no longer in the habit of preferring to other kinds." (*The Spirit of Conquest and Usurpation and their Relation to European Civilization* [1814]: Constant, 1988: 53–55).

Making a thinly-veiled allusion to Napoleon—that "man from another world"—Constant wondered what a modern people would have to say to the likes of Cambyses, Alexander, or Attila. Most probably, and most appropriately, it would be: "Like the leopard you belong to another climate, to another land, to another species from our own. Learn civilization, if you wish to reign in a civilized age. Learn peace if you wish to rule over peaceful peoples." (*The Spirit of Conquest and Usurpation and their Relation to European Civilization*, [1814]: Constant 1988: 83). From this it followed, he told the members of the Athénée Royal in 1819, with the last would-be world conqueror now safely out of the way, "that an age must come in which commerce replaces war. We have reached this age." ("The Liberty of the Ancients compared with that of the Moderns" [1819]: Constant 1988: 312).

Constant was drawing upon almost a century of generally up-beat reflections on the pacifying properties of commercial exchange. But not all the major figures of the enlightenment had been prepared to put so much trust in the long-term properties of commerce. David Hume, for one had famously insisted that what he called "the jealousy of trade," that "narrow and malignant opinion" rather than drawn the otherwise bellicose peoples of the world together in a happy exchange of goods and opinions had, in reality, only led all those states that had made "some advances in commerce. . . to look on the progress of their neighbors with a suspicious eye, to consider all trading nations as their rivals, and to suppose that it is impossible for them to flourish, but at their expense" ("Of the Jealousy of Trade" [1759] in Hume 1994e: 327–28). Furthermore, as Rousseau had argued against Saint-Pierre, "princes" did not necessarily see any conflict between "commerce," expressed as wealth and "empire." Since every prince "wishes to command in order to enrich himself and enriches himself in order to command," he required both ("Jugement sur le projet de paix perpétuelle," in Rousseau [1760] 1964: 594). Honor and embarrassment, not the rational calculation of interests, private or public, wrote the Dutch physician, Bernard Mandeville in 1723, had always been the prime motives for war. Even in the "age of enlightenment" nations sought for the first and feared the latter as surely as they had in the less enlightened past; when it came to privileging "commerce" over "empire" empire was always likely to win.

It was not, however, only the calculation of the interests of individuals that the rise of the international commercial society had changed. Even if it were not especially *doux*, commerce, since it depends upon "the good understanding of nations with each other," could in Constant's view, "be sustained only by justice; it is founded upon equality; it thrives in peace."[8] Like Montesquieu, he also believed that it had been responsible for creating a broadly global culture. It had "brought nations closer together and has given them virtually identical customs and habits." Monarchs, he added optimistically, "may still be enemies, but peoples are compatriots" ("Des réactions politiques": in Constant 1998: 493).

No matter how uncertain its pacifying properties might eventually turn out to be, all were agreed that commerce had indubitably created a far more interconnected, interdependent world than had existed in the past. It was a world in which even monarchs had to think far more carefully than they had about the consequences of their actions. "A war among commercial nations is a fire that destroys them all," wrote Diderot in one of the passages which he inserted into the Abbé Guillaume-Thomas-François Raynal's best-selling *History of the Two Indies* (1780), "The time is not far off when the sanctions of rulers will extend to the individual transactions between the subjects of different nations, and when bankruptcy, whose impact may be felt at such immense distances, will become affairs of state. . . and the annals of all peoples will need to be written by commercial philosophers as they were once written by historical orators." (Diderot 1994: 689).

This very interdependence, however, also had its dangers. Trade wars, unlike territorial conflicts would inevitably come to involve nations that might have no immediate stake in their outcome. Far from encouraging a universal and perpetual peace, as the proponents of "sweet commerce" anticipated, a globalized commercial world could just as easily lead to the creation of universal state of emergency. "Experience," Vattel had written in a more somber tone in 1757,

> shews what a train of calamities war entails even upon nations that are not immediately engaged in it. War disturbs commerce, destroys the subsistence of mankind,

raises the price of all the most necessary articles, spreads just alarms, and obliges all nations to be upon their guard, and to keep up an armed force.

—Vattel 2008: 653–54

It followed, therefore, that any state which "without just cause breaks the general peace, unavoidably does an injury even to those nations which are not the objects of his arms; and by his pernicious example he essentially attacks the happiness and safety of every nation upon earth. He gives them a right to join in a general confederacy for the purpose of repressing and chastising him, and depriving him of a power which he so enormously abuses" (Vattel 2008: 653–54).

And even if it were the case that commerce made men sufficiently gentle, and more plausibly perhaps sufficiently interdependent to create the possible conditions for peace, this still could not determine how, much less when, such a peace could or would be brought about. The person who provided the most compelling answers to these questions, the one that was to have a lasting impact on all subsequent peace proposals from the Congress of Vienna to the creation of the United Nations, was Immanuel Kant.[9] Kant's best-known and most influential work on the subject was "Toward perpetual peace, a philosophical project" of 1795; but it is evident that he had been thinking since the mid-1780s about not merely the means to achieve a perpetual peace among humans, but also of peace itself as the highest objective of mankind, and continued to do so until his death in 1804.

Like most of the peace theorists of the period Kant was no pacifist. War might well be "the source of all evil and the corruption of morals" but it had had its uses (Kant [1798] 1992: 155). Not only had it been responsible for forcing humans to settle and cultivate the planet ("Towards perpetual peace," Kant 1996b: 333), it was also a means to an end, "a deep-seated, maybe far-seeing attempt on the part of supreme wisdom, if not to found, yet to prepare the way for a rule of law governing the freedom of states, and thus bring about their unity in a system established on a moral basis" (Kant, [1790] 1991: 96). If for Saint-Pierre and others the union of states—whatever form it might take—had been a means to secure perpetual peace, for Kant perpetual peace was a means to secure a union of states or, what he called, variously a "cosmopolitan whole," "a universal *cosmopolitan existence*," the fulfillment of a "cosmopolitan right." Of course once this cosmopolitan world order had been created it would continue to ensure a future and lasting peace, but for Kant this was far more than the simple conditions for safety and prosperity. It was to be nothing less than the final end of human existence, "the end . . . which nature has as its aim," and the "womb in which all original predispositions of the human species will be developed" ("Idea for a universal history with a cosmopolitan aim," Kant [1784] 1999b: s118).[10]

First, however, a lawful condition, one in which all the nations of the world would be able to exit from the state of nature just as individuals had once done, had to be brought about. How? Clearly not by means of any external law. The law of nations in which past generations had placed such hope, had, in Kant's view, been "simply an idea," and a useless one at that, because no legal code could possibly have any force in a world in which "states are not subject to a common external constraint" ("Towards perpetual peace," Kant 1996b: 326). Because there did not exist any such thing as an international court, and since *all* warfare must necessarily take place in a "lawless condition," the very concept of a *law* (*Gesetz*)—or right—of war would, he claimed, seem to be so inherently meaningless, that "it is difficult even to form a concept of this or to think of law in this lawless state without contradicting oneself." (*Metaphysics of Morals*, Kant [1797] 1996b: 485). All that the law of nations demonstrated was that each human being possess the "moral disposition" required to overcome the "evil principle within him" ("Towards perpetual peace," Kant 1996b: 327).

Encouraging though this might be, it did nothing to set limits on the condition of war that existed between states as they were currently constituted. The only contracts that had ever existed between sovereign bodies rather than individuals, were treaties, or ceasefires, and these had only ever put an end to a "current war . . . but not a condition of war, of always finding pretexts for a new war" ("Towards perpetual peace," Kant 1999b: 356). And if a law of nations, however conceived, could not secure any kind of real peace neither could the much-vaunted balance of powers, in which, in the end Vattel had put his best hopes. The quest, said Kant, for a "an enduring universal peace by means of the so-called *balance of powers*" was a "mere fantasy, like [Jonathan] Swift's house that the builder had constructed in such perfect accord with all the laws of equilibrium that it collapsed as soon as sparrow alighted on it" ("On the common saying: that it may be correct in theory but is of no use in practice," Kant [1793] 1999b: 309).

For Kant, too, commerce—or the *right* to commerce—played a crucial role in creating the possible conditions for peaceful interactions between peoples. All nations, he wrote in the *Metaphysics of Morals* "stand... in a community of possible physical interaction (*commercium*), that is in a thoroughgoing relation of each to all the others of offering to engage in commerce with any other; and each has a right to make this attempt." (Kant [1797] 1999b: 489). But this could only ever be a condition of possibility. On its own it could achieve nothing. (He was also highly suspicious of the increasing association between commerce and colonialism, and thus with the ever-present threat of universal monarchy.[11])

If none of the panaceas in which past generations had pinned their hopes could possibly be made to work in any real-world situation, what could? Kant's answer, was to insist that no union of nations could be brought about unless all its members had the same system of government. None of the jurists whom he had famously dubbed "the sorry comforters of mankind," or the authors of the various peace proposals that had preceded his, recognized that the success of their plans might depend upon the nature of the constitutions of the states involved. Only Sully's *Grand Design* seemed to have recognized the problem, by grouping them according to regime type—hereditary monarchies, elective monarchies and republics—and thereby showed an awareness that there were any significant constitutional differences. But this too amounted to little more than a reliance on another version of the "balance of powers," and as Vattel remarked it could never have been put into practice without "injustice and violence" nor maintained by lawful means. "Commerce, industry, military pre-eminence would soon [have] put an end to it." (Vattel 2008: 497).

Furthermore, for Kant, it would not be sufficient for all nations to live simply under the same kind of regime—they would all have to live under one particular kind of regime: what he called a "representative republic." By this he did not mean a "democracy"—at least in the ancient sense of the term—nor even a state with a republican constitution as such. (In general he believed that monarchs made better, more efficient representatives than elected assemblies.)[12] What he meant was simply a society in which no individual should be constrained by any external—that is, purely human—law other than those to which he *could* have given his consent. ("Towards perpetual peace," Kant 1999b: 327) This would make of all citizens "co-legislating members of a state (not merely as means but also as ends in themselves)" (*Metaphysics of Morals*, Kant [1797] 1999b: 484). Only under these conditions would it be possible to give "complete justice to the rights of man." This was not, he insisted, in itself a moral principle (although its fulfillment would have clear moral consequences). It required only rational calculation and what he called the "mechanism of nature," which would balance out the conflicts that always arose between individuals without eradicating the naturally "self-seeking energies" of the human ("Towards Perpetual Peace," Kant 1996b: s366). It could therefore be as easily the creation of a "nation of devils" (assuming devils to be, like most men, rational self-interested creatures) as human beings.

Under such a constitution of society a man, "even if he is not good in himself . . . [is] nevertheless compelled to be a good citizen." A republic is also the only form of government that "offers a prospect of attaining the desired result, i.e. Perpetual Peace," since only under such circumstances would citizens be in a position to "give their free assent, through their representatives, not only to the waging of war in general, but also to each particular declaration of war." (*Metaphysics of Morals*, Kant [1797] 1999b: 484) Great powers, Kant observed, are "never shamed before the judgment of the masses, but only before one another." In a representative republic, however, it is these common masses (or at least their representatives) who have to decide whether to declare war or not, and since their honor is not at stake they have nothing to be ashamed of in front of other powers, great or small ("Towards Perpetual Peace," Kant 1996b: 342). For them, going to war inevitably means not only "taking upon themselves all the hardships of war" but, "to make the cup of troubles overflow," also, once the war is over, assuming the "burden of debt that embitters peace itself, and that can never be paid off because of new wars always impending" ("Towards Perpetual Peace," Kant 1996b: 351). Clearly if they are rational beings, diabolical or otherwise, they are only likely to do that if they are certain there can be no solution other than war. Little wonder that Kant has been hailed, as the ancestor of "democratic peace theory," the hopeful notion that liberal democracies—the nearest modern equivalent to his "representative republics"—do not wage war upon each other.[13]

From this it followed that once the generally despotic, authoritarian monarchies of the late eighteenth century had been transformed into representative republics, they would acquire a moral obligation to unite together, to create "a league of a special kind which can be called a *pacific league (foedus pacificum)*" ("Towards Perpetual Peace," Kant 1996b: 327) For without what he calls this "*cosmopolitan* whole," and "with the obstacle that ambition, love of power and avarice, especially on the part of those who hold the reins of authority, put in the way even of the possibility of such a scheme, *war* is inevitable" (Kant [1790] 1991: 96). Kant changed his mind frequently as to exactly what form this "pacific league" would take from a full "league of peoples," "an international state," a "universal union of states," a federation, to a confederation, and a partnership. By 1797, however, he had come to the conclusion that it could only be "a voluntary coalition of different states which can be dissolved at any time not a federation (like that of the American states which is based on a constitution and therefore cannot be dissolved)" (*Metaphysics of Morals*, Kant 1996b: 488).[14] Kant, it would seem, became increasingly concerned, as the French Revolution unfolded, to avoid the pitfalls into which so many previous proposals for some kind of European federation had fallen and would fall—that one state comes to dominate all others, thus transforming a federation into an empire. This, as Kant would have been well aware was the fate that had befallen the Delian League, founded in 477 BCE with the objective of protecting all of Hellas from Persia but which had rapidly become the Athenian Empire. It has, of course, been the fear that has dogged most federal unions, and in the charges so often leveled against the EU by its enemies, dogs them still.[15]

But no matter how uncertain its final political form might be this cosmopolitan union remained a condition of future time. Kant believed that people had mocked Saint-Pierre and (as he seems to have read him) Rousseau, "only because they believed its execution was too near" ("Idea for a Universal History with a Cosmopolitan Purpose," Kant [1784] 2007: 114). It was for this reason that he had insisted on the word "towards" (*zur*) in the title of his essay. But even if it was a "dream of perfection," an "archetype, in order to bring the legal constitution of mankind nearer to its greatest possible perfection" it should not, like all such ideas, be abandoned, as Kant had said of the Platonic republic, "under the very wretched and harmful pretext of its impracticability" (Kant 1998: 397).

We might not ever get there—in Kant's view we almost certainly would not. But we should always keep it before us as an objective, since for Kant, the very fact that we are able to *imagine* such a state makes it our duty "to work toward this (not merely chimerical) end." (Kant, "Towards perpetual peace", 1999b: 337) Certainly no heterogeneous group of peoples would ever be likely to act simultaneously. And like Rousseau, Kant had a general horror of revolution as means of political transformation, since it violated what he called that "law of continuity (*lex continuo*)," which is precisely what separates civil society from the lawless condition of the state of nature (*Metaphysics of Morals*, Kant 1999b: 480). It was example that would do the trick. Some one nation would have to show the way. And once "one powerful and enlightened people can form itself into a republic (which by its nature must be inclined to seek perpetual peace), this would provide a focal point of federative union for other states." It was not the threat or coercion, but imitation that would finally alter the political institutions of the world, since all humans, given enough time, are clearly able to see what will be of most benefit to them. Slowly thereafter all the states of the world would follow suit. All would become republics and, abandoning their "savage (lawless) freedom," would "accommodate themselves to public coercive laws, and so form an (always growing) state of nations (*civitas gentium*) that would finally encompass all the nations of the earth" ("Towards Perpetual Peace," Kant 1999b: 327–28)

No one would know, he reflected, just when and how it would happen if at all but we could take heart from the fact that "[e]ven one single example can be sufficient sign in the course of events that it [a republic constitution] must happen one day. One cannot foresee that it will be accomplished, but only that [men] will try it so often that it must eventually be realized." (*Reflexionen zur Rechtsphilosophie* in Kant 1902–19: 609). That was written in 1781. Eight years later, on 14 July 1789, that "single example" seemed finally to have manifested itself. On learning of the fall of the Bastille, Kant is said for the first time in his adult life to have abandoned his daily walk (he was a man of fixed habits) so that he could read every newspaper available, and when in 1792, he heard of the creation of the French Republic, he is said to have declared: "Lord let your servant depart in peace, for I have lived to see this remarkable day." Six years later, by which time the worst excesses of the Terror were over and France was stable, for the while at least, in the hands of the Directory, he wrote cautiously, in the last work he ever published: "The revolution of a gifted people which we have seen unfolding in our day may succeed or miscarry." It might, he conceded, in the end turn out to have been so costly, so "filled with misery and atrocities," that "a sensible man, were he boldly to hope to execute it successfully the second time, would never resolve to make the experiment at such a cost." But what mattered for Kant, what made the Revolution an outward indication of something far larger than itself, was the "wishful participation which borders closely on enthusiasm" that was to be found "in the hearts of all spectators" (*Metaphysics of Morals*, Kant [1798] 1992: 153–54).[16] This was a clear sign that sooner or later others would follow suit.

In the end, of course, whatever hopes the French Revolution might have aroused in those who lived through it, its aftermath turned out to be not the glimmerings of any future cosmopolitan order, but six long years of the most costly and devastating wars Europe had ever experienced. It was the precise inversion of what Kant had hoped for. "Representation"—as embodied in Napoleon—had led not to perpetual peace, but to total war. War, wrote the Prussian Carl von Clausewitz, after witnessing the destruction of his homeland at the battle of Jena in 1806, had now become "a war of all against all. It is not the King who wars on a king, not an army which wars on an army but a people which wars on another, and the king and army are contained in the people" (quoted in Bell 2007: 241).

Yet for all that, when it was over and the Great Powers assembled in Vienna in 1815 to create what Maine described as "a peace. . . which was as long as any which existed since Modern Europe" (Maine 1888: 8): they, too, placed their hopes, once again, in the idea of a political union. It was, nonetheless, one controlled exclusively by them, which Gentz described—over-optimistically, it is true—as "a true federative body, in which no member can be mutilated, wounded or poisoned without the harm penetrating more or less deeply into all the others" (quoted in Holbraad, 1970: 2). In the end, however, Europe would have to live through more than a century of what Maine dismissed airily as "intervals of petty local war" (Maine, 1888: 4) and then twenty-seven more of two devastating "civil wars," before anything quite like this would be achieved.[17]

CHAPTER TWO

Human Nature, Peace, and War

THEODORE CHRISTOV

Between the early seventeenth and early nineteenth centuries, major political thinkers conceived for the first time the possibility of a world of states, where a multitude of sovereign political bodies would eventually emerge from a former world of empires. The formation of early modern theories of the state occurred during a period in which the rights of persons—whether natural or artificial—to govern themselves were affirmed in the idea of autonomy. The sovereignty of the state was subsequently modeled after the autonomy of the individual: each arose from the need to provide protection and establish independence.[1] Through arguments about the inclinations of human nature, political thinkers theorized an international state of nature comprised of sovereign states as morally equivalent to autonomous persons: to many of them, the most meaningful way to understand the state—what provokes one to wage a war and what makes one seek peace—was to construct an analogy between persons and states.

Once instituted as an artificial person, a commonwealth, in Hobbes' fine language, "hath the same Right, in procuring the safety of his People, that any particular man can have, in procuring his own safety" (Hobbes [1651] 1991: 224). Commonwealths analogously take on the qualities and attributes of the natural individuals who comprised them in the first place: the intellectual move is always from the natural to the artificial person, rather than the other way around. To wish to describe the characteristics of pre-civil persons by way of transposing those of states back to the very individuals who originally constituted them would assume the very conclusion of the argument to be proven. The analogy between natural and artificial persons, while essential in its capacity to evoke the qualities and attributes of sovereign states from those of human beings, remains at the same time incomplete in its deficiency to make the reverse analogous move.

While the analogy helps characterize the domestic nature of the state, it also places the distinctly human inclination to the pursuit of peace, especially within the context of inter-state relations, at the very center of debates over the moral basis for international warfare. From Grotius, through Hobbes and Pufendorf, to Rousseau, Vattel and Kant, the relations between states instantiate the rights and duties of the individual writ large. The international domain of sovereigns without a sovereign above them all is empirically observable and manifests the interactions between autonomous agents, except on a much larger scale. These authors were all keenly aware that, while their arguments emerged in response to the calamities of internecine conflict and civil war, they also sought to solve the international state of nature, where states themselves take on the characteristics of self-defensive and fearful individuals. The absence of conflict outside contributes to the cultivation of peace at home.

The quest for peace, they observed, was not limited to the domestic sphere, but extended to the foreign domain as well: the symbiosis between "home" and "abroad" would naturally become a major preoccupation in the thought of early modern political thinkers. The idea that the international arena is itself a state of nature defined the development of the modern concept of the state, and Hobbes' view on the subject is generally drawn in its support and regarded as foundational. Artificial persons are analogous to natural persons: states stand in relation to one another parallel to how individuals act outside sovereignty, and, in the absence of a common superior to enforce the rules of conduct, war is the natural state of affairs. Hence the most viable political project is to pacify the state; the proliferation of tamed leviathans would, in turn, ameliorate the international arena. The close association between a state's domestic organization and how it conducts itself externally lies at the heart of the early modern history of peace: the construction of the commonwealth proceeds from the larger view of ameliorating the international domain by way of pacifying the domestic realm. A peaceful international order is best promoted through domestic peace.

As an intellectual creation central to the history of natural jurisprudence beginning with Hugo Grotius, the idea of the state of nature can be said to serve at least three distinct purposes: to alarm, by remaining vigilant in the face of a believable threat of an imminent civil war; to historicize, by providing an account of how most, though not all societies may have generally evolved; and to enable the human mind to derive the source of man's natural rights and duties. The specific use that Grotius makes of the analogy between persons and states is built upon their common absence of a superior. Drawing upon a "clear similarity" between a natural body and the "artificial body" of the state, in his *De Jure Belli ac Pacis*, Grotius relates persons and states in order to illuminate the character of their interaction (Grotius [1625] 2005: 667). Their autonomy can be conceptualized within the context of individual entities striving to preserve their existence in a world of no overarching authority. In this context, states relate to one another not merely as natural individuals outside sovereignty, but most of all, as interdependent entities whose interaction is guided by a set of general precepts of mutual respect and notions of right conduct in accordance with the law of nations.

In his earlier work *De Indis* (1609) (also known as *De Jure Praedae*), Grotius makes use of the analogy to make an argument about the nature of and necessity for state sovereignty in a world without a global sovereign. The prominent feature of the analogy is not only to make an analytical move from the more readily observable (inter-state interaction) to the more obscure (individual rights), but also to describe just how individual persons relate to one another outside the conditions of civil society and the establishment of authority. In this sense, the analogy serves not merely as a heuristic device intended to provide a more thorough account of the natural life of man, but also makes a claim to moral agency. Outside the artifice of sovereignty, natural persons are more than just hunting animals seeking their own survival at all costs and fulfilling their drive for self-preservation in a hostile and belligerent environment. They are also rights-bearing and autonomous individuals capable of exercising moral judgments. Chief among their natural rights is the right to self-preservation, generally, and self-defense from malicious and potentially deadly attack, specifically. Interpreted as a basic blameless right with a set of other rights that flow from it, the principle of self-preservation could be seen not only as a philosophical attack against the Skeptics.[2] It could also be viewed as a natural response to the political turmoil in which the Dutch people found themselves at the time, in the aftermath of their revolt against the Spanish monarchy.

The immediate context in which Grotius writes *De Indis* was in fact the Dutch revolt against the King of Spain: such a revolt was justified, he argues, on grounds of sovereignty since the United Provinces did represent the people. In light of the particular historical circumstances, then, it is hardly surprising that Grotius defended a strong conception of state sovereignty, so that he might properly justify the people's power of representation. The argument required a notion of sovereignty that would consequently carry over its force in constructing the rights-bearing autonomous individual. The most significant implication of Grotius' argument is the departure from previous political discourse and the assertion that, even in their natural state of no political authority, individuals are entitled to certain rights.

The three fundamental rights, which are argued analogously from those of sovereign states, are the right of dominium [*ius imperii*], the right of punishment [*ius gladii*], and the right to assert power over one's enemy [*ius victoriae*]. Since the state is the subject of civil dominium, the individual is similarly the bearer of natural dominium, whose character is loosely a primitive form of property rights.[3] The second of these rights—and one that can be viewed as an extension of the first—is the right of punishment. Because the natural right of dominium implies the need for protection of what is considered one's own, any threats of dispossession are seen as a "legitimate" means of doing so. Hence in its most radical claim, *ius gladii* "was held by private persons before it was held by the state" (Grotius [1609] 2006: 136).[4] Finally, to assert the *ius victoriae* is a fundamental right of a state to assert its strength in subjecting weaker states to domination as prescribed by the right of conquest. If individuals can reduce each other to subjection, Grotius argues, then it should not be surprising that states can do the same, "whether that Subjection be merely Civil, merely despotical or mixt" (Grotius [1625] 2005: III, 1374).

Once victory of the stronger over the weaker becomes the basis for dominion and a legitimate means of establishing territorial entities, disputes can be settled only by the laws of war. Indeed, Grotius goes so far as to argue that the right of conquest extends to the conqueror-king's complete subjection of the defeated state by establishing absolute, rather than limited sovereignty over it. "But sovereignty may be acquired by Conquest, either so far as it was in the King, or another Governor, and then all the Power he had passes to the Conqueror, and no more." Patrimonial kingdoms get established thereby, so that "the Conqueror has the same Right to alienate it [sovereignty] as the People had" (Grotius [1625] 2005: III, 1376–77). Similarly, a stronger individual outside sovereignty (or one who has allied with others in acquiring greater strength) has all the means at one's disposal to subdue the weaker and would not be blamed for doing so. The immediate implication of the right of conquest for man in the natural condition is that, in its relations with other states, a state may rightly and blamelessly engage in war to reduce other states to subjection. The radicalism of Grotius' claim, that the civil state does not wield any rights that had not already been possessed, in some form, by natural man, would provoke Hobbes' own thinking on human nature in relation to the origin of the state and how we should organize ourselves politically. As a direct intellectual descendant of Grotius, Hobbes is similarly committed to understanding the inclinations of human nature and whether such inclinations manifest themselves differently in times of war and in times of peace.

Already well into his fifties (when the average lifetime was mere mid-thirties), Thomas Hobbes had not produced a single major work of political philosophy before *De Cive*.

Living during political turmoil, he had spent decades studying human nature and what remains constant in the human condition, either in times of war or in times of peace. What motivations, in particular, tend to incline us to form political societies, even in presence of irreconcilable differences of opinion? The starting point of such deliberations is, naturally, the individual, with all the passions that animate our desires to pursue actions. While no one can possibly deny the most obvious fact of human development, that we are all born under the dominion of our parents, very few of us would be able to provide a reasoned account for why we should subject ourselves to the rule of another. The question of how to submit ourselves voluntarily to rightful and legitimate authority, rather than remain in fear of sheer and brute force, would become central to all his political writings. Despite hostilities directed against his core argument about the centrality of human relations, Hobbes remained steadfast in his insistence that he sought to derive truth, rather than assert facts. Natural solitude, widely seen as synonymous with Hobbes, is "such a monstrous Paradox and absurdity," the Royalist Roger Coke objected, that no "Ingenuous man should assent to it" (Coke 1662: Preface). In his assertion that nature abhors the solitary, Coke in fact proved, rather than dispelled Hobbes' main argument that humans are not dissociated monads waging a war of extermination, but calculative pursuers of peace, inextricably tied in covenantal bonds.

In his attempt to describe the state of men without civil society, Hobbes numbers "solitude" as one of "the incommodities" of that "Warre, where every man is Enemy to every man," and despite this single use in the entire corpus of Hobbes' works, it is widely seen as an easy synonym for the state of nature. "[T]he life of man" outside sovereignty, as the infamous description in chapter thirteen of *Leviathan* makes clear, is "solitary, poore, nasty, brutish, and short." Rather than being the cause of war, and hence antecedent to it, "solitude" in fact follows the destruction of peace and is, therefore, "consequent to a time of Warre," especially civil war (Hobbes [1651] 1991: 89). Natural persons find themselves as no lone solitaries: they passionately congregate and eagerly "seek ayd by society: for there is no other way by which a man can secure his life and liberty" (Hobbes [1651] 1991: 101). Not incidentally, the observation of our love for company is included under Hobbes' general discussion of the passions. Unlike the motivating faculties of fear and aversion, or the pleasures of the senses, the love for human association is a passion of the mind according to Hobbes. Glory and "diffidence" (or fearfulness), as two of the "three principall causes of quarrel" along with "competition," are also numbered among the passions of the mind: they all presuppose an associative character of human interaction, which proceeds, in large, from "need" [*indigentia*], the desire for protection in order to survive (Hobbes [1651] 1991: 101). A social environment, mediated primarily by families and life protectors, is essential for materializing the human passions even outside civil society.

Clearly, the passions, as characteristic of men in general—whether they find themselves within or outside a commonwealth—necessitate the presence of others for their manifestation, and Rousseau's criticism of "Hobbes' error" on this point could not be more insightful. The Hobbesian "state of war among men" does not proceed from the savagery of solitaries, "who are independent and have [subsequently] become sociable." Hobbes' theory, instead, assumes all along, in Rousseau's apt formulation, "this [sociable] state to be natural to the species and to have given it as the cause of the vices of which it is the effect" (Rousseau [1756–59] 1997: 159). From the moment of birth, solitude is our greatest enemy and a multitude of servants and their saviors (whether victors, parents, or masters) is our natural state: nature's habitants, covenanted in a dominion, are "allies" united against those outside, "so that if we must have *war*, it will not be a war against all men nor without aid" (Hobbes [1642] 1998: 30). The state of nature is a state of war precisely because men stay firmly united into groups seeking to incorporate the weaker into their grouping.

Moreover, their state of war does not originate in any presumed inherent human aggression, or a personal struggle over limited resources; rather, it proceeds from the imperative to secure their own preservation, which is possible only with the augmentation of the number of servants within a grouping. The salvation of oneself requires the salvation of others: the saved and their saviors find themselves continually in a state of war against outsiders for no other reason than their perpetual quest for peace. In the absence of a single authority to unite them into one person, natural men instinctively band together "by means of reciprocal agreements made with each other" for their common defense (Hobbes [1642] 1998: 102). A natural multitude of restless security seekers, strengthened in great numbers, rather than reclusive solitaries, characterizes the condition outside civility. Inextricably tied into a thickly stratified web of covenantal bonds that vary in their strength and duration, natural habitants continually establish contractual bonds according to the dictates of nature's necessities. Far from being a solitary condition, the state of nature persists as a complex arena of rights transferals among calculative pursuers of peace.

As descriptive of the life of man outside civility, the Hobbesian state of nature presents, in part, an ahistorical and purely fictional situation as a condition of the social contract: it is intended to serve as a conceptual apparatus for imagining how autonomous agents would act outside the contingency of human experience. But it also can be said to manifest the historical (rather than cultural) development of societies: Hobbes frequently draws on the example of the small families of North America as existing in a state of nature not on account of their primitivism, but because of their absence of full-fledged sovereignty. He also imagines the international domain of autonomous states as the best instantiation— and not merely a manifestation—of the natural condition: the international state of nature follows the interpersonal one. The foreign domain also reveals the most fundamental tenet of Hobbes' civil science: that the state of war and the state of peace cohabit the same space and that enmity and amity exist side by side. The links between nature and sovereignty, savagery and civility, war and peace, death and life itself remain fragile and tenuous.

The frontispiece of Hobbes' *De Cive* (1642) captures the central message of his political project: the distance between the state of war and the state of peace is far narrower than their opposition might suppose and their relationship is invariably tense. Comprised of three equal panels, the middle of which is—crucially—veiled, the lower half of the engraving illustrates the contrast between the anarchy of nature and the order of the city. *Libertas*, on the right, is an Algonquian woman of Carolina whose long arrow in her right hand points downward, as if anticipating the damnation of Christ's final judgment depicted in the upper panel, *Religio*. The state of war behind *Libertas* impresses precisely with the absence of everything that *Imperium* on the left makes possible. Barren uncultivated lands with a few scattered huts fill the background of the state of war: frightened men, chased by hunters with arrows, run for their lives. Their anxious faces express the agonizing experience of survival in a warlike environment, where everyone is free to exercise their natural right to self-preservation, even if that entails the killing of another in order to remain alive. Far removed from any ordinary experience Hobbes' European reader might have been familiar with, the visual depiction of war includes its

FIGURE 2.1: Frontispiece of Thomas Hobbes' *De Cive* (Paris, 1642) reproduced with the kind permission of The William Andrews Clark Memorial Library, University of California, Los Angeles.

most extreme form: cannibals have gathered around a fire roasting human flesh from the hanging limb of a human victim. Primitive savagery distinguishes life outside sovereignty: unbounded in their natural right to take the life of another in extreme cases of survival, natural men are perpetual warriors who fight simply to remain alive. Life in the state of nature is not only precarious, but it also defines war itself.

Outside of nature, life could not be any more peaceful: order and serenity reign on the left panel. The toga-clad and regal-looking *Imperium*, reminiscent of a free Roman citizen, balances the scales of justice in her right hand in the embodiment of orderliness and legitimacy. Holding a sword in her left hand pointing upwards, she dispenses justice not only through wise judgment but also through fear of punishment, as if to indicate that no one who disobeys her authority will be spared. Unlike the barrenness of nature, life in the *civitas* abounds in the cultivation of civic life: industrious people till the land, while the spires of the churches in the background beckon them to rise above their daily chores in the experience of the divine. Through religion and agriculture, the primitivism of war and the solitude of fighting have been banished and nature has been transformed into an oasis of peace and prosperity.

While nature and civility reinforce the usual opposition between war and peace, they seemingly overlap in the middle panel. The space between *Libertas* and *Imperium*, occupying an equal third of the lower half of the panel, is veiled by a curtain: were one to lift it, it would appear that no radical break exists between war and peace, and their dichotomy is largely imaginary. How can, then, nature and sovereignty, savagery and civility, war and peace, co-exist in the same space? The question of their relationship will become the central question of the entire tradition of natural law, originating with Thomas Hobbes and his Dutch predecessor Hugo Grotius at the beginning of the seventeenth century through their followers Samuel Pufendorf and John Locke to the middle of the eighteenth with the Swiss Jean-Jacques Rousseau and Emer Vattel.

These thinkers used interpersonal relations analogously to the international affairs between sovereigns and thereby laid the foundation for how we have come to regard modern politics. Eminently observable in inter-state interaction, the international domain is an expanded illustration of how individuals would interact in the absence of any intervening authority over them. Rather than being derived from the rights and duties of individuals from such an analogy, political agency writ large is merely described through their actions, since states need individuals in the first place. In turn, war and peace—the subject of the relations between states—provides the domestic theory of the state with the most compelling example for how independent agents act interdependently.

The intellectual transition from the war of savagery to the peace of the commonwealth requires the idea of a state of nature: it alone can possibly justify the establishment of the modern state. Outside of any political commitments or social environment, a bare individual, stripped of any prior obligation, can be imagined to consent to submission to authority and to enter into a social contract. For many, if not all, contractarian thinkers, the laws of nature as applied to natural persons—or the laws of nations when enacted by artificial persons—circumscribe the minimalist character of the natural rights tradition. Outside of sovereignty, all individuals mutually recognize the basic meaning they ascribe to the protection of the self. In fact, if there were no such minimal consensus on the primary proposition of what constitutes self-preservation as a natural right, any attempt to come to an agreement over secondary ones would not be possible. The interaction of individuals, with the capacity to exercise their own wills, can be applied to that of states. Commonwealths emerge as persons writ large: the international state of nature follows the interpersonal one.

In this common narrative, the radical dissociation of nature's war and sovereignty's peace eliminates the possibility for their mutual coexistence: the institution of the sovereign is largely regarded as the irreversible end of the state of nature, and where the state enables all the commodities of life that peace brings. But for many early modern political thinkers, the relationship between war and peace should be seen less as diametrical and more as coextensive, as Hobbes' frontispiece of *De Cive* indicates: a state may be at peace internally and yet in conflict externally. As a sovereign over its subjects, the state commands peace, whereas as a sovereign among sovereigns, the state remains in a state of nature internationally.

The international arena, which not merely manifests but preeminently instantiates the state of nature, is the domain where the state of war and the state of peace cohabitate the same space: enmity and amity exist side by side in a world of states. The institution of leviathans by no means ends the state of war, as international relations reveal: it simply solves the domestic dilemma of peace, while it simultaneously creates an international state of nature, where states themselves take on the same qualities of self-preservation that had defined those of natural individuals. The leviathan may save us from ourselves, but it cannot save us from other leviathans. For this reason, Rousseau, in *Émile* (1762), would even pose the question of whether "it would not be better to have no civil society than to have several... Is it not this partial and incomplete association which is the cause of tyranny and war? And are not tyranny and war the two worst scourges of mankind?" (Rousseau [1762] 1915: I, 96). The state of nature is, *par excellence*, observable in international relations: even as citizens of states—and because of—we remain in a perpetual state of war. While sovereignty emerges in response to the miseries accompanying the natural condition and solves conflict between private individuals, it simultaneously creates an international state of nature among states without a sovereign either between them or over them.

And yet, the analogy between men and states, while essential, remains only incomplete: unlike natural persons, who remain vulnerable because of their perfect equality, artificial states do not face the same level of insecurity (and hence any argument in favor of extending the leviathan to a global one fails on account of the safety provided by states themselves). The urgency of constituting a civic commonwealth has no equivalent in establishing a global or a world state, were it even possible to construct one. Any peace between states, however long-lasting, marks only a temporary cessation of hostilities, rather than a permanent solution to their warlike disposition. The Prussian philosopher G. W. F. Leibniz perceptively captures the volatile character of international peace as "a breathing-space of two gladiators" (Leibniz [1693] 1988: 166), reflecting Hobbes' infamous reflections how "in all times, Kings, and Persons of Soveraigne authority, because of their Independency, are in continuall jealousies, and in the state and posture of Gladiators; having their weapons pointing, and their eyes fixed on one another; that is, their Forts, Garrisons, and Guns upon the Frontiers of their Kingdomes; and continuall Spyes upon their neighbours, which is a posture of War" (Hobbes [1651] 1991: 90). In his *Codex Iuris Gentium Diplomaticus*, a major work on the law of nations, Leibniz concludes that the assertion made by "the subtle author of the *Elementa de Cive*" of warlike international relations "is not altogether absurd, provided it refer not to a right to do harm, but to take proper precautions." Among nations, inclined to pursue peace even by means of war, "breathing time" and "breathing space" is the surest peace that can be obtained in a world competing for more security (Leibniz [1693] 1988: 166).

The war that defines the natural condition imposes the imperative to exit from it, whereas the gladiatorial posture among sovereigns makes no such demand. Even the character of war and peace—whether among natural or artificial persons—would seem to differ on the basic level of how each is experienced. The state of nature, for Hobbes, manifests itself variously, and, depending on the nature of the conflict, it ranges from the more familiar and less violent to the less common and more warlike. Whether it can be eminently observed among some Amerindian tribes, or mercenary soldiers, or factions during civil war, or among irreconcilable ideological doctrinaires, what characterizes such a condition is the absence of any sovereign authority: outside sovereignty, reign the miseries of war. Unique among all manifestations of the state of war, international relations alone serve more than a mere example of the miseries that accompany the state of war: they are themselves the state of nature in its most original and actual sense, for they always are, regardless of how secure domestic sovereignty may be. All other manifestations simply show the state of war as a possible and contingent condition: we may fall into it (as in the case of civil war), or we may exit from (as Amerindians may do so eventually). As a permanent state of war, on the other hand, international relations stand out as both an actual and ongoing state of affairs: precisely because sovereigns seek to organize themselves in a world of independent states, they will continually find themselves in a condition of enmity.

The state of war in the international domain stands out as categorically distinct from any other instantiation of the state of nature. The experience of war and peace, correspondingly, differs from Hobbes' "perpetuall *War*" (Hobbes [1642] 1998: 30) found among natural individuals and the "publique Peace" (Hobbes [1651] 1991: 133) maintained internally by each leviathan. The realm of international relations does not suffer from an impending all-out war, although neither does it ever hope to attain the security of peace that is possible domestically. It merely functions as an armed peace. The analogy between men and cities (and for Hobbes cities are artificial persons endowed with the same attributes as natural men) affirms the claim that both natural and civil persons are virtually indistinguishable with respect to how they interact with one another: they are all in a state of nature among themselves. The international arena populated by sovereigns can be described in exactly the same way as the domain of natural persons: the same characteristics that define self-defensive natural men and the same natural laws that operate among them can be transferred to civil persons.

"As for the law of nations," Hobbes concludes his *The Elements of Law*, "it is the same with the law of nature. For that which is the law of nature between man and man, before the constitution of the commonwealth, is the law of nations between sovereign and sovereign, after" (Hobbes [1640] 1969: 190). His understanding of the law of nations, and how it relates to the law of nature and civil law, reflects his commitment to locate the fundamental precepts of—what has later come to be known as—"international law" firmly within the boundaries of natural law. Hobbes was certainly not the first one to situate the province of *jus gentium* within the domain of *jus naturalis*. His contemporary, Richard Zouche (1590–1661), similarly sought to establish the foundations of the law of nations within a natural law framework and the language of ancient Roman law, and by the middle of the seventeenth century, the shift from *jus commune* to *jus naturalis* had already taken place.

Hobbes' naturalist theory of *jus gentium* would later earn him Vattel's accusation that he was ultimately mistaken for his straightforward application of the law of nations exactly as the natural law when applied to nations, because the law of nature must "suffer" a "necessary change" once "applied to states or nations" (Vattel [1758] 2008: 8–9). "[T]he Law of Nations, and the Law of Nature," Hobbes observes in *Leviathan*, "is the same thing" and the two are indistinguishable only by virtue of their subjects, whether natural individuals or artificial persons (Hobbes [1651] 1991: 244). His firm division of natural law into that of men and that of commonwealths would become standard in all of his mature political writings and lead to strengthening the analogy between the interpersonal and international domain.

Regardless of whether persons are natural or artificial, the precepts dictating their conduct derive their force, crucially, from the same natural law of self-preservation. While individuals have a primary obligation to care for their basic necessities and physical survival, all sovereigns have the secondary duty to abide by the law of nations and provide for their citizens' flourishing and improvement. As the principal actors under the law of nations, commonwealths emerge not simply as guarantors of domestic peace but also as promoters of a commodious life. The development of the arts and sciences, which distinguishes "the modern world from the barbarity of the past," contributes to "a commodious living": the condition, where "the enormous advantages of human life have far surpassed the condition of other animals" (Hobbes [1651] 1991: 4, 39). It is the duty of sovereigns not only to establish the safety and security of citizens and to promote peace, but also to pursue growth and prosperity through robust commerce as a vehicle for peace. Robust commercial relations with other states and a general openness of international trade are all part of the universality of the law of nations and practiced as a right of nations.

While frugality and economic foresight determine domestic prosperity, commercial relations with other states transform a state from a self-sufficient political entity into a partner for peace and a strategic ally: states would far more likely engage with it in the quest for international peace. The law of nations dictates the promulgation of free traffic in the conduct of indiscriminate commerce and a universal observance of equality in dealing with diverse states. A failure to apply the law of nature of impartiality in international affairs is manifestly a declaration of hatred, which is effectively a condition of war: "For he that alloweth that [free commerce] to one man, which he denieth to another, declareth his hatred to him, to whom he denieth; and to declare hatred is war" (Hobbes [1640] 1969: 87). The laws of nature compel states to have their ports open and their markets free to all equally with a certain guarantee of safety for a peaceful interaction. In general, those states that respect the dictates of the law of nations can expect a high degree of cooperation, and, in a world of competing states with conflicting interests, economic exchange can be beneficial for peace through demands for mutual respect and the reciprocation of trade agreements.

Communication, in consequence to commerce, must be free and equally accessible to all regardless of citizenship "for without this there would be no society among men, no peace" (Hobbes [1651] 1991: 40). As communicative creatures, endowed with the capacity to engage peacefully with others, all humans have a right by nature to roam the corners of the world unhindered as long as they respect the laws and customs of the first inhabitants and do not dispossess them of their land against their will. The natural right of free passage for Hobbes is part of the law of nature, "[t]hat all messengers of peace, and such as are employed to procure and maintain amity between man and man, may safely come and go," and allows for negotiation to occur (Hobbes [1640] 1969: 87). "By the mere law of nature," as Samuel Pufendorf later echoed Hobbes' view on peaceful settlement, "envoys … are inviolable" and, as messengers of peace, they should be allowed free access, not least in times of war (Pufendorf [1688] 1934: 228). Especially during conflict, when violence cannot obliterate the basic laws of humanity, "Mediators of Peace should have immunity" and be allowed to reach an agreement, for "Peace cannot be had without mediation, nor mediation without immunity" (Hobbes [1642] 1998: 51). The natural right of free passage, both in unhindered crossing in peaceful times and for mediation during conflict, extends to all nations across the globe, since it is derived as a dictate of natural reason, and hence exerts the same force everywhere. It, therefore, properly belongs to *jus gentium*, which reason alone, in the observance of justice, prescribes to everyone in general. In their pursuit of the "Fundamentall Law of Nature; which is, to seek Peace, and follow it," sovereigns enter into alliances for mutual protection without instituting a common power above them all (Hobbes [1651] 1991: 92).

Hobbes not only discounts the extension from a single to a global leviathan as illogical; he also ardently defends the proposition that states remain in the international state of nature by all means necessary. The need for self-preservation, which requires a natural person to enter into a contract with another solely for their survival, carries no compelling obligation when extended to civil persons. Since for Hobbes the primary duty of sovereigns is to procure the survival of their citizens and to "have their industry protected," any transfer of rights to an entity outside one's own state amounts to renouncing one's allegiance to the sovereign (Hobbes [1651] 1991: 189). And if all citizens were to renounce their state allegiance, they would find themselves in a condition of self-inflicted despotism and a return to the state of war. A sovereign above all sovereigns, as desirable for world peace as it may seem to be on account of its broad appeal to global security, is greatly resisted by both Hobbes and Pufendorf, who remain fearful of any claims to universal authority, whether political or religious.

Eighteenth-century critics of Hobbes, including the Prussian Christian Wolff (1679–1754), dismissed the inconvenience of rival polities and the inevitable proneness to a politics of war among them. Their proposals for a world state—such as Wolff's *civitas maxima*—would only lead to the fragmentation of sovereignty and result in the compromising of states' liberty in the external domain. Firmly rejecting the Wolffian idea of a world superstate with an authority over the component member states, Vattel affirmed the principle of equality as consistent with the law of nations and relied on Hobbes to make "clear that there is by no means the same necessity for a civil society among nations as among individuals" (Vattel [1758] 2008: 9). The rejection of a supreme sovereign and reaffirming the voluntary practice of the law of nations underlie Hobbes' tenet: just as individuals in nature interact in accordance with the laws of nature—especially the "Fundamentall Law of Nature; which is, to seek Peace, and follow it"—even outside any juridical authority, so do commonwealths follow the laws of nations in the absence of a common power above them all (Hobbes [1651] 1991: 92).

Even in the most extreme circumstances of warring princes, where "every Soveraign hath the same Right, in procuring the safety of his People, that any particular man can have, in procuring his own safety," the law of nations prescribes the duties and obligations of states not only in times of peace, but also during war (Hobbes [1651] 1991: 244). In Hobbes' view, the perennial quest for international peace frames the relations between commonwealths, rather than any foreign aggression for the sake of aggrandizement, which would likely endanger their own preservation. Should defensive wars become necessary when survival itself is at stake, they also ought to be conducted in accordance with the law of nations and generally recognized duties in warfare. While sovereign states may not have the assurance of permanent security in their external relations and may at any time resort to defensive war in providing for their own safety, they yield a great advantage in the active engagement with other states for mutual benefit and peaceful relations. Samuel Pufendorf, one of Hobbes' successors, espouses the general position that the international arena instantiates the state of nature among sovereigns. Similar to most thinkers in the tradition of *jus gentium*, Pufendorf does not regard the state of natural liberty of states as descriptive of extreme isolationism: instead, the foreign mirrors the domestic, where each individual is part of a web of agreements and alliances.

Pufendorf's argument for sociability emphasizes its radical departure from Hobbes' solitary individual and positions itself in the principle of benevolent *socialitas* as the engine of human interaction. "The natural state of men," Pufendorf counters the Hobbesian war of all against everyone else, "even when considered apart from commonwealths, is not one of war, but of peace." The relative peace outside sovereignty is precarious because of the many inconveniences that the pursuit of self-preservation demands. The law of nature dictates bodily preservation as an imperative according to reason and "is commended to every man by his most ardent love of his own and by reason to itself" (Pufendorf [1688] 1934: 171, 264). The insertion of the language of "self-love" articulates the centrality of nature's laws in circumscribing a set of common duties toward ourselves and toward others. The object of such self-love (*amour propre*) is the self-interested pursuit to care for one's bodily integrity, rather than practice benevolence as expressed in love of the self (*amour de soi*). Clearly, benevolence does not awaken our preservationist instinct.

While the impulse to preserve ourselves proceeds from self-love, it easily tends to overtake any other-regarding passion, and only right education and discipline can maintain their balance. Pufendorf sanctions "that boundless self-love (*amour propre*) whereby every man regularly leans toward himself and his own," but warns against unbridled passions over reason since "the mass of men order their lives not by reason but on impulse, and trust their lust as reason, chiefly by fault of their education and habits." The binding passion of excessive self-love obscures ratiocination, for "the majority [of men] are led by the violence of their passions wherever their lust or a false idea of their advantage may take them" (Pufendorf [1688] 1934: 827, 965, 964). Outside sovereignty, natural men contract under the dominion of their savior, where the acquired habit of discipline in obedience—such as that practiced by children toward their parents—is replicated in the obedience to civil authority.

Man's unrestrained acquisitive impulses, such as the desire for power, cannot be bridled unless one recognizes the predicament of one's own "imbecility." "It is the custom of all men to be hunting perpetually and with no set purpose for one power after another," Pufendorf argued, closely following Hobbes' own view, "not because a person is always hoping for a greater power than he now enjoys, or because he cannot rest content with only a little, but because he cannot preserve his present power and resources for a life of comfort save by acquiring more." In their perpetual struggle to gain more power by subduing others, men realize the limitations of the human condition, where "the weakness of their own resources makes their safety hang by a thread" (Pufendorf [1688] 1934: 955, 163). Universal imbecility renders mutual assistance not only necessary for survival itself, but also beneficial for the advancement of one's own interest.

Human weakness, when coupled with the desire to further one's interest in common with others, can indeed mitigate those human passions tending to dissociate the self from the community. Prompted by the need for self-preservation, one enters into an association with the stronger and yet remains vulnerable to those destructive elements that constantly gravitate toward personal gain and ambition. Imbecility necessitates active congregating, but unbridled passions continually erode it and leave it vulnerable to dissociation. Concern for the self, however, produces actions whose effects are consistent with a sociable disposition. Men act sociably not because they altruistically grant beneficence to other fellow human beings, but because it is in their vital interest to outweigh their natural weakness with the remedy of increased assistance from others.

As an act of habituating oneself to the mutual rendition of advantages, the insertion of *socialitas* into the discourse on sociability seemingly repairs the damage done by Hobbes: the starkness of naked personal advantage can be clothed in the garb of enlightened self-interest, or the "pretended love of our species," as Bernard Mandeville rendered it (Mandeville [1729] 1924: 183). By its own nature, self-interest in no way precludes some degree of mutual effort and joint forces. "Self-love [*amour propre*] and a sociable attitude [*socialitas*] should by no means be opposed to each other," Pufendorf affirms, "but rather that their tendencies should be restrained in such a way that the latter be not checked or destroyed by the former" (Pufendorf [1688] 1934: 210). On this account of reinforcement, *socialitas* seems to sit comfortably alongside any passion for personal gain or benefit.

Despite his explicit and persistent efforts to isolate *socialitas* from any self-regarding motivations, Pufendorf is under no illusion that even our most selfless acts are, in some way, ultimately prompted by self-interest. In their quest for self-preservation and constant improvement, men self-reflectively pursue their advancement and they "seek and love a certain thing according as they think it has something for their advantage" (Pufendorf [1688] 1934: 56). We socialize for the simple reason that social exchange with others brings advantages that we could not obtain otherwise. The self-interested individual pursuing their own advantage in common with others is no longer the problem, but comes closer to being the solution for the problem of socialization. The practice of *socialitas* begins to resemble the pursuit of active self-interest. Insofar as it establishes minimalist dictates for human interaction, the law of sociability emerges as an imperative limiting the unrestrained license over violent conflict (Pufendorf [1688] 1934: 211). The preservation-based utility of *socialitas* furnishes a multitude of security seekers in their quest for peace: the advancement of one's security is possible only in concert with the equally vulnerable, particularly those of the same family. The artificial formation of great states proceeds from the natural domain of families, for all commonwealths originate in the natural sovereignty of families (which itself is replicated in the artifice of the commonwealth, except on a larger scale). Families serve prototypically for the generation of the commonwealth.

Families in the natural condition seek to surround themselves with the most protection they can gain, while continually facing the many inconveniences of the absence of civil sovereignty. Their common fear of being subdued by outsiders serves as a principal motive for "why the fathers of families left their natural liberty and established states" and "surround[ed] themselves with defense against the evils which threaten man from his fellow man" (Pufendorf [1688] 1934: 959). Fear, rather than any inclination for war, motivates the banding together of equally vulnerable individuals in confederacies while at the same time it sustains their mutual agreement. Sociality is merely symptomatic of their desire to associate for protection, but it may never on its own give rise to a civil state. Unlike Hobbes, however, for whom civil association does not eradicate the effects of fallen human nature, Pufendorf upholds the state as performing a quasi-salvific function. As the son of a Lutheran pastor and a former student of theology, he held no illusion about redeeming fallen human nature by man's own efforts, but he certainly found it realistic that self-regarding inclinations can be successfully curbed. The establishment of states, motivated by fear, comes to the rescue of fallen creatures in search of permanent security and peace. Civil sovereigns seem to exercise a transformational effect over their citizens, and "in fact states," as he observes, "are a sort of remedy for human imperfection" (Pufendorf [1678] 1990: 111). States act as crutches that support the faults of fallen human beings.

Pufendorf remained keenly sensitive to Europe's new political configuration and his attempt to distinguish between military growth for state power and military preparedness for self-preservation led him to a more robust foreign policy. Similarly to Hobbes who had argued that forearming is the best defense, Pufendorf affirms a state's need for constant vigilance and readiness to forestall, and if necessary, to repel a foreign attack, for "that state is properly considered wise which thinks of war even in times of peace" (Pufendorf [1688] 1934: 273). The peace he has in mind, however, is clearly not the irreversible eradication of conflict, but only a temporary cessation of hostilities: "one should not be the aggressor, even when there is just cause for war, unless there is a very fair occasion, and the condition of the state easily allows it" (Pufendorf [1688] 1934: 1126). Pufendorf must have incurred Kant's indignation that his proposal for international peace does not exercise any legal force externally and for that reason he is merely a "sorry comforter" (Kant [1795] 1991: 103). But the parallel Kant draws between Pufendorf and Grotius, another of his sorry comforters, can be potentially misleading and even mask a fundamental difference between the two on the nature of peace among states. The Grotian appeal to the right of war in the name of universal justice has been largely abandoned in the era after the Peace of Westphalia. It is this new geopolitical reality that is clearly reflected in Pufendorf's view of war and peace as pragmatic diplomacy.

The real strength of a state consists in its skillfulness in avoiding unnecessary wars waged out of ambition and glory. The uncertain outcome in the conduct of any war requires that states utilize non-military tactics, rather than rely on their armies alone. They have a duty to surround themselves "with innocent means of defense, . . . find allies for [themselves], carefully observe the undertakings of others, and take similar precautions" (Pufendorf [1688] 1934: 273). If the essential analogy between the interpersonal and the international state of nature were to hold true, as Pufendorf maintains, then states could indeed live relatively peacefully: they act according to the dictates of reason in avoiding unnecessary war, and make agreements in order to mitigate the scope for conflict.

While states may avoid the conduct of international war, they nevertheless engage in warfare in order to solve conflict when all other possible means have been exhausted. The persistence of war, even if diminished, poses a profound challenge to Hobbes' own project of peace, as Rousseau's reflections in his unfinished manuscript on "The State of War" show. The tragedy of modern politics reveals itself as a "manifest contradiction" in the constitution of the human race: the very solution to natural inconveniences in the creation of a civil state domestically became simultaneously the source for perpetual conflict internationally. Subject to "the evils of both without gaining the security of each," we are constantly being thrown in a "continual vacillation [which] makes our situation worse than if those distinctions [between home and abroad] were unknown" and "put ourselves in the worst possible position" (Rousseau [1755-56] 1990: 186). The distinction between the inside and the outside, as advanced by both Hobbes and Pufendorf, troubles Rousseau because it intentionally obliterates a line between pre-civil humans and their civil(ized) counterparts.

Both Hobbes and Rousseau disagree on how to characterize *ab initio* the relations between natural individuals outside the artificiality of state sovereignty. Rousseau's natural man is devoid of any kind of social interaction, which would have struck Hobbes as inconceivable, if not irrelevant, since the basic passions of competition, diffidence, and glory clearly operate within the state of nature. Rousseau's isolated individual, "naturally peaceful and shy," rather than constantly battling the dangers of war, as Hobbes would have him, remains unperturbed by the passions. "[H]onor, self-interest, prejudice, and vengeance" emerge only "by force of habit and experience" and "after having associated with one man" (Rousseau [1755-56] 1990: 188). Apart from this radical isolationism in Rousseau's initial construct, there is little divergence in the rest of their accounts of the growth of human conflict and the persistence of warfare.

For Rousseau, as for Hobbes, the depiction of natural man is much less an account of the personal qualities of private individuals under duress of basic survival than an attempt to create a social construct. In a significant way, Rousseau's narrative about natural man is not a story about individuals naturally inclined to peace and between whom no war could ever take place (after all, men become soldiers only after having associated as citizens). Rather, it is a political argument about how artificial bodies constituted by the social compact—and acting with a general will (*volonté générale*)—wage lawful war among themselves. The question is not what establishes war as an advantageous affair of the one who wages it, but what renders it legitimate.

Rousseau has already stated this question in one compelling form when he examines the origin of inequality with the rise of social relations in his *Second Discourse*. In his insistence that we must not confuse "savage men with the men we have before our eyes," he not only wishes to distinguish himself from Hobbes, but also to refute prevalent arguments that inherent unsociability can generate societal cohesion (Rousseau [1755] 1997: 138). "It would be absurd to suppose," he observes in his *Essay on the Origin of Language*, "that the means of uniting them [can be] derived from the cause of their separation" (Rousseau [1781] 1986: 11–12). Radical unsociability would come to characterize natural man and become the hallmark of his *Second Discourse*, which subsequently became the object of intense criticism by his Swiss contemporary Emer de Vattel.

Rousseau's portrayal of natural man, Vattel complained, reduces him to a brute animal, if not even "more stupid than various species of animals." His natural man is incapable of "thoughtful awareness of self" and hence deprived of perfectibility: "[t]he entire bliss of Mr. Rousseau's natural men," Vattel concludes, "seems to come down to idleness and apathy." Awareness of oneself presupposes the natural duty to care for one's own preservation. It also implies a disposition for human interaction, which only "society" and "communication between men" can realize. By removing "perfectibility" as an essential attribute of human nature, Rousseau in effect denies "the principle of sociability, from which Grotius and other great writers deduced all Natural Law." It is not sufficient for men to come together as a group, for "beavers, bees, ants and other animals" are similarly predisposed to form groupings, and some of them even "have a kind of language of their own." It is also necessary to explain the products of their association. Through the use of language—which developed naturally, first through "abstractions" and then through "halting words"—men have removed themselves from their original condition to a superior moral state. For Vattel language is what makes men truly human by declaring their presence to others not by "sounds of sadness" or a "cry for scolding," as brute animals do, but through reasoned intelligibility in "communication between men" in order to "perfect their reason and knowledge" (Vattel [1760] 2008: 97, 99).

The problem with Rousseau's inability to explain the "simple and natural origins of language" runs much deeper than just being an ignorant observation about the brutish solitude of humanity (Vattel [1760] 2008: 97). His denial of a sociable disposition, which for Vattel is innate and stems naturally from our moral composition, deprives us of the medium to pursue our most basic inclination, that of self-love. It "causes us to desire and seek for our happiness or the perfection of our condition,. . . of our soul, the well-being of our body, and the prosperity of our fortune," as he asserts in his major work (Vattel

[1758] 2008: 753). The origin of self-love, "the first principle of all obligations, and in particular of the obligation to keep natural law," lies both in the frailty of the human condition and in the drive to improve our nature only with the assistance of others (Vattel [1758] 2008: 754). The instinctual formation of social groups out of security seekers is driven as much by a desire "to band together to make a stand against violence" as by the recognition that our happiness lies in "our well-being, our expediency, our advantage" (Vattel [1760] 2008: 99). Sociability follows the dictates of right reason coupled with self-interest in the pursuit of utility; its sources lie within the bounds of the laws of nature, "whose rationale is found in the essence and nature of man, and of things in general" (Vattel [1758] 2008: 747). It stems from our obligation to them even in the absence of any external punitive superior, establishing common justice, or a general will, affirming unity. It is from this obligation to oneself primarily, in the attainment of the highest degree of one's happiness, and to others only secondarily, that requires men to enter into "communication and commerce with each other" (Vattel [1758] 2008: 15). The spirit of commerce not only contributes to the growth of modern civil liberties, but it also animates the pursuit for peace, even among hostile and rival powers. The advancement of commerce and the progress of the enlightened individual go hand in hand.

Vattel's solution to the asceticism of Rousseau's natural man lies in the conflation of man's inherent propensity for self-preservation and his capacity to procure it only in association with others. What Rousseau fails to notice is that our natural inclination for perfection is inseparable from our duty to care for the self only in common with others: men advance sociability not out of considerations for enhancing general benevolence, but merely for the sake of securing their own safety and proper advantage. Cooperation through enlightened sociability, Vattel concludes, holds the key to solving the fundamental moral question of how to displace war and maintain peace and freedom. The kind of international order that would be able to accomplish such a high task is the one based on an understanding of natural man as the only moral and political agent capable of providing a blueprint for how states can build peace among themselves.

The analogy between the interpersonal and the international state of nature served as a central intellectual preoccupation during a period when major European thinkers conceptualized for the first time a political universe of independent sovereign states without a common superior over them. Their intellectual efforts relied on getting a clear picture of how individual human agency acts outside the artifice of sovereignty. They did so by placing international relations at the very center of debates over the nature of violence and conflict and the conditions for establishing lasting peace. The formation of the civil state could come about only after a profound re-examination of human nature: how its natural tendencies to wage war could be harnessed and brought to the service of peace. We may be constantly torn between our "propensity to enter into society" and our "thoroughgoing resistance" to this tendency, but we only stand to benefit from such an antagonism. Kant's "unsocial sociability" pits each against the others, who simply cannot do without one another in a common struggle for peace (Kant [1795] 1970: 44). It is precisely this antagonism that, far from being an unfortunate condition of humanity, in fact functions as a spur to the cultivation of the potentials of the species, according to Kant.

The lesson for us, living in a more ordered, and yet—arguably—less enlightened age than that of Kant, is unambiguous: considered as a whole, humankind has its own purpose of attaining peace, which cannot be fulfilled by any single individual, or, for that matter, any particular group or nation. As pursuers of peace, our purpose is to realize human potential all at once and all the time, and not simply only in parts of the globe at certain times. Moreover, it is only the realization of peace globally that enables human beings to reach their fullest potential. The attainment of peace is indeed a collective effort of all humanity unimpeded by warfare and strife. Such a conception of development in the entire human species but not in the individual is based on a presupposition of world peace. "However wild and fanciful this idea [of world peace] may appear," as Kant was fully aware, "it is nonetheless the inevitable outcome of the distress in which men involve one another" (Kant [1784] 1970: 48). The discourse on human sociability, developed earlier by Grotius, Hobbes, Pufendorf, Mandeville, and Rousseau, reaches its culmination in Kant's succinct Fourth Proposition in his *Idea for a Universal History*. What makes sociability so difficult for us is the radical evil in the human will and yet it is the impulse to regulate antagonisms that draws us closer to perpetual peace and accelerate our progress to reaching the end of history. The motive force of the movement away from warfare towards the end of history in the fulfillment of human potentials is the realization of "good out of evil" (Schneewind 2009).

CHAPTER THREE

Peace, War, and Gender

SYLVANA TOMASELLI

The long eighteenth century was rich in proposals for securing enduring peace between nations. The age was that of the Abbé de Saint-Pierre's *Projet de paix perpétuelle* (1713), Emer de Vattel's *Le Droit des gens; ou, Principes de la loi naturelle appliqués à la conduite et aux affaires des nations et des souverains* (in English, *The Law of Nations or the Principles of Natural Law Applied to the Conduct and to the Affairs of Nations and of Sovereigns* [1758]), Jeremy Bentham's *Plan for an Universal and Perpetual Peace* (1789, composed posthumously by his editor),[1] and Immanuel Kant's *Perpetual Peace: a Philosophical Sketch* (1795). This means neither that authors such as these thought human beings as naturally peaceful or, more importantly for what follows, that peace was necessarily deemed an undisputed good and war an unqualified evil in that period. While striving for lasting peace was considered to be a duty by some, most notably by Kant, this was by no means a universally shared assumption. Nor was it the case that peace and war were conceived solely as conditions between nations or entire societies; the idea of war, or at least some form of struggle, was extended to, amongst other areas, the relation between the sexes as well as among races.

Even within the parameters of questions of gender, what follows can only touch on a few aspects of the wealth of views held within the period about war and peace and the associations of ideas they generated. The conflicting thoughts on these subjects include positive conceptions of war, of its merits in relation to the development of personality and on the strengthening of bonds between men or between women; they also comprise ideas of peace that link it to effeminacy and moral corruption. As a consequence, the case for peace tended to have to be *made* in this period, and life under prolonged peace had to be shown not only to be achievable, but desirable within the terms set by a discourse in which martial spirit and its attendant virtues were extolled and often valued above all else. In depictions of peaceful idylls, or at least of a world in which violent conflict would gradually recede into the past or be displaced to other parts of the globe, we see how various authors sought to present peace in an attractive light, seeking to convince readers of its plausibleness and appeal. In these wrangles sexuality was rarely left far off the canvas or the page.

WOMEN, WAR, AND PEACE

While the writings of women on the topics of war and peace are of particular interest to a chapter such as this, the many women who engaged in wars in this period as soldiers, sailors or pirates, whether in positions of command or not, whether dressed as men or not, can only be briefly remembered here.[2] It is important to do so, however, before narrowing our focus, as we will in a moment, on the writings of two prominent and distinguished theorists, Margaret Cavendish and Mary Wollstonecraft.[3] We must also recall that female soldiers and fighters were by no means unknown to the long eighteenth-century mind itself; they featured in ballads and other forms of folklore as well as in eye-witness reports such as those of "visitors," mostly involved in the slave-trade, to the Kingdom of Dahomey, famous for its corps of female warriors (Goldstein 2001: 60–64). Nor were earlier heroines laid to rest. Thus, in his satirical and rather lewd poem, *La Pucelle d'Orléans (The Maid of Orléans* [1762]), Voltaire ruthlessly exploited the life of Joan of Arc (1412–1431) for his own polemical purposes and as an exercise in lampooning a famed seventeenth-century epic, *La Pucelle* (1656), by Jean Chapelain (1595–1674).[4] At least two conscientiously very different other epic poems about her were to follow, an eponymous one by Robert Southey in 1796, the other by Friedrich Schiller, *The Maid of Orléans*, in 1801. Except for Southey's, the aforementioned texts drew attention to Joan's sexuality, her virginity, in their very title. Schiller's is notable for having her fall in love, but significantly for portraying her as pitilessly killing men in battle prior to her being affected by her passion for one of them. His Joan is powerful, though temporarily weakened by her feelings, not lascivious, and ultimately victorious. Sex and war, but often also love, seem inevitably entangled in these and other works of the period, the bodies and lives of women providing the terrain on which writers fought their ideological battles. By devoting several pages to her life in his *History of England* (1754–61), David Hume gave a most sympathetic account of her achievements and indicted those powerful men who used and destroyed her for their own political ends. She was a prisoner of war and ought to have been treated with "all the courtesy and good usage, which civilized nations practise towards enemies" (Hume 1983: II, 407). She was guilty neither of military nor civil misconduct, he argued, adding:

> Even the virtues and the very decorums of her sex had ever been rigidly observed by her: And though her appearing in war, and leading armies to battle, may seem an exception, she had thereby performed such signal service to her prince, that she had abundantly compensated for this irregularity; and was on that very account, the more an object of praise and admiration.
>
> —Hume 1983: II, 408

If he thought that some might think of her warring as a want of female virtue, Hume himself did not. His *History*, especially of the mid-fourteenth century, is rich in example of such heroines. As J. G. A. Pocock has noted, what was remarkable about Hume's account of the rise of chivalry and its "protective gallantry towards 'the fair sex'" was that, for him, "it produced a series of viragos admirable in policy and war: the Countess of Montfort, the Countess of Blois, and Edward III's Queen Philippa of Hainault, who defeats the Scottish king at Neville's Cross before displaying mercy to the burghers of Calais" (Pocock 1999b: 249). As Hume put it: "if any thing could justify the obsequious devotion then professed to the fair sex, it must be the appearance of such extraordinary women as shone forth during that period" (Hume 1983: II, 408; Pocock 1999b: 249 n. 6).

More ubiquitous perhaps still in the epoch's imaginary than historical figures were the Amazons. Famously depicted by Peter Paul Rubens and Jan Brueghel in the later part of the sixteenth century, they remained a very alluring subject for a variety of authors, such as the Abbé Guyon, whose *Histoire des Amazonnes Anciennes et Modernes* (1740) was translated by Samuel Johnson the year after its original publication, as well as a number of artists in this period, such as the Austrian Rococo painter, Johann Georg Platzer (1704–1761)

FIGURE 3.1: Pierre Mignard, *Alexander the Great and Thalestris, Queen of the Amazons*. Peter Horree. Alamy Stock Photo.

and the German Johann Heinrich Wilhelm Tischbein (1751–1829), most famous for his portrait of his friend Goethe. It needs to be said that not all pictorial or literary depictions of the Amazons highlighted their fighting character or portrayed them in battle. Representations such as that of the French painter Pierre Mignard (1612–1695) "Alexander meets the queen of the Amazons" (*c*. 1660), brought to mind their encounter with men, not in physical combat, but for the purposes of reproduction, and, one might add, suggested a serene intimacy. Likewise, in Hobbes' *Leviathan* (1651), the Amazons feature solely as an illustration of the possibility of dominion of female children residing with their mothers (Hobbes [1651] 2012: vol. 2, 308).

But if some depictions portrayed them with the smooth face of peace, as lovingly sensual or in a maternal light, Amazons also often stood for female carnal rapacity, their bodies combining physical strength, martial spirit and daring, sexual prowess and unadulterated lust. This was particularly true in Britain. Their imagined wantonness thrilled some, but it also made them a favorite subject of mockery, the essence of sexual depravity, and a staple of misogynist and antifeminist works of the Restoration and the early eighteenth century.⁵ Amongst many farces and satires that used them in this way, Alexander Pope's *The Rape of the Lock* (1712) is one of the mildest, in that he chose Thalestris, the Amazon queen, as the character to embody "subdued aggression" and "concomitant and conflicting sexual desire" (Weinbrot 1988: 40).

Women adopted a variety of strategies in their responses to what were intended and perceived as a slur on their sex as a whole or individuals within it. One form of retort was the long-standing conception of "the chaste Amazon" "[r]ejecting all congress with men, prudent, courageous, and self-governing [. . .] the obverse of the misogynist stereotype" (Green 2014: 43). This view had its roots in Christine de Pizan's (1364–1430) *La Citta delle dame* (Book of the City of Ladies) (1405), which took the kingdom of the Amazons as having endured for at least eight centuries and depicted its women as brave, noble and invincible. This is not to say that every woman who took up the pen to write in their sex's defense or praise approved of the idea of female warriors. "[H]owever gallant Amazons may appear in paintings," Madeleine de Scudéry (1607–1701), herself the author of *Illustrious Women* (1642) for one, admitted, "they do not appeal to me," though she envied their freedom from men and marriage (cited in Broad and Green 2009: 190).

Far from being disliked, let alone denigrated in the German-speaking Protestant courts, Amazons had appeared in pageants and tournaments in celebrations of stately christenings, birthdays, and weddings, but they were still played by men for much of the seventeenth century. Women could assume their role in the *ballet de court* after 1650 and the notion of an Amazon state was the basis of a lavish five-act opera, *Hercules unter denen Amazonen* (Hercules Amongst the Amazons), staged in Braunschweig in 1693 and 1694 (Watanabe-O'Kelly 2010: 51–55). Though the Greeks were attributed virtues, such as magnanimity and constancy, denied to the Amazons, all are treated as equals by the end of the opera (Watanabe-O'Kelly 2010: 55). Each side did tussle with the divergent calls of love and war, but neither was seen as depraved either for their desires or their martial character. Nor were Amazons the object only of Germanic male fantasy. While "[i]t is not until the late nineteenth century that women writers and thinkers begin to imagine for themselves what an Amazon state would be like," there is at least one example of a chamber opera composed by an eighteenth-century woman—Maria Antonia Walpurgis, the electoral Princess of Saxony (1724–1780)—*Talestri regina delle Amazzoni* (Talestri, Queen of the Amazons), premiered in Dresden on 24th August 1763, "just at the moment when the Seven Years War between Prussia and Saxony had come to an end," and in which she sang the title role before her family, thereby projecting herself as the kind of ruler Europe then needed, one both able to engage in warfare and maintain the long-sought peace (Watanabe-O'Kelly 2010: 29, 239–41). One need only to be reminded of Richard Wagner's Valkyries to appreciate that the helmeted, shield-bearing woman was to remain a firm fixture of the Germanic cultural imagination for a long time to come.

Apart from the stage and literature, and as comments in such works as John Millar's (1735–1801) *The Origin of the Distinction of Ranks* (1771) or the *Encyclopédie* entry "Amazone" attest, the existence of Amazons in Antiquity and contemporaneously in various parts of the world, especially in the area of the great river that bore their name, continued to be a topic of scholarly and scientific discussion in the eighteenth century. Whether portrayed in a positive or negative light, the naturalness or otherwise of female warriors was mostly not at issue in these various European discourses. What, if anything, seemed disputed was their sexual morality rather than their bellicosity. The eighteenth-century turn of mind was not set against associating women and war, far from it. Indeed, portraiture of women in this extended period reveals a fashion not only for showing huntresses, but also women in military armor and as the Goddess Minerva.[6] At its height in the seventeenth century, the trend continued well into the next. By comparison, ladies did not seem to favor sitting as Pax, or with her. To be sure, as the Greek and Roman goddesses of peace, Eirene, Pax, and Concordia, do not have male counter-parts, unlike most other mythological deities, personifications of peace perforce assumed female bodies. However, while peace was represented frequently, it was as an impersonal allegorical figure, such as the engraving in *The London Magazine* showing the Goddess of Peace bringing an olive branch to America and Britannia (January 1775).

MARGARET CAVENDISH

A line drawing (*c.* 1655–58) of Margaret Cavendish, Duchess of Newcastle (1624?–1674) by Pieter Louis van Schuppen (1627–1702) shows her between a male and a female figure: the former, Apollo, holds a sun and a lyre, the armed figure is the woman, presumably Pallas Athena, goddess of war and wisdom. Cavendish herself was to write a series of orations for and against war as well as for and against peace. A prolific author of plays, poems, letters, and treatises of natural philosophy, rich in social and political observations, she placed these orations at the beginning of her *Orations of Divers Sorts, Accommodated to Divers Places* (1662). Whilst these were intended to display her rhetorical skills and toss her invented and actual readers back and forth on various subjects, they demonstrate that even in the wake of the English Civil War and writing for a readership that would have lived through its horrors, the idea of peace as inherently good and war as evil was by no means self-evident, neither was the notion that all forms of physical violence between individuals in a society needed to be eradicated. Cavendish, for one, defended dueling with swords, but not with pistols, though this is not discussed in *Orations* (Susan James, in Cavendish [1662] 2003: xxv). What her speeches show are a number of conceptions allied to both war and peace, deployed and re-fashioned well into the nineteenth century, if not beyond. This makes her particularly interesting for our present purposes.

Speaking to the just and wise, Cavendish's unconvincing self-deprecatory preface asked that they "observe that most of my orations are general orations, *viz.* such as may be spoken in any kingdom and governments; for I suppose that in all, at least in most kingdoms and governments there are soldiers, magistrates, privy-counsellors, lawyers, preachers, and university scholars" (Cavendish [1662] 2003: 117, 118). Still in this preface, she invited readers to an imaginary market place, where they would hear orations concerning war and peace. "But the generality of the people being more apt to make war than to keep peace," she noted,

> I desire you to arm yourselves, supposing you to be of the masculine sex and of valiant heroical natures, to enter into the field of war, and since wars bring ruin and destruction to one or some parties if not all, and loss causes men to desire peace, out of war I bring you into great disorders caused by the ruins wars have made, which I am sorry for, yet it must be so, the Fates have decreed it. And misery causing men to be prudent and industrious, by which they come to flourish again, at least their successors, and to show you their industry, I bring you out of the field of war into a new-built city, where you must stay the building of it, for it will be built soon, having many labourers; and after it is built, there being a large market place, you may stand or sit with ease and hear the orations that are there spoken.
>
> —Cavendish [1662] 2003: 119–20

FIGURE 3.2: Margaret Cavendish, Duchess of Newcastle (1624–1674). Private Collection. Bridgeman Images.

Her fictional audience was to progress in this way to peace *through* war. Rather than deeming war an inherent human desire, mankind needed the very experience of it to become their erstwhile yearning; that warfare was an essential part of the forward march towards the kingdom of peace was to be an enduring idea, now more especially associated with Kant. In this imaginary tale, peace became the sphere of disputations, petitions, and speeches in courts, followed by "good agreement, unity, and love," which in turn would allow for rest, charity and further opportunities to hear orations, including those by women. The idyllic citadel Cavendish sketched in these opening pages appears to be one in which warring with words replaced battling with swords, though she made allowances for those who did not care to listen to the views of their fellow citizens, or indeed those of women at all. Those citizens could seek the company of country gentlemen and hear their discourses, but, were they not to like their pastimes, they could "walk into the fields of peace to receive the sweet and healthful air, or to view the curious and various works of nature" (Cavendish [1662] 2003: 120).

Thus even before embarking on her actual orations, Cavendish's preface had already drawn on many of the images evoked by ideas of peace in her own as well as the next century, not least that of man, seemingly solitary, walking through sunlit fields or resting under the shade of a tree in a quiet and benign countryside, in which peace, nature and beauty are conceptually intertwined. Jean-Jacques Rousseau and Goethe were to depict themselves and be depicted by others against such backgrounds. Peace and nature, and a nature conceived as rich and benevolent landscapes, were to prove an enduring association in the period. For her own immediate purposes however Cavendish had provided a rather more urban fictional space for her orations to be delivered. Addressing the imaginary members of her community in the different temporal frames they were to live through prior to and following the establishment of peace, the orations were grouped into fifteen parts, and included a call to arms, one speech for and one against breaching the peace with a neighboring nation, one to deserters, another from a general to mutineers, one on the need to build a church, one each for and against taxes, several funeral orations, and a number addressed to sleepy undergraduates, thus marking the gradual change in the subjects that the imagined public in her fictional city would be debating as they went from the state of war to that of peace.

Sluggishness was the first idea that peace conjured up in Cavendish's initial oration, "An Oration for War"; indeed, it did so in its very first sentence:

> Be not offended, *Noble Citizens*, if I labour to persuade my country to make heroic war, since it is neither safe, profitable, nor honourable for it to live in sluggish peace: for in peace you become ignorant of the arts in war, and living sluggishly you lose the courage of men and become effeminate, and having neither skill nor courage, you cannot expect safety: for should you chance to have enemies, you would not have abilities to help yourselves, having neither experience by practice, nor courage by use and custom; for custom and use work much upon the nature of men.
> —Cavendish [1662] 2003: 130

Peace, she continued, was a spoiler of youth and age, making the one covetous, cowardly and the other wanton and foolish. In times of peace, what ought to be councils of the wise became "gossiping meetings," rather than proper debating and advisory bodies: "[t]hey propound many things but resolve not any, debate not, but conclude, and sometimes find faults, but never help to mend them." As for the young, their "heroic spirits and noble ambitions" were quenched; they warred only with women, and in their "love-skirmishes" were "shot through their hearts with glances from their mistress' eyes" (Cavendish [1662] 2003: 130). Peace degenerated men, rotted bodies with excess, corrupted with idleness, which softened minds, made for vacant lives, and eternal oblivion. Once linked to lethargy, peace became linked to indulgence and its handmaiden effeminacy—effeminacy, as we will have cause to see again, being one of the very greatest afflictions that could befall a society.

While Cavendish's brief, but sharp, opening salvo might contain some conceptual links that are now familiar, it remains arresting for a number of reasons. First, in this oration, she reserved the register of corruption associated with peace for men of wealth. When it came to the poor, Cavendish's argument was of a different nature. Her claim was that war opened a door firmly shut in peacetime: it makes for the possibility of advancement and what, Cavendish appeared to have valued above all, glory: "for the meaner sort, it is better for them to wear honourable arms than to bear slavish burdens, and how happy is that man that can raise himself from a low birth to a glorious renown?" (Cavendish [1662] 2003: 131). Whatever else was to be said about war, the glory it could afford was irrespective of social rank. This, she reiterates in "An Oration to stay the Soldiers from a Mutinous return from the Wars":

> Can any man live, act, or die more honestly than in the service of his country? . . . And let me tell you, to be a soldier is the noblest profession; for it makes mean men as

princes, and those princes that are not soldiers are as mean men; and though fame doth not mention every particular soldier, but generally all together, yet the memory of every particular solider and their particular actions never die, as long as their successors live, for their children mention their fore-fathers valiant actions with pride, pleasure, and delight, and glory that they descended from such worthy ancestors and as for scars gotten in wars, they are such graces and becoming marks as they woo and win a mistress and her favour sooner than wealth, title, or beauty doth.
—Cavendish [1662] 2003: 149

Thus, while "An Oration for War" is more of a defamation of peace, of what it does to man and his nature (and in most, though by no means all, of her orations, Cavendish writes as belonging to the male sex) than an extolment of war as such, other speeches continue to present war as ennobling. Later ages, especially our own, might take for granted that peace is a good, war an evil and that they self-evidently lead to all that is good and evil respectively. This was not always so.

That said, "An Oration for Peace" follows "An Oration for War" and endeavors to redress the balance. Presuming that readers were now stirred towards warring, the oration began by decrying unjust wars, rather than war itself, before noting that "[b]esides, wars corrupt all good manners, nay, even good natures, making the one rude and the other cruel; and though long wars may make men martial, skilful, and may heighten their courage, yet neither skill nor courage can always bear away victory, especial from a powerful enemy, unless fortune be on their side" (Cavendish [1662] 2003: 131–32). Even when Cavendish disparaged it, war was not denied its edifying potential: it made men greater. Though she made war out as the corruptor of "good manners, nay even good nature," her critique of war came from another angle altogether. It was its uncontrollable nature that dammed war in her account. As fortune was the decisive factor in war, the wise could not favor it. War was depicted here as a "great devourer" and the bearer of ruin. Given its relation to uncertainty, peace became tied to steadiness and continuity:

Wherefore, let me persuade you not to follow unjust and inconstant fortune to the wars, but to live at home in peace with Minerva and Pallas. The one will defend you, and both will make you happy in present life and will give you fame and renown according to your desert, that your memory may live in after-ages.
—Cavendish [1662] 2003: 132

The speech thus appealed to the prudence of its audience. Its tone was less arousing. Fame could be had in peace, according to this oration, and could be obtained by meriting it. But what remained unsaid was that it was not glory. Nor was it feared that such a speech for peace would lead to a frenzy for it. To the degree that it enticed, it did so by evoking home and tranquility. It was not made out to be the stuff of passion. It conjured domesticity, not grandeur: all virtues, perhaps, but the less illustrious ones. Battlefields provided the true stage for the display of greatness.

In her "Oration against War," the third of Cavendish's speeches, and those that made up the rest of the collection, war, provided it be not unjust, did not shed the noble features in which it was adorned in the first, "Oration for War," rather its consequences were deplored. Thus to the degree that it was denounced, it was for the devastation it was most likely to bring in contrast to peace, which was allied to abundance in Cavendish's words (e.g. Cavendish [1662] 2003: 201, 278), an association that had a long history, and one that would prove enduring as demonstrated by Elizabeth Vigée Lebrun's "Peace

Bringing Back Abundance" (1780), both personified as women, which she submitted on her entry to the Académie royale de peinture et de sculpture (see Figure 5.2 in this volume). While war was portrayed by Cavendish as the toy of uncontrollable and fickle fortune, peace appeared as a state that could be managed, regulated, and indeed enhanced; it was the work of men, good counsel, and government, not the fates. Whatever her true beliefs and the interpretative challenges her deployment of her rhetorical skills might create for the reader, Cavendish in her Orations showed peace arrayed in its benefits, stability and wealth, for which it was the essential precondition. It was tranquil. It could make for honorable lives, but war or warlike conditions was the field of gloriousness. This could, however, never be true of civil wars, which Cavendish, unsurprisingly, utterly condemned and for which she suggested the conquest of other nations and the establishment of colonies as preventative (Cavendish [1662] 2003: 136–37). While her text is especially open to interpretation given its rhetorical genre, it seems fair to say that, possibly given the importance considerations of honor and glory held for her, she was unable to exert herself wholeheartedly in demonstrating the unattractiveness of war.

Also striking is that the Orations did not speak of "death and destruction," but "ruin and destruction" in relation to it. The absence of war, peace, in this work did not signify the absence of death. How could it, when throughout Europe so many died of bubonic plague in this period? How could it, given the high rate of child mortality and the great number of women who died in childbirth? Several of Cavendish's orations are funeral orations. Intermingled with orations to soldiers were orations to dead women, old and young, amongst which is "A Child-bed Womans Funeral Oration." For women, peace did not distance death as it did for men, though of course women died in wars and men died in peace time from natural and other causes. The oft dire reality of childbearing was underscored by women in this period in arguments for the parity of courage between the sexes. "The truth is," Cavendish lamented,

> That although all women are tender creatures, yet they endure more than men, and do oftener venture and endanger their lives more than men, and their lives are more profitable than men's lives are, for they increase life when men for the most part destroy life, as witness wars, wherein thousands of lives are destroyed, men fighting and killing each other, and yet men think all women mere cowards, although they do not only venture and endanger their lives more than they do, but endure greater pains with greater patience than men usually do; nay, women do not only endure the extremity of pain childbirth, but in breeding, the child being for the most part sick and seldom at ease; indeed, Nature seems both unjust and cruel to her female creatures, especially women, making them endure all the pain and the sickness in breeding and bringing forth of their young children, and the males to bear no part of their pain or danger; the truth is nature hath made her male creatures, especially mankind, only for pleasure, and her female creatures for misery; ... wherefore those women are most happy that never marry, or die whilst they be young, so that this young woman that died in childbed is happy in that she lives not to endure more pain or slavery, in which happiness let us leave her after we have laid her corpse to rest in the grave.
> —Cavendish [1662] 2003: 226

Even a woman such as the Duchess of Newcastle, who was herself childless and relatively unburdened by marital and other forms of servility, could see that peace, however necessary to a people's security and agricultural and commercial prosperity, did not usher the end of physical and emotional suffering, let alone freedom from domination, for her sex. War, in her view, could bring honor to men, indeed, we saw, also to "the meaner" sort of them. Yet, even if we discount as rhetoric much of the force of what she claims, it seems that in peace, the pleasures and happiness of man increased, but not clearly so those of woman.

The case was made across the Channel in 1673, when François Poulain de la Barre (1647–1725) entered the fray of attacks and defenses of women and published his *Discours Physique et Moral de l'Egalité des deux Sexes, ou l'on voit l'Importance de se défaire des Préjugez*, translated in to English in 1677. He claimed that women could do everything men did, in statecraft, the military, religion, philosophy, and science, not only as well, but better. He went further by arguing that once "states are completely at peace, the majority of the people who exercise authority seems to be almost dead or useless. Women, however, never cease to be necessary" (Poulain de la Barre [1673] 1990: 79). Women, unlike soldiers, always protected the vulnerable and never did so for their personal gain, adding, "the pains and care, the fatigue and consideration which women assume are unmatched in any other office in civil society" (Poulain de la Barre [1673] 1990: 80).

MARY WOLLSTONECRAFT

For all the differences between them, putting Mary Wollstonecraft in conversation with Cavendish more than a century later highlights continuities in ideas of peace, gender, and war. Wollstonecraft, who not only was not a Duchess, but disliked the aristocracy,

FIGURE 3.3: John Opie, *Mary Wollstonecraft*. DEA PICTURE LIBRARY, Contributor. Getty Images.

and might be thought to share very little with Cavendish, held comparable views of women and men in times of peace. Peace did not offer much of a reprieve from death and self-sacrifice for women in her view, any more than it did not only for Cavendish, but for Wollstonecraft's contemporaries, such as Olympe de Gouges (1748–1793). Wollstonecraft's best friend, Fanny Blood, died in childbirth, and although she herself was delivered relatively easily of her first daughter, Fanny Imlay, she was to die of septicemia a few days after the birth of her second daughter, Mary Godwin, later Shelley. It was crucial to Wollstonecraft's case for the re-evaluation of the involvement of her sex in society that its self-sacrifice, courage, and devotion be fully recognized. In a world in which mothers would dedicate themselves to the upbringing of children as the virtuous citizens of the future, and non-married women be enabled to pursue those professions, such as midwifery, that contributed to the wellbeing of their communities, their entitlement to civic participation could not be disputed.[7] Though there were clearly exceptional pockets of "domestic happiness," even, as Wollstonecraft put it, in Paris, such was not the world as it was, but it was the world that she strove for in vindicating the rights of men as well as women (Wollstonecraft [1794] 1989: 147–48). Were it to be realized, it would see the end of what both Cavendish and she described as the enslavement of women to men. Where they differed was that for Wollstonecraft such an age was within reach (though she could be overwhelmed by doubts at times as her *Introductory To A Series of Letters on the Present Character of the French Nation written in Paris on 15th February, 1793* exemplifies) (Wollstonecraft [1798] 1989: 444–45), and importantly that the peace it entailed would not lead to degeneration or any form of what Cavendish had referred to as "sluggishness":

> It is a vulgar errour, built on a superficial view of the subject, though it seems to have the sanction of experience, that civilization can only go as far as it has hitherto gone, and then must necessarily fall back into barbarism. Yet thus much appears certain, that a state will infallibly grow old and feeble, if hereditary riches support hereditary rank, under any description. But when courts and primogeniture are done away, and simple laws equal laws are established, what is to prevent each generation from retaining the vigour of youth?—What can weaken the body or mind, when the great majority of society must exercise both, to earn a subsistence, and acquire respectability?
> —Wollstonecraft [1794] 1989: 22

The fears for the vigor of youth raised by Cavendish were assuaged thus by Wollstonecraft. It was riches, the "selfish enjoyments of the senses" that emasculated. Writing from Paris some month before the Terror, she wondered,

> Seeing how deep the fibres of mischief have shot, I sometimes ask, with a doubting accent, Whether a nation can go back to the purity of manners which has hitherto been maintained unsullied only by the keen air of poverty, when emasculated by pleasure, the luxuries of prosperity are become the wants of nature?
> —Wollstonecraft [1798] 1989: 445

In Wollstonecraft's view, emasculation and effeminacy was in the present, especially in France, the flag-bearer of heightened sophistication and artificiality (Wollstonecraft [1798] 1989: 444). A future society in which needs would be curbed or at least not hyperinflated and in which most would earn their living would be an energized one. It would not be a placid community. It would be an active one. Energy mattered in the eighteenth century. Individuals and peoples were measured in terms of it, for instance, by Montesquieu when he wrote approvingly of the Germanic hordes that conquered Roman Europe or the Abbé Raynal and the contributors to his *Histoire des deux Indes* when they wrote contemptuously of the indolence of various societies encountered by Europeans.[8]

Wollstonecraft's confidence in the vitality of her imagined new world did not make Wollstonecraft a pacifist. Like Cavendish, she thought defensive wars admissible. Indeed, she thought that, once these were to become the only ones to be fought, the true valor of women would shine anew:

> . . . if defensive war, the only justifiable war, in the present advanced state of society, where virtue can shew its face and ripen amidst the rigours which purify the air on the mountain's top, were alone to be adopted as just and glorious, the true heroism of antiquity might again animate female bosoms.
> —Wollstonecraft 1995: 236

Clearly, Wollstonecraft did not wish women to be denied heroic virtues, what she saw as true masculine virtues. She was convinced that they naturally neither lacked physical or moral courage, fortitude or the readiness to sacrifice themselves for their country, quite the contrary. She did have to make the case for their patriotism, however, and her case inevitably took its shape from those she sought to challenge.

Wollstonecraft had come to speak of women and war in *A Vindication of the Rights of Woman* (1792) because of Jean-Jacques Rousseau, whose thoughts on nature, education, man and woman had an enormous influence on the second half of the eighteenth century. It was he who had derided the idea of women at war in *Émile* (1762): "I know that, as a proof of the inferiority of the sex, Rousseau has exultingly exclaimed, How can they leave the nursery for the camp!" (Wollstonecraft 1995: 236). Wollstonecraft was to make her readers ponder the reality of this nursery and motherhood more generally. But before turning to the condition of women, she had challenged the axiomatic notion that military life was home to virtues. "And the camp," she thus continued,

> has by some moralists been the school of the most heroic virtues; though, I think, it would puzzle a keen casuist to prove the reasonableness of the greater number of wars that have dubbed heroes. I do not mean to consider this question critically; because, having frequently viewed these freaks of ambition as the first natural mode of civilization, when the ground must be torn up, and the woods cleared by fire and sword, I do not choose to call them pests; but surely the present system of war has little connection with virtue of any denomination, being rather the school of finesse and effeminacy, than of fortitude.
> —Wollstonecraft 1995: 235–36

For Wollstonecraft, effeminacy was not the bugbear of demilitarized society, but was actually taught at the very heart of masculine quarters. Garrisoned soldiers were not the stuff of fabled heroes in her view. They were as women pathetically caring only for the figure they cut at balls and parading in the park avenues of provincial towns. There was no honor for either of the sexes in that. If she ever thought at all well of warriors, the soldiers of her day were an altogether different breed of beings in her estimation. Her diatribe against those who dichotomized the camp and the nursery, men and women, consisted principally in showing army life and soldiering in her time perhaps more than war itself, as it was, and de-glorifying it. Unlike, Germaine de Staël, for instance, who "acknowledged the achievements of the French army, and almost marveled at their docile loyalty to a corrupt and unstable civil government," Wollstonecraft had nothing positive to say about armies of any nation, referring to the military as "a pest in every country" (Wollstonecraft [1794] 1989: 50). Yet soldiers did not entirely stand out of the rest of contemporary society. The corruption was general. But the effeminacy that prevailed was not the product of peace itself, it was the result of an ill-ordered society governed by the desire to please and shine and fueled by a luxury economy.[9] Still targeting Rousseau some four years later, she argued that the arts and sciences that modernity enjoyed were not themselves nefarious, quite the contrary:

> Men exclaim, only noticing the evil, against the luxury introduced with the arts and sciences; when it is obviously the cultivation of these alone, emphatically termed the arts of peace, that can turn the sword into a ploughshare. War is the adventure naturally pursued by the idle, and it requires something of this species, to excite the strong emotions necessary to rouse inactive minds.
> —Wollstonecraft [1794] 1989: 23

Luxury had to be severed from the body politic. The arts and sciences were needed for this and to fight the inertia, the sluggishness, which worried Wollstonecraft as it had Cavendish. Though she was not one to praise war even in jest, Wollstonecraft shared Cavendish's concern with the potential lethargy of peace. Idleness, especially as she saw it combined with ignorance, was the ill and industry the cure. Here as elsewhere Wollstonecraft was wont to make her point by tying warring men to women as if to prick her readers to attention: "[i]gnorant people, when they appear to reflect, exercise their imagination more than their understanding; indulging in reveries, instead of pursuing a train of thinking; and thus grow romantic, like the croisaders; or like women, who are commonly idle and restless" (Wollstonecraft [1794] 1989: 23).

But fearing her comparison between eighteenth-century women and soldiers be misunderstood, she had added in *A Vindication of the Rights of Woman*,

> But fair and softly, gentle reader, male or female, do not alarm thyself, for though I have compared the character of a modern soldier with that of a civilized woman, I am not going to advise them to turn their distaff into a musket, though I sincerely wish to see the bayonet converted into a pruning-hook.
> —Wollstonecraft 1995: 236

In Wollstonecraft's vision of a much better world, wars, if unavoidable, would be followed by a return to the land, to ploughshares and pruning hooks, not urban centers in which social inequality made all victims to vain aspiration for admiration. Heroes in Ancient Greece had tilled fields as Ulysses had on his homecoming. But such was not the condition in eighteenth-century Europe:

> As soldiers, I grant, they can now only gather, for the most part, vain glorious laurels, whilst they adjust to a hair the European balance, taking especial care that no bleak northern nook or sound incline the beam. But the days of true heroism are over, when a citizen fought for his country like a Fabricius or a Washington, and then returned to his farm to let his virtuous fervour run in a more placid, but not a less salutary, stream. No, our British heroes are oftener sent from the gaming table than from the plow; and their passions have been rather inflamed by hanging with dumb suspense on the turn of a die, than sublimated by panting after the adventurous march of virtue in the historic page.
> —Wollstonecraft 1995: 233

Yet, however critical she might have been of her society, she did not seek a return to a mythical past. Her ideal world would share some of its features, such as that just cited, but she looked to the future, to a kind of world-wide America, and of men like Washington. Domestic happiness could now be had. "Fortunately," she wrote in her reflections on the French Revolution,

> the blessings of society have been sufficiently experienced to convince us, that the only solid good to be expected from a government must result from the security of our persons and property. And domestic felicity has given a mild lustre to human happiness superior to the false glory of sanguinary devastation, or magnificent robberies. Our field and vineyards have thus gradually become the principal objects of our care—and it is from this general sentiment governing the opinion of the civilized part of the world, that we are enabled to contemplate, with some degree of certainty, the approaching age of peace.
> —Wollstonecraft [1794] 1989: 147

The more representative and consensual governments became, and the more they became supported by the "sweat and blood" of their people, the less frequent "wars and their calamitous effects" would become (Wollstonecraft [1794] 1989: 222).

The age of peace could only dawn in the wake of a total transformation of society, indeed a moral revolution. Some of the political changes alluded to already would be required, such as a form of representative government and a society in which all labored, but political alterations even if combined with social ones would be insufficient, as Wollstonecraft thought the revolution in France was demonstrating in its first two years. Not even greater economic equality would usher in the age of peace, though it would contribute to its advancement. What was required was an entirely different form of social organization, the implementation of decentralization so as to dismantle the accumulation of power, wealth and the opportunity of their display, a stop to the intensification of the division of labor, and an end to the luxury economy. Though these points were not put forward systematically by Wollstonecraft, they can be garnered from her writings from her *Vindications* onwards. What is even clearer is that none of this could be had without "a REVOLUTION in female manners," which in turn required for women to be educated and to enjoy the rights of citizenship (Wollstonecraft 1995: 117, 292–94). Wollstonecraft's imagined age of peace was one in which both the sexes, having undergone a complete change away from the hall of mirrors that characterized eighteenth-century Europe, were educated and worked together in "the mild lustre" of domestic happiness. Yet, always seeking not to alarm her readers, she had written as reassuringly as she could in *A Vindication of the Rights of Woman*:

> I only recreated an imagination, fatigued by contemplating the vices and follies which all proceed from a feculent stream of wealth that has muddied the pure rills of natural affection, by supposing that society will some time or other be so constituted, that man must necessarily fulfil the duties of a citizen, or be despised, and that while he was employed in any of the departments of civil life, his wife, also an active citizen, should be equally intent to manage her family, educate her children, and assist her neighbours.
> —Wollstonecraft 1995: 236

Rights led to peace, the rights of woman as well as man, but a peace conceived as life in interdependency and the fulfillment of duties to one's family and community in a radically different kind of social and economic order than that of late eighteenth-century England

and France. The virtues it would afford would be those of self-command, diligence, industriousness, dedication to others and the like. Wollstonecraft did not advertise the prosperity it would bring, much less the necessity of peace to the development of commerce given her strong reservations about commercial society and its attendant luxury.

Though within sight, peace would be not the automatic by-product of the progress of civilization. The means of peace had to be chosen. Society crafted in such a way as to be both peaceful and dynamic. While Wollstonecraft's views of historical development were to be modified by her travels through what she deemed the less advanced stages of human society in Northern Europe, thereby making her more forgiving of contemporary French culture (Wollstonecraft [1798] 1989: 327, 346), the road on which Europe was advancing would not in itself lead to genuine and meaningful peace, neither between nations, nor between its peoples, nor between the sexes. In this as in other respects, she both resembled and differed from some of her contemporaries as well as those who had influenced her.

Just as Wollstonecraft was wont to compare soldiers to women, so she almost always compared the condition of women to that of slaves. Like Olympe de Gouges, who was guillotined in November 1793 whilst Wollstonecraft was still in Paris, she understood the importance the slave trade assumed for the wealth of Europe. Her ever more profound critique of commercial society was partly due to her understanding that it was underpinned by the "infamous" traffic in slave and slave labor. Whilst the revolutionary wars raged in Europe, a quieter war continued the world over and would do so when these would end thereby telling the lie of peace. "During my present journey," she wrote from Hamburg,

> And whilst residing in France, I have had an opportunity of peeping behind the scenes of what are vulgarly termed great affairs, only to discover the mean machinery which has directed many transactions of moment. The sword has been merciful, compared with the depredations made on human life by contractors, and by the swarm of locusts who have battened on the pestilence they spread abroad. These men, like the owners of negro ships, never smell on their money the blood by which it has been gained, but sleep quietly in their beds, terming such occupations lawful callings; yet the lightning marks not their roofs, to thunder conviction on them, "and to justify the ways of God to man."
>
> —Wollstonecraft [1798] 1989: 344

War, as Wollstonecraft realized, took more forms than one. The advancement of civilization, from her point of view, did not mean a concomitant diminution of violence and an end to barbarism, as these could assume hidden practices within it, as was the case with slavery and the domination of women by men.

THE SCOTTISH DEBATE

The question of whether the progress of the arts and sciences and the development of commerce was marked by diminishing levels of violence and an improvement in human relations, including between the sexes, was widely debated in the eighteenth century, and particularly so in Scotland from the 1740s onwards. Partly inspired by Montesquieu's *De L'Esprit des Loix* (1748) in which the condition of women was made the single most important index of the overall nature of their society, many eighteenth-century writers were particularly attentive to their status throughout the world and in the conjectural history of civilization. Adam Smith, whom Wollstonecraft read and engaged with, thought humanity became less violent as it became more polished. Whilst he was far from exalting war, Smith could nonetheless say that it "is the great school both for acquiring and exercising [a] species of magnanimity," adding,

> In war, men become familiar with death, and are thereby necessarily cured of that superstitious horror with which it is viewed by the weak and unexperienced. [. . .] It is this habitual contempt of danger and death which ennobles the profession of a soldier, and bestows upon it, in the natural apprehensions of mankind, a rank and dignity superior to that of any other profession.
> —Smith [1759] 1976: 239 [VI.iii.7]

Though he believed later stages of society to be less brutal than those preceding them, he did not appear to subscribe to the possibility of perpetual peace. Wars, for whatever reason or of whatever nature, were a feature of human existence for him. Unsurprisingly given their frequency in his own time, Smith's analysis of the moral sentiments of his time was replete with examples from military life. These were discussed in a language that drew on concepts of masculinity and femininity with which Wollstonecraft might well have agreed. She could easily have written, as Smith did, that "[i]n quiet and peaceable times . . . [t]he external graces, the frivolous accomplishments of that impertinent and foolish thing called a man of fashion, are commonly more admired than the solid and masculine virtues of a warrior, a statesman, a philosopher, or a legislator" (Smith [1759] 1976: 63 [I.iii.3.6]). She would also have been sympathetic to his claim that

> [t]o compare [. . .] the futile mortifications of a monastery, to the ennobling hardships and hazards of war; to suppose that one day, or one hour, employed in the former should, in the eye of the great Judge of the world, have more merit than a whole life spent honourably in the latter, is surely contrary to all our moral sentiments; to all the principles by which nature has taught us to regulate our contempt or admiration.
> —Smith [1759] 1976: 134 [III.ii.45]

However, although "a long peace is," he noted, "very apt to diminish the difference between the civil and the military character," Smith gave a more sympathetic account of life in and out of camps, arguing that given the effort it took "to conquer the fear of death" it was natural that soldiers "plunge themselves, for this purpose, into every sort of amusement and dissipation" (Smith [1759] 1976: 317 [VII.iii.I.4]). This said, the index of masculinity and effeminacy was used by him and Wollstonecraft in much the same way, approving with the one, condemning, indeed loathing, with the other. And while he could write of "useless outcries and womanish lamentations," when referring to a man who sinks under pain and torture, he did not forget women in labor: "A man may sympathize with a woman in child-bed; though it is impossible that he should conceive himself as suffering her pains in his own proper person and character" (Smith [1759] 1976: 317 [VII.iii.I.4]).

Amongst Smith's friends and pupils, Adam Ferguson and John Millar were to provide penetrating studies of the relationship between violence and civilization in their respective histories of society. A friend of both David Hume and Smith, Ferguson tackled the question of effeminacy directly in *An Essay on the History of Civil Society* (1767), his history of civilization.[10] Very much a Highlander and a onetime chaplain to the 42nd (Black Watch), Ferguson knew both the community of the clan and the reality of modern society (Forbes 1966: xxviii, xxxix). He knew both the lost world of loyalty and self-denial, and what appeared as the inevitable future of a society governed by self-interest and luxury. His sources were varied, and included the *Letters* of Lady Mary Wortley Montague and Joseph-François Lafitau's *Moeurs des Sauvages Amériquains* (1724). Having traced the development of civilization, he was eager in the last part of his book to differentiate between luxury and corruption, defining the one as "that accumulation of wealth, and that refinement on the ways of enjoying it, which are the objects of industry, or the fruits of mechanic and commercial arts" whereas the other was "a real weakness, or depravity of the human character, which may accompany any state of those arts, and be found under any external circumstances or condition whatever" (Ferguson [1767] 1966: 248–49). In polished societies, degeneracy did not come from luxury as such but from the absence of devotion to a common good, and an inequality resulting not from merit but from wealth. In those circumstances, regardless of the form of government, republican or monarchical, "men of every condition, although they are eager to acquire, or display their wealth, have no remains of real ambition"; "they have changed into effeminate vanity, that sense of honour which gave rules to the personal courage" (Ferguson [1767] 1966: 251). Effeminacy and self-preoccupation away from the public good went hand in hand, according to Ferguson, and in this Wollstonecraft resembled him. "In this condition," Ferguson thought,

> mankind generally flatter their own imbecility under the name of politeness. They are persuaded, that the celebrated ardour, generosity, and fortitude, of former ages, bordered on frenzy, or were the mere effects of necessity, on men who had not the means of enjoying their ease, or pleasure.
> —Ferguson [1767] 1966: 256

Such societies paved their way to despotism and to their utter ruin and devastation. Ferguson's account of its causes and trajectory was complex. It suffices to note here that extended territories, leading to the centralization of power and the combination of militarized regimes over unarmed peoples were some of its key features. Yet, when they were at their most corrupt and broken stage such states would again see "that personal confidence and vigour, that social attachment, that use of arms, which, in former times, rendered a small tribe the seed of a great nation" (Ferguson [1767] 1966: 279). The spirit of the militia was essential to keeping dreaded effeminacy at bay.

Whilst Millar, Smith's pupil, also noted the abatement of martial ardor with the improvement of the arts and manufactures, which "by introducing luxury, contributes yet more to enervate the minds of men, who, according as they enjoy more ease and pleasure at home, feel greater aversion to the hardships and dangers of a military life, and put a lower value upon that sort of reputation which it affords," he did not express the degree of anxiety we saw in some of his contemporaries (Millar [1771] 2006: 230). Indeed, Millar's *Origins of the Distinction of Ranks* (1771) showed that although the development of the art of war in the Middle Ages had led to an improved relationship between the sexes as men adopted a chivalrous code in their dealings with women, it was the arts of peace that, by bringing men in the frequent company of women, heightened the latter's standing as their abilities became increasingly recognized and valued. If the replacement of militia by standing armies evoked any regret in Millar, he did not speak of the corruption of the people, but remarked instead, as had Ferguson, on their potential use in suppressing the liberties of the people. However, he concluded his work by rejoicing in the condemnation of slavery that the latter part of his century was witnessing in the judicial courts as well as from campaigners. The arts of peace were good to women and to slaves.

This did not make for peace between nations, however, for Millar pointed out that standing armies and increased wealth meant, amongst other things, that wars were now much longer than ever before.

CONCLUSION

One of the striking differences between our age and that examined above is that those living in it and supporting liberal democracies take peace to be an assumed good. The case for wars, not peace, needs to be made in our day. Rightly or wrongly our fear is not of corruption and effeminacy, but of violence and death. Though we only glimpsed this idea here and there during the long eighteenth century, it would seem that this was not quite so then. The idea of peace did not immediately conjure up the idea of non-violence or the avoidance of death, especially not for women and slaves. It evoked the idea of sluggishness, enervation, and weakness. Those who foresaw a different world had to think through ways of avoiding these forms of emasculation in both the sexes. They had to make the case that peace could be the theater of a new greatness, the advancement of science, widely understood, and the development and strength of mind, not just of the body. Peace did not need to lead to degeneration and corruption. It could, if genuine, be the place for perfecting human nature. For this, however, hidden wars, such as those among races through enslavement and between the sexes for the subjugation of women, had to be exposed and terminated. True peace required grand virtues, not least courage to end inequities.

ACKNOWLEDGMENT

Very special thanks go to Fredric Smoler, and to Alexandra Campbell and Laura Worsley, as well as Erika Ingham, of the National Portrait Gallery, for their help with matters of art.

CHAPTER FOUR

Peace, Pacifism, and Religion

MURAD IDRIS

INTRODUCTION

The year 1648 was not a year of pacifism. This is the case whether pacifism is understood expansively (as in this chapter) as an avowed commitment to peace, or more narrowly as an individual's principled or conscientious refusal to resort to violence, be it absolutely or only in certain circumstances. 1648 is best known for the myth of the Peace of Westphalia and 1814–15 for the Congress of Vienna; they are rarely invoked as having much to do with pacifism. The treaties of Münster and Osnabruck are often held up as having ended a series of religious wars by formalizing—if not inaugurating—the idea of coexisting, sovereign nation-states, where each state would possess exclusive authority over deciding on its religion, and where "war" would come to describe violence between such "sovereign" states. The European representatives of the treaties may have momentarily ended some of their hostilities against one another in Europe, but the year 1648 is also important to the history of peace and war for other, less-known events that bring into view a broader, more global view of empire. For example, in 1648, European powers continued their colonization of the Americas, as with the wars between Portugal and the Netherlands over Brazil; France and the Netherlands reached an agreement to divide the Caribbean island of Saint Martin; and in the Arabian Peninsula, Oman continued to push Portuguese forces from the area (eventually signing a treaty that restored to Oman control over a Portuguese colonial fort, as Portuguese power in the region declined, and Oman became, for a time, a sea power). Examinations of the commitment to peace from 1648 and after should have a global scope in view, even though this periodization is already burdened by a number of Eurocentric historical and theoretical commitments. The "Age of Enlightenment" was an age of empires, but much of the work on pacifism in this period remains thoroughly embedded in Europe. The language of "pacifism" would travel to other parts of the world in later centuries, as colonized thinkers and non-European subjects adapted it, transformed it, or unmasked it.

While *pacifism* was, between 1648–1815, commonly invoked as a religious or ambiguously secularized European Christian commitment, *peace* and *religion* also formed other nexuses, both within Europe and outside it. The majority of this chapter focuses on European thought, but a handful of illustrative examples outside the West, drawn especially from various genres of Islamic thought, will sketch out some other religion-and-peace cultural constellations, both during this period and beyond it.

The currents and events mentioned above do not represent distinct lenses so much as layers of political and cultural history; depending on how one understands the relationship among discourses about peace in Europe, Christianity, and imperialism abroad, these currents might appear complementary or contradictory, arising out of similar impulses or inconsistent commitments. The privilege afforded to the European state in prevailing discourses—telegraphed in the later centuries by compulsive reference to the "post-Westphalian state"—also restructured discourses surrounding commitments to universal peace, often construed as the abolition of what the myth of Westphalia had ostensibly inaugurated. Pacifism in European thought thus became, for the most part, about three modes of thought that reflect the rise of discourses about states, whether by accepting the state, working within it, or seeking to overcome it. These different strands of pacifism did not yet offer distinctions between various domains, such as economic, individualist, or cultural pacifism; the emphasis often was alternately on condemning war, on individual conscience, or on pacifist organizations based on Christian theological doctrines and appeals to individual conscience.

These three key strands of European and American pacifism that developed between 1648 and 1815 are: (i) a commitment to peace either within the state or between sovereign nation-states; (ii) conscientious objections to wars waged by such states, or in some cases, a more expansive objection to numerous kinds of violence; and (iii) a critique of the state as the locus and agent of war, and its boundaries as facilitating war, which would have to be transcended, eroded, or removed altogether. The first strand was often state-centric. In some cases, the formation of the modern "Westphalian" state constrained understandings of war as being either within the state or between states. Imperial violence, in this way, often fell outside this frame, though there are important exceptions in which the commitment to peace went beyond European political formations. The second strand of pacifism, running parallel to and sometimes intersecting with the others, presented war as the origin of all human ills but also sought a collective form of resolution. Such resolutions most often were presented as going beyond the form of the nation-state, whether in continuing the earlier history of congresses, or in calling for world republics or world federations. The third strand represented a conscience-based refusal of war. This strand, continuing earlier understandings of Christian pacifism, often invoked principles like turning the other cheek. From this perspective, war was inconsistent with religion. It was most often Quakers who offered these religion- and conscience-based objections. The distinctions across these strands are obviously imperfect, but they are nonetheless useful as heuristics for organizing the history of pacifism and religion in the West, and in working through their resonances, parallels, or adaptations beyond.

Corresponding to each of these three, the next sections begin, respectively, by considering Thomas Hobbes' *Leviathan* (1651), George Fox's peace testimony of 1651 and his *Declaration* (1660) and William Penn's *Essay Toward the Present and Future Peace of Europe* (1691), and texts from the organized peace movements of the early nineteenth century. The latter two sections will also briefly consider how alternate themes linked to peace and religion appear in contemporaneous non-European texts, mostly drawn from Muslim contexts.

PEACE, PACIFISM, AND THE STATE

The first strand of pacifism, as a general commitment to peace, encompasses a large segment of philosophical, literary, and cultural production during this period. Hobbes' *Leviathan* (1651) appeared three years after the Peace of Westphalia (for a critical discussion, see Armitage 2013: 73). It is usually regarded as an exemplary cultural artifact for the relocation of peace to the state's territorial boundaries and the naturalization of

FIGURE 4.1: Thomas Hobbes, 1676 (1588–1679). Ian Dagnall Computing. Alamy Stock Photo.

war to all that lies beyond those boundaries. Many have found in Hobbes a "true philosopher of peace" (Bull 1981), a "peace-lover" (Gert 2010), and even an advocate of certain kinds of secular pacifism (May 2013).

But the relationships of *Leviathan* to peace, pacifism, and religion are far from straightforward. First, some have argued that Hobbes' state of nature is, counterintuitively, without any actual acts of physical violence (Foucault [1997] 2003: 92), meaning that the state does not end or limit violence so much as extend or even inaugurate it. Second, as is commonly recognized, Hobbes identifies both religious controversy and the infiltration of the Church into sovereignty as among the major reasons for war. In other words, religion demands peace, but religious disagreement produces war. It is perhaps for this reason that Hobbes not only calls for the sovereign to dictate public religion, but also reduces Christianity to a bare minimum. For the sake of peace, he reduces Christianity to the idea that "Jesus is the Christ" (Hobbes [1651] 1994: 291, 340, 348, 402), where "no other article is necessary" (ibid: 404). Finally, as Hobbes repeatedly insists, the laws of nature incline men toward the pursuit of peace. These laws arise, in part, from Hobbes' reading of religious sources, and from his re-presentation of these sources in generally secularized guise, in opposition to the preferred language of Christian natural law. Indeed, he describes the second law of nature as being a mere restatement of the Gospel: "This is that law of the Gospel: 'whatsoever you require that others should do to you, that do ye to them'" (Hobbes [1651] 1994: 80). In making one's adherence to the scriptural Golden

Rule conditional upon whether others follow it, Hobbes' understanding of the commitment to peace builds on a religious doctrine while radically transforming it. As one commentator observed, Hobbes' claim that the second law of nature restates "the Gospel law" without its "insignificant sounds" implies that he "must certainly have been conscious of the irony of the transmogrification (and the horror it would inspire in the bishops)" (Krook 1959: 107 n.1).

These three elements—non-violence in the state of nature, religious controversy and war, and the ambiguously secularized Christian underpinning of desiring peace—come together in Hobbes' discussion of preaching the Gospel outside Europe. Just as one would not want a man from the Indies preaching his religion in Europe, he explains, so a European ought not to preach his religion in the Americas (Hobbes [1651] 1994: 191–92). And yet, later in the text, Hobbes imagines himself preaching in the Americas, considering it unnecessary to have the Church's approval (Hobbes [1651] 1994: 466–67), but he does not describe it as a breach of the Golden Rule, as an act of stirring up religious controversy that can elicit war, or as an irony that the spread of a doctrine of peace might itself be inconsistent with the demand for peace. Peace and religion, then, undercut each other in that religion calls for following peace, but the spread of religion can be against peace. Hobbes' commitment to peace, in other words, is derived from religion, but then, in passively following the spread of "Jesus is the Christ" elsewhere, brings into view its own limits and its expansion of violence, empire, and settler colonialism (for a full discussion of these dynamics in Hobbes, see Idris 2019: 226–48).

If Hobbes' *Leviathan* exemplifies the idea that the *desire for peace* should lead to the militarized state, and if it also exemplifies this desire's ambiguous relationships to religion, empire, and war, a different strand of cultural production took aim at the state from a pacifist perspective. Indeed, throughout the Age of Enlightenment, pacifist criticism, as often expressed in literature, satirized militaristic culture and sometimes forthrightly criticized rulers as fundamentally irreligious and anti-Christian for waging war. Consider the following three examples that span the period. John Milton (1608–1674) in *Paradise Lost* (1667) simultaneously undermines and parodies the "conventions of military heroism in epic poetry" by repeatedly emphasizing "peace of conscience" and "peace within man"—thereby redeploying the idea of the Christian subject's inner, ethical core of peace (see White 2008: 132–38).

Jonathan Swift (1667–1745) later captured the appeal to religion in condemnations of militarism and praise of peace. In *Gulliver's Travels* (1726), Swift satirizes militaristic people as "Houyhnhnms," a race of rational horses who created an apparently stable or even "peaceful" society. However, they have no religion; they have little respect for the intrinsic value of life, be it among their own or among the humanoid "Yahoos."

In a third illustrative example, Mary Shelley, in one of her early poems, titled "War" (1810), folds her condemnation of war into a condemnation of monarchs. The poem begins by surveying the atrocities of war; as a "hero" of war dies, he bemoans his fate and prays to God. By the end of the poem, it becomes clear that war's devastation—from destruction and death to "ruined towns and smoking cities"—is "thy work, Monarch," which is "the work of Hell." The poem's religious imagery, like that of Milton and Swift, condemns war out of a pacifist sensibility, but here Shelley explicitly puts the blame not on society at large or historical processes; she identifies war and monarchs who wage war as servants of Hell, which is to say, devils (see White 2008: 195; also see Cox 1998).

FIGURE 4.2: Jonathan Swift, *The Tale of a Tub* (1721). Traditionally, sailors throw a tub to divert a whale from attacking their ship. This whale symbolizes Thomas Hobbes' *Leviathan* and the tub is intended to distract Hobbes and others from scuttling the ship of state. Engraving after drawing by Bernard Lens II. Private Collection. Bridgeman Images.

PEACE AND PACIFISM BEYOND STATE BOUNDARIES

Christianity, as we saw above, called for peace, and religious disagreement undermined it. Religion, at the same time, offered an ethics and a language from which to criticize war or, as we see below, to call for pacifism. While the discussions above limited the realization of peace to the state, discussions of peace and pacifism during this period also appeared in the genre of the "peace plan," or works that purported to offer guidance on how peace between states would be attained. The most famous of these works focus on Europe, and in the case of some plans, the very call for peace, and the hope for its realization, derives from a religious mold.

In the earlier part of this period, John Amos Comenius (1592–1670), a Czech theologian and philosopher of education, combined his call for peace with a call for universal education and universal language. Comenius worked from the theologically grounded belief that the present age was coming to an end and a new age of peace was coming. He "used the Old and New Testaments to buttress his belief in the dawning of a new age, when the world would return to the original blessings of Eden" (Atwood 2009: 373). The narrative structure here is explicitly based on and derived from religion. This is not surprising, as he belonged to the Unity of the Brethren, a Protestant sect, which was "not always dogmatically pacifist, but its members avoided violence as inconsistent with the ethic of love" (Atwood 2009: 18; for the earlier history of the Brethren, see Brock 1957). As Comenius wrote in the *Consultatio* (*De rerum humanarum emendatione consultatio catholica*; or "General Consultation on the Reform of Human Affairs") of 1666, "Mankind has had enough of folly and war, and it is to be hoped that the time will come when all men are exhausted with wars and return to peace, and the state of this world nearing its end becomes one of peace and tranquility" (as quoted in Atwood 2009: 374). A year later, he wrote his "classic statement" on peace, *Angel of Peace*, against war between England and the Netherlands (see Atwood 2009: 373 n.17; Polišensky 1970, 1979; for the text of *Angel of Peace*, see Comenius [1667] 1945). He put forward a pedagogical view of religious faith and its role in securing peace.

But the history of European and American pacifism is tied to the rise of a different contemporaneous sect, namely the Quakers. This is the case in a number of ways, and the literature devoted to this connection is vast (see especially Weddle 2001; Angell and Dandelion, 2013, ch. 1–4; also see Ingle 1994; Yoder 2009; Ziegler 2001). Like Comenius, the Quakers used theological arguments to assert the importance of peace. George Fox (1624–1691), the founder of the Religious Society of Friends, or Quakers, had a profound impact on peace discourses first in England then in New England. One of the most important documents along these lines was the Quakers' 1660 *Declaration from the Harmless and Innocent People of God, called Quakers, against all Plotters and Fighters in the World* (for the full text of the *Declaration*, see Weddle 2001: 234–37), which George Fox and eleven other Quakers issued. The declaration laid out peace as the primary principle of Quakers, and it condemned war as proceeding from sin: lust, envy, and greed. It declared the principle and practice of nonresistance as the foundation of religious belief and conscience, reinterpreting various parts of the Hebrew Bible and the New Testament.

The Quaker position on violence was again set forth in 1676 by Robert Barclay (1648–1690): "All their teaching followed conclusively from the fundamental belief that each man's life was guided by an 'inner light' which transcended even the Bible, in virtue of which there could be no right to constrain men; wherefore nonresistance and pacifism were axiomatic" (Beales 1931: 31). Barclay's writings, from statements of the Quaker position and Christian divinity (for example, Barclay 1676), to his *Theological Theses* (1675), *An Epistle of Love and Friendly Advice to the Ambassadors of the several Princes of Europe* (1677) and *Treatise on Universal Love* (1677), elaborated the basic tenets of Quakerism, Christian love, and pacifism. But there have been important debates about the origins of the peace testimony among Quakers, as well as its extent (Weddle 2001: 6–8; also see ibid. 245–54 for Weddle's discussion of the historiography of pacifism; see Cockburn 2012 on pacifism and gender; Bell 2011 on religion and pacifist masculinity). For some, it was understood as an integral part of Quakerism from its inception, and should be understood exclusively in religious terms; while for others, it arose out of political considerations, as a "self-defensive, reactive, strategic phenomenon arising out of political necessity" (Weddle,

FIGURE 4.3: George Fox (1624–1691) preaching to a crowd in Maryland, America in 1671 during a four-day meeting of local Quakers. Classic Image. Alamy Stock Photo.

2001: 7). Both views ultimately downplay the diversity among Quakers and disagreements of how the peace testimony was understood, utilized, and adapted.

William Penn (1644–1718), an early Quaker and the founder of Pennsylvania, took the Quaker idea of the divine, inner light within each person as the basis for combining a condemnation of war, an appeal for liberty of conscience, and a promise of greater economic prosperity. He wrote *An Essay Toward the Present and Future Peace of Europe* (1693) against the backdrop of war between the alliance of Holland, Spain, and England against France. Penn's plan, however, is largely devoid of Quaker theological language. It emphasizes a link between peace and economic prosperity. The idea was not only that war is unprofitable, but that liberty of conscience would produce civil peace and prosperity, while religious persecution by Christians and the pursuit of violent means only brought about war and economic devastation (see Murphy 2016: 217–20). While there is debate about the extent to which the plan reflects a bourgeois sensibility and the degree to which it reflects Quakerism (Beales 1931: 32), this theme of identifying peace and prosperity was a common maneuver throughout this period. Penn's explicit identification of *religious liberty* with economic prosperity seems to anticipate affiliated secularized iterations of this claim in later periods, namely that freedom more generally brings prosperity.

Not all peace plans were pacifist in orientation, and Penn's plan stands out because of how it combines Quaker pacifist commitments and diagnoses of war with its own brand of limited internationalism. Penn proposed a parliament with representatives from across Europe, and he entertained the possibility of at least two non-European nations joining them: "the Empire of Germany to send Twelve; France, Ten; Spain, Ten; Italy, which comes to France, Eight; England, Six; Portugal, Three; Sweedland, Four; Denmark, Three; Poland, Four; Venice, Three; the Seven Provinces, Four; The Thirteen Cantons, and little Neighbouring Soveraignties, Two; Dukedoms of Holstein and Courland, One: And if the Turks and Muscovites are taken in, as seems but fit and just, they will make Ten a Piece more. The Whole makes Ninety" (Penn 1693: §7; also see Murphy 2016: 219). While Penn disavows any "Exactness," describing the numbers as "by Guess, being but for Example's Sake," the disparities in number of representatives across each group correspond rather strikingly to economic (rather than religious or political) forms of difference, power, and inequality (see Mikkeli 1998: 50–52). This would reinforce the integral character of "prosperity" and production for peace in Penn's imaginary.

Nonetheless, Penn's inclusion of the Ottoman Empire and Russia—as among "the Best and Wealthiest Part of the Known World; where Religion and Learning, Civility and Arts have their Seat and Empire"—does lend it distinctiveness on the question of religion. Whereas other plans were either explicitly about Europe or implicitly for Christians, and thereby re-entrenched religious difference, Penn generalizes a Quaker interest in peace to non-Christians. In this sense, it is helpful to note that the Duc de Sully's "Grand Design" of 1638 named as one of its benefits the ability of united Christian states to present a unified military front against the Ottoman Empire (Murphy 2016: 221). Likewise, some of the other peace proposals during this period—as in John Bellers' *Some Reasons for an European State* (1710), the Abbé de Saint-Pierre's *A Project for Settling an Everlasting Peace in Europe* (1713), King James III's *Declaration for a Lasting Peace in Europe* (1722), Rousseau's assessment of the Abbé de Saint-Pierre's plan (1756), and Charles Alexandre de Calonne's *Considerations on the Most Effectual Means of Procuring a Solid and Permanent Peace* (1796)—confined themselves to European Christendom. The exclusion of the Turk or Muslim, then, from the peace plan was also his exclusion from the imaginary of peace. Indeed, Voltaire's ([1761] 2005: 50–52) *Rescript of the Emperor of China on the Occasion of the Plan for Perpetual Peace* ridiculed Jean-Jacques Rousseau and the whole genre precisely on this count. He ventriloquized a letter from the emperor of China, asking why China had not been included, as well as "the Great Turk neighbor of Hungary and of Naples, the king of Persia neighbor of the Great Turk, the Great Mogol neighbor of the king of Persia, similarly have the same rights." This is no less the case if attacks by Muslims—from the Turks to the Moors—could "disturb the perpetual peace."

Penn's elisions of the links between economy, power, and violence should, nevertheless, not be downplayed, just as his plan's inclusion of the Ottoman Empire should not overstate its universal hospitality. Penn justifies some aspects of his plan by reference to prudential concerns, not ethical commitments. One of the reasons he gives for including the Turk, which he gives as one of the eight advantages of his European parliamentary proposal, is that it would offer Christians *security from Turkish attacks*. The inclusion of the Ottoman Empire would thus be not strange if Penn's stated aims are not simply peace or peace through justice, but ending the Ottoman threat to European Christian principalities and states. For Sully, the advantage was a united military front; while for Penn, it was instead diluting the threat through inclusion. Both cases, however, turn a pacific imaginary into a weapon against a religio-political enemy. Furthermore, the

FIGURE 4.4: Benjamin West, *William Penn's Treaty with the Indians* (1771–72). Reproduced with the kind permission of the Pennyslvania Academy of Fine Arts, Philadelphia, USA.

Christian core of the plan remains, and Penn (and most commentators) leave unaddressed what the political and theological implications might be for generalizing the specifically Quaker idea of the divine, inner light within each person, through a peace plan, to non-Christians. Of the other seven advantages that Penn lists in his conclusion, three are about Christians and their image among non-Christians: ending human and especially Christian bloodshed; the improved reputation of Christianity among "infidels"; and personal friendship among Christian rulers (Penn 1693: §10).

Comenius, as we saw, approaches the coming of peace through a theologically laden view of history, and emphasizes education and communication as its vehicles; Penn, by contrast, places the emphasis on the interior of the person and on the presence of an international parliament. These two different strands of how religion informs pacific imaginaries combine in an ambiguously secularized form, in Immanuel Kant's *Toward Perpetual Peace* (1795) when read alongside his *Idea for a Universal History with a Cosmopolitan Aim* (1784). First, rather than locating the divine in each person, Kant locates a metaphorical devil. Second, this metaphorical devilishness is part of the grand design of "nature" or "providence." Third, in this pacific imaginary, religious disagreement functions so as to keep people separate and to provide a pretext for war, but it is gradually abolished. This final view that the single core of all religions is for peace, in other words, denies the particularistic religious basis from which the teleology emanates.

Kant's philosophy of history is providential in structure. In that sense, his understanding of how peace can be realized continues a religious understanding of time and universal order. While some of the other thinkers mentioned above displayed a great deal of optimism in the belief that *people* could bring about peace if they reform themselves and

FIGURE 4.5: Immanuel Kant (1724–1804). FALKENSTEINFOTO. Alamy Stock Photo.

their institutions, Kant begins more pessimistically on that front, with the supposition that men are too short-sighted and selfish. And yet, his pessimism is a cover for a deep optimism in "Nature" and its providential course. Even "a nation of devils" ultimately contributes to and unwittingly works toward peace (Kant 1996b: 335).

The entire course of history, in other words, has been working through wars toward peace. Kant explains in *Idea for a Universal History*, without the view that man's history of wars has been perfecting him for peace, "the natural predispositions [of man] would have to be regarded for the most part as in *vain* and *purposeless*; which would remove all practical principles and thereby bring nature, whose wisdom in the judgment of all remaining arrangements must otherwise serve as a principle, under the suspicion that in the case of the human being alone it is a childish play" (Kant 2007: 110). At other crucial moments in this essay (e.g. Kant 2007: 115), he raises the specter of a purposeless nature and a non-teleological history as a nightmare in which there is no meaning. Kant thus attempts to resolve the theodicy of nature and history, which stand in as secularizations of God in this providential narrative. It is no coincidence that Kant identifies the "justification of nature" with "providence" in the earlier essays (Kant 2007: 119); he claims to distinguish them in *Perpetual Peace*, noting that "nature" is about theory rather than religion, and that its course is "cognizable for us" whereas "providence" is not (Kant 1996b: 332). In both cases, then, nature is providence made knowable. One should not blame the course of history for the evils of war, for the result is fundamentally good. He explains in *Idea for a*

Universal History: "All wars are therefore only so many attempts (not, to be sure, in the aims of human beings, but yet in the aim of nature) to bring about new relationships between states, and through destruction or at least dismemberment of all of them to form new bodies" (Kant 2007: 114). Through a series of wars, "Nature has therefore once again used the incompatibility of human beings, even of great societies and state bodies of this kind of creature as a means to seek out in their unavoidable *antagonism* a condition of tranquility and safety." Kant would repeat this faith two years later in the 1786 essay "Conjectural Beginning of Human History," affirming that war supplies the conditions that make peace possible, desirable to people, and perhaps inevitable: "at the stage of culture where humankind still stands, war is an indispensable means of bringing culture still further; and only after a (God knows when) completed culture, would an everlasting peace be salutary, and thereby alone be possible for us" (Kant 2007: 173–74; for later articulations of this theodicy, see Kant 1996a: 79–85, 153, 302). He displaces faith in God's peace onto faith in nature's peace, and nature works less in "mysterious ways" than ones that are circuitous and violent, but purposive and comprehensible.

At the end of his "First Supplement" to *Perpetual Peace*, Kant describes religious and linguistic difference as bringing "with them the propensity to mutual hatred and pretexts for war," and yet he also suggests that "the gradual approach of human beings to greater agreement in principles" will bring about peace (Kant 1996b: 336). In a footnote, he maintains that all religions at their core are ultimately "only one single *religion*" with varied expressions. We can thus see across the course of this period how peace plans were at times expressed *for* followers of a given religion, *from* an explicitly religious perspective, or as an ambiguously secularized form of religious thinking, one informed by a theological structure that treats religious difference as a problem to be resolved. Furthermore, the notion of religious difference as a problem to be overcome for the attainment of universal peace would find other expressions in this period, as in a less-known peace plan by the Russian thinker, Vasily Malinovsky (1765–1814; also Vasilii Malinovskii). The peace plan appears in his *Dissertation on War and Peace* (1807). It called for a reshaping of European borders through the radical reform of religion, education, and property, as well as the idea that each religiously, ethnically, linguistically, and religiously homogeneous group would have a state (see Ferretti 1998: 93–130, 223)—an earlier statement of contemporary understandings of Wilsonian self-determination.

If we see, as I proposed, a tension in Penn's incorporation of the Muslim into his peace plan, there is also a problem in Kant's body of work as a whole with the non-Christian and non-European. Those who, for Kant, are struggling peoples either waiting to catch up to Christian Europe or whose incorporation into universal peace is fundamentally impossible, seem to contribute even less to peace than Kant's "nation of devils" (see Idris 2019: 271–86). On the one hand, this would raise questions about the extent to which non-Christian religions are only assimilated as variations on Christianity and as non-European variations on Europe. On the other hand, these ideas of world or international parliaments would find resonances outside European thought in later centuries. While such plans were rarely pacifist in the strict sense of the term, they mixed religion and peace in ways resonant with European thought. They suggest the non-synchronous manner in which themes are elaborated across cultural and political history. For example, K'ang Youwei (1858–1927), in his *One-World Philosophy*, predicts the regionalization of the world into a handful of large states and proposes a constitutional parliament. He reads the Confucian principle of harmony and "Great Unity" into the ordering of universal peace—though he is unsure if Muslims will be able to join (K'ang 1958: 69,

146–48). During the inter-war period, the South Asian thinker the Aga Khan, in *India in Transition* (1918) called for a "South Asiatic Federation" as a way of managing religious, ethnic, racial, and other forms of difference, and as an alternative vision of empire (see Devji 2013: 69–74). Meanwhile, in the Middle East of the early 1950s, Sayyid Qutb would call for the formation of an Islamic federation, bringing together all Muslim-majority states and mini-states into a bloc, one that is infused with Islamic principles, upholds humanitarianism, and polices the globe against colonial aggression (see Idris 2019: 287–306).

THEOLOGIES OF PEACE

Pacifism and religion would come together in the late 1810s through the "peace movements" of the period. Peace movements in Europe and the United States are usually said to have been "formally" established in the final year of this volume, 1815 (for example, see Beales 1931). Central to this history of religious pacifism are specific sects, foremost among which are the Quakers, as well as the Anabaptists and the Mennonites.

The American Revolution (1765–1783) tested Quaker loyalties and pacifist principles. Mary Knowles (1733–1807), the English Quaker poet, abolitionist, and "a great favorite" of the English royal family, had her five-year-old son, George, recite to the monarchs in 1778 a poem she had written:

> Here, royal pair, your little Quaker stands,
> Obscurely longing to salute your hands;
> Young as he is, he ventures to intrude,
> And lisps a parent's love and gratitude.
> Though with no awful services, I'm come,
> Forbid to follow Mars' dire thund'ring drum;
> My faith no warlike liberty hath giv'n,
> Since "peace on earth" sweet angels sang in heav'n
> Yet I will serve my prince as years increase,
> And cultivate the finest arts of peace:
> As loyal subjects, then, great George, by thee
> Let genuine Quakers still protected be.
> Though on me as a nursling mamma doats,
> I must, I will, shake off my petticoats;
> I must, I will, assume the man this day
> I've seen the king and queen! Huzza! huzza!
> —quoted in Anon, *The Female Instructor*, 1811: 101

The poem upheld the Quaker principles of peace, but it was "stated in classical language with a broad Christian appeal." In the poem, Knowles characterized "Quaker pacifism as a restraint on 'warlike liberty' rather than a sectarian dictum" (Jennings 2006: 73–74).

The first American Peace Society, the New York Peace Society, was established by David Low Dodge (1774–1852), and nearly at the same time, Noah Worcester (1758–1837) created the Massachusetts Peace Society. Conscientious objection during the eighteenth and early nineteenth centuries had been "confined almost exclusively to the peace sects: Quakers, Mennonites, Dunkers, and several smaller bodies" (Brock 1968: 3). David Low Dodge's growing concern with the justifiability of violence stemmed from his reading of the Gospels and reflections on the American Revolution. The American Revolution

FIGURE 4.6: A meeting of the Religious Society of Friends, a Christian movement founded by George Fox *circa* 1650 and devoted to peaceful principles. Central to the Quakers' belief is the doctrine of the "Inner Light," or sense of Christ's direct working in the soul, which led them to reject both formal ministry and all set forms of worship. De Luan. Alamy Stock Photo.

represented the hard case for him; if the revolution was justified, how could violence never be just? However, he came to support a full nonresistant position and published anonymously *The Mediator's Kingdom Not of this World, but Spiritual, Heavenly, and Divine* in 1809.

During their early period, peace societies were primarily composed of "Unitarians, Presbyterians, Congregationalists, Baptists, and Methodists," while "Episcopalians, Roman Catholics, and curiously, Quakers, were not so active," perhaps because the peace societies, and Worcester specifically, did not condemn all wars. One of Dodge's supporters, Samuel Whelpley, took his early ideas "a step further and argued that if countries disarmed and refused to fight they could be protected by international arbitration interpreting and applying the law of nations" (Janis 2010: 75–78). Dodge was a "pacifist hardliner who repudiated all wars," and it is possible that his uncompromising stance and refusal to cooperate with "either moderate pacifists or Quakers" explains why his peace society did not last; Noah Worcester, meanwhile, opted for a "big tent" approach to "both pacifists and just war advocates" (McKanan 2002: 77). Dodge's most famous book is a short text titled, *War Inconsistent with the Religion of Jesus Christ* (1812), which proceeded to make accessible arguments along three fronts, as discussed below. Worcester published his *A Solemn Review of the Custom of War* (1814) shortly thereafter.

Worcester's text "blended reason and evangelical Christianity into an argument for organized social action against war" by emphasizing "the importance of 'human agency' to achieve divine purposes" (Cortright 2008: 27). For Worcester, "progress resulted from a mixture of human effort and divine purpose" (Janis 2010: 77). Like Dodge, he attacked the depravity of war and argued that it was contrary to Christianity. Worcester's *A Solemn Review* underwent numerous printings, including in *The Friend of Peace*, the Massachusetts Peace Society's quarterly periodical; the 1817 volume included *A Solemn Review* and also reprinted the letters of American politicians, news of war, extracts from parliamentary speeches, discussions of universal peace, and anti-war literary culture, including selections from the English poet William Cowper (1731–1800).

Against the idea that only God can end war, Worcester argued, "If ever there shall be a millennium in which the sword will cease to devour, it will probably be brought about by the blessing of God on the benevolent exertions of enlightened men" (Worcester 1814: 5). But the problem, he writes, is that it is *Christians* who have posed the greatest obstacles to peace, and it is therefore incumbent upon Christians to enlighten themselves. When responding to different positions in defense of war—Biblical precedent, the disposal of "vicious and dangerous characters," redress, and displaying strength to deter enemies— he moves from theological arguments about the nature of God's will to humanist arguments about prudence, experience, and the morality of a nation (Worcester 1814: 9–13). His arguments continuously point back to the idea that Christianity is the religion of peace, but that Christianity is "not a powerful intelligent agent. It is not a God, an angel, or a man. It is only a system of divine instructions relating to duty and happiness, to be used by men for their own benefit, the benefit of each other, and the honor of its Author." In other words, Christianity can put an end to war "by the efforts of those who are under its influence," that is, "by enlightening the minds of men as to the evil of the custom, and exciting them to an opposite course of conduct." In this vein, Worcester seems to combine Enlightenment humanism with an evangelical spirit, ending *A Solemn Review* with a call for spreading Christianity. This, for him, meant abolishing war so that true Christianity will "convert the heathen from their idolatry," and eventually "the natives of India" once they are "more improved in their idolatrous customs"—but first, before heathens or idolaters, the "heathen and savage custom" of war must be shed by Christians, and emphasis should be on the "conversion of Christians" (Worcester 1814: 30–33). These rhetorical maneuvers were widespread during this period, and they have important earlier resonances in the Renaissance (see Idris 2014 on Erasmus).

Although their political theories of the individual, the state, and the international differed dramatically, Dodge, like Hobbes, discussed peace in terms that were partly moral and partly prudential. Both sought to draw out the prudential significance of theological tenets and to recast arguments based in prudence using language that would appeal to Christian morality. Dodge gave seven reasons that war is "inhuman," eight reasons that war is "unwise," and eleven reasons that war is "criminal." In the first section, Dodge's understanding of the human is inextricably tied to an understanding of humanity as the creation of the Christian God. "Inhumanity" across the text refers at times to the un-Christian or anti-Christian, and at times to cruelty; in this way, Dodge, too, combined a humanistic and a religious perspective. When Dodge presents war as the oppression of the poor, the creator of widows and orphans, the abuse of God's creatures, and the hardening of men's hearts, he explicitly draws on the authority of Christian texts and principles. When he also describes the mutilation of soldiers' bodies, the scene of a battle, and war casualties, he appeals instead to his readers' sense of horror, separately from Christian doctrine (Dodge [1812] 1905: 2–22). The discussion of war as unwise similarly mixes humanist and theological claims. At times, Dodge appeals to the Christian injunctions to remain meek, to protect property, liberty, and happiness because they are God's gifts, and to prioritize "eternal things" over "temporal things" (Dodge [1812] 1905: 28; also see ibid. 30, 34, 43). At other instances, he appeals to the logic of expediency. He brings these together in key moments, as when he recasts the logics of military buildup, arms races, and preparations for self-defense in both terms: he critiques these structures because they have the effect of inciting jealousy and envy, and because they are rooted in sins like pride, avarice, and vengeance (ibid. 23–24). Finally, when Dodge gives eleven reasons why war is criminal, his use of the language of "criminality" operates both on the register of Christian moralism and the register of law. The differences between the various kinds of reasons are thus blurry throughout the text. They seem to provide a catalogue of variegated justifications and arguments intended to appeal to a broad and diverse audience.

Worcester and Dodge, then, both represent a particularly Christian understanding of pacifism and the conscience. On the one hand, during Europe's Age of Enlightenment, religion and peace formed a series of other constellations, and both inside and outside Europe, some of these constellations exceed pacifism while others are not recognizable today as pacifism in either its expansive or narrow senses. This is not because they do not come with normative commitments. Three brief examples suffice for drawing out some of these other textures. First, one of the most important works of Arabic lexicography, *Taj al-'Arus* was compiled by Murtada al-Zabidi, from south-central India, in the eighteenth century. The word most often translated as "peace," *salām*, is defined here by reference to theological questions. In the background of these definitions is that *salām* is one of the 99 names of God. Second, it was also during the eighteenth century that a collection of Hanafi legal opinions was compiled, also in India, under the title *al-Fatawa al-Hindiyya* (Indian Legal Opinions), and which has been a basis for normative Sunni Islam in India. This code's discussions present reconciling or making peace between a quarreling buyer and seller as a religious obligation. Third, the Pashtun leader Khwushhal Khan (1613–1689) wrote the *Dastarnamah* as a text of advice in which he presents the maintenance of reconciliation or peace (*ṣulḥ*) as the religious duty of a just sovereign (see Ahmed 2016: 479–80). In these examples, peace and religion are braided in a register that is neither focused on the limits of the modern state nor Christian morality.

On the other hand, as the later examples of K'ang Youwei and Sayyid Qutb discussed above suggest, there are some important resonances—or broad world-altering discursive shifts—between the above discussions and various episodes of non-European political and religious thought. One might also add the examples of modern Sufism and of the Ahmadiyya movement in South Asia, which at various points in its history reinterpreted the idea of *jihad* to mean a brand of evangelism, and, according to some accounts, sometimes invoked the Prophet Muhammad's own refusal to fight back when he suffered at the hands of others (see Aydin 2017: 74; Hafez 2010: 208–09; Jackson 2011: 36). Such examples push against comfortable periodization and draw attention to the non-synchronous manner in which concepts are made and themes elaborated, and to the dynamics of power that structure their emergence, global travels, and publicity into today's well-known structures and discourses of pacifism in the nineteenth and twentieth centuries. Whether this reflects the particularity of peace, pacifism, and religion, or the reinterpretation of classical doctrines of quietude and forbearance and their assimilation into these categories, or the workings of empire in the dissemination, creative reworking, and reading back of these ideas and ideals into other archives and traditions, all remains an open but important question.

CONCLUSION

Across most of these currents of thought, pacifism appeared during this period at times as an (ambiguously) secular set of commitments, drawing on humanist sources and impulses; and at others, it was clearly derived from interpretations of Christian doctrinal texts and commitments. During this period, discussions of ideas analogous to peace appear in, for example, Muslim contexts, but they operate differently. In later centuries, whether it is the religious inflection of the peace plan or the theological commitments inflecting pacifism and non-violence, some of the structures surveyed in this chapter resonate or perhaps are indirectly reworked.

It is also clear that the various positions that go under the broad umbrella of pacifism were sometimes inconsistent or indeed in contradiction with one another. The idea that peace is demarcated by the boundaries of the state, and that war exists beyond its borders, demanded that citizen-subjects exercise a form of pacifism within the state and among one another but remain ready to defend these borders. Meanwhile, peace plans that emphasized prosperity expanded the idealization of peace so as to include a number of states, and for some plans, all states. Such plans turned on imagining pacifism not only as a rejection of war, but as an optimistic philosophy of history, and an active embrace of global capitalist imaginaries, liberal regimes, and apparently secular forms of governance. On the other hand, the condemnation of war, not as a "necessary" evil but as an altogether objectionable and unjustifiable form of killing, gave rise to conscientious objection, as an individuated act of resistance and as a collective form of pacifism with the peace societies. Along this spectrum, different commitments to peace could justify war, condemn some forms of violence while eliding others, or offer a set of theological or humanist critiques based on war's sources, practices, and effects. The question would, however, remain twofold. The first is whether pacifism's historical particularities and theological peculiarities as a doctrine place limits on attempts to universalize it. This would include such questions as its construction of the conscience and disobedience or its religious and theological baggage. The second, and most urgent, is how one should judge the idea that everyone desires peace and should demonstrate their commitment to it—that is, how to adjudicate across appeals to pacifism and the corollary insistence on the "peace-loving" basis of humanity: as important moral convictions, empty platitudes, or alibis for war and dispossession.

ACKNOWLEDGMENT

I wish to acknowledge the support of the Institute for Advanced Study, where I was AMIAS Member in the School of Social Science, 2018–2019.

CHAPTER FIVE

Representations of Peace

JENNIFER MILAM

In 1776, when Pompeo Batoni completed his painting *War and Peace*, Europe was enjoying peaceful times. The first Partition of Poland, agreed to by Catherine II of Russia, Maria Theresa of Austria and Frederick II of Prussia in 1772, restored the balance of power in Central Europe. France and England had not yet become embroiled in the War of American Independence, which broke out later in the year. It was an opportunity for sovereigns and heads of government to represent themselves as enlightened rulers, supporting the arts and bringing prosperity to their countries, rather than pursuing costly warfare. Batoni's work is a visual allegory of this ideal. Mars, the Roman god of war, is shown in Classical armor, with sword drawn and shield ready, as he is waylaid by Pax, the Roman goddess of peace. Gently touching the hilt of the god's sword with her left hand, Pax reaches upwards with her right to offer an olive branch to the warrior. His pose of action has the potential to be turned into an embrace, with the scene suggesting visually through the exposed breast of Pax that the pleasures of love will follow if Mars frees his hands by releasing his weapons.

FIGURE 5.1: Pompeo Batoni, *Peace and War* (1776). The Art Institute of Chicago, IL, USA. Gift of the Old Masters Society. Bridgeman Images.

The painting was viewed by Pietro Graneri, the House of Savoy's Ambassador in Rome. His critique of Batoni's composition exposes the diminished effectiveness of allegorical devices in the representation of peace in Western art at the end of the eighteenth century:

> Peace is shown as a young woman, half naked, who with one hand embraces a warrior who represents War, and with the other presents an olive branch to him—the only symbol to make her credible as Peace—otherwise she would be taken as a temptress who would tame a ferocious man through her charms and cajolery. . .[1]

A highly successful history painter and portraitist popular with Grand Tourists in Rome, Batoni was following a well-established tradition of personifying peace in female form. His painting attempts to persuade the viewer of the pleasures of peace through the seductive power of the female nude. Yet, as Graneri's reading of the figure as "temptress" confirms, viewers were increasingly disenchanted with this allegorical language of embodiment. While the personifications and symbols were well known, when viewed as real bodies, the allegories appeared tired and failed to live up to the expectations of a visualized history. From the first half of the seventeenth century onwards, alternative modes of representing what might be called "current events" developed and challenged the visual conventions of allegory. As artists and audiences came to appreciate the historical importance of events taking place around them, art began to engage with history in new ways, largely focused on the men who made peace, rather than on the female bodies that personified its pleasures.

FIGURE 5.2: Elisabeth Louise Vigée Le Brun, *Peace Bringing Back Abundance* (1780). Heritage Image Partnership. Alamy Stock Photo.

Less than a decade after Batoni portrayed *War and Peace*, Elisabeth Vigée-Lebrun submitted her *morceau de reception* to the *Académie royale de peinture et de sculpture*. The subject of her painting was *Peace Bringing Back Abundance*, a choice that demonstrated her education, training, and ambitions as a learned history painter.[2] Thematically, the work responded to contemporary events. It was executed in 1780, while France was engaged in the American War of Independence, but exhibited in 1783 at the time of the signing of the Treaty of Paris. Although Vigée-Lebrun's allegorical treatment of the subject followed established conventions of pictorial representation, the connection with the political present was foregrounded by certain writers. In the *Mémoires Secrets*, for example, the figure of Peace is described as "noble, decent, modest like the peace that France has just concluded" (Bachaumont 1780–89: 24: 4–5). Other critics, however, reportedly judged her work as derivative and "nothing more than a copy" beholden to the examples of seventeenth-century masters.[3] This chapter explores the diverse handlings of allegorical depictions of Peace, and the alternatives offered by the devices of realism, to consider how the visual representation of peace involved a response to history and the role of men and women in its making.

THE POLITICS OF PEACE IN BAROQUE ALLEGORY AND DUTCH REALISM

Like many representations of Peace dated between 1648 and 1815, Vigée-Lebrun's painting was created with politics in mind and it was equally interpreted with political inflections. Artists in this period drew from an extensive repertoire of allegorical pictorial traditions that involved personifications, symbolic objects and attributes derived from Classical antiquity and developed during the Renaissance by humanist scholars, artists and emblematists. Widely used in prints, sculpture, painting and other forms of architectural and interior decoration, pictorial allegories were understood by educated viewers as subjects that engaged the mind as much as the eye. At the same time, particularly in the hands of Dutch realists, representations portrayed as eyewitness accounts of actual events emerged as an alternative to Baroque allegories. A comparison of two paintings from the beginning of this period, *The Ratification of the Treaty of Münster* (1648) by Gerard ter Borch and *Minerva Protects Pax from Mars* (1629–30) by Peter Paul Rubens, provides a clear indication of the contrasts between the two approaches that informed representations of Peace during the Enlightenment.

Ter Borch's *Ratification of the Treaty of Münster* engages the viewer through the principles of verisimilitude. Between May and October of 1648, the year in which this work was painted, a series of peace treaties were signed in the Westphalian towns of Osnabrück and Münster. Known as the Peace of Westphalia, these treaties simultaneously brought to an end the Eighty Years' War between Spain and the Dutch Republic and the Thirty Years' War in the Holy Roman Empire. Most importantly to the intended audience for this image, the Peace of Westphalia signaled the official recognition of the Dutch Republic by the Habsburg crown. While Dutch artists are well known for their depictions of everyday life and realistic portraiture, it was unusual at the time to depict a contemporary event of such political significance. There was no established visual tradition of representing current events in the seventeenth century anywhere in Europe. Instead, in a manner similar to Rubens' use of allegory, artists working in the Dutch Republic represented contemporary political subjects through allegorical allusions and metaphors

FIGURE 5.3: Gerard ter Borch, *The Ratification of the Treaty of Münster* (1648). Reproduced with the kind permission of the National Gallery, London, UK.

FIGURE 5.4: Peter Paul Rubens, *Minerva Protects Pax from Mars* (c. 1629–30). Reproduced with the kind permission of the National Gallery, London, UK.

based on stories taken from the Bible and Classical antiquity.[4] In what was something of a revolutionary move, ter Borch turned to the conventions of group portraiture in Dutch seventeenth-century painting to depict the historic moment of oath swearing at Münster. By so doing, he merged the genres of history painting and portraiture to stake a claim for the truthfulness of his representation of peace secured through the actions of men.

Ter Borch's painting has been characterized as an eyewitness account of the actual event.[5] As a member of the entourage of Count Peñaranda, the chief Spanish negotiator, ter Borch was personally present when the oath of ratification was sworn. To claim his position as an eyewitness, he includes a self-portrait on the far left side of the composition. Like Rubens, ter Borch blended his diplomatic interests into his representation of the event. Grouped loosely around the table at the center of the composition, the six Netherlanders swear their oath with raised fingers, while the two Spanish delegates place their hands on the cross and a bible, an opposing gesture that reinforces the different beliefs and political associations of the main actors in the scene. Yet, these figures are also part of the larger group, which is now unified within the great hall of Münster.

To enhance the specificity of place, ter Borch depicts the hall with scrupulous attention to detail, a handling that is particularly noticeable in the minute brushwork used to delineate the woodwork on the stalls and paneling, as well as the ornate features of the candelabrum. The importance of the documents is signaled by their placement on the table, in the center of the painting, with the viewer's attention drawn to them through the use of red in the seals and on the precious box. The green velvet cloth sets off these papers and objects, while at the same time providing a further link to written descriptions of the scene that specifically mentioned this detail. Visual elements that are supplied by art (the painterly handling of the velvet, for example, and the use of bright red coloring in specific sections of the composition guide the eye around the scene and provide a sense of order that breaks up the monotony of black and white dress at the center) undermine the naturalism of the scene. This has the effect of elevating the event, as represented, so that it is recognized as a moment of historic importance. The painting is clearly composed and artfully arranged. It is the detailed realism of the scene, rather than its naturalism, that convinces viewers of the veracity of its representation. Moreover, by placing himself within the image, ter Borch claims authority for himself as an eyewitness capable of representing the facts and importance of this historic event. He captures the event as a moment in time and portrays it as a moment in history. Furthermore, as an historical scene that eschews allegorical devices, it places greater emphasis on the actions of men who made history, in marked contrast to the prominence of nude female bodies within Baroque allegorical representations of peace.

Peace continued to be portrayed as an allegorical figure linked to ideas of good government and magnanimous sovereignty. Through allegorical pictorial language associated with the themes of war and peace, Baroque artists addressed current political concerns using visual modes of persuasion to carry meaning. Those modes of persuasion were largely centered on the lavish portrayal of the human body engaged in dynamic movement. Figures such as Minerva, Venus, Pax, and Mars personified the abstract ideas of wisdom, love, peace, and war, which Rubens deployed in scenes of compelling narrative action.

During his lifetime, Rubens was widely regarded as the leading European painter of his generation and his approach to allegorical representations of peace remained influential throughout the seventeenth and eighteenth centuries. Trained in Antwerp, Rubens combined his artistic career with diplomatic missions to Spain and England, on behalf of the Netherlands.[6] In 1629, he travelled to the court of Charles I of England at the request of Philip IV of Spain. His task was to negotiate a truce that would cease hostilities between their respective allies, the Protestant forces of the Dutch Republic and the Catholic forces of the Spanish-ruled southern Netherlands.[7] The Stuart court was far more interested in Rubens' artistic skills than his diplomatic mission to secure peace. It was during this time that the painter progressed one of his major decorative schemes, the Banqueting House at Whitehall. The ceiling celebrates the peaceful reign of James I, father of Charles I, and sits above the throne where the latter king received ambassadors and presided over state occasions. It provided a pictorial model of ideal rule, in which the good monarch has overcome his personal weaknesses and enemies of the state to secure peace and prosperity for his subjects. During the nine months that he remained at the Stuart court, Rubens completed several other paintings for Charles I, including *Minerva Protects Pax from Mars* (1629–30), which he presented as a gift. Both this painting and the ceiling of Whitehall demonstrate the extent to which art and diplomacy were intertwined in Rubens' career as an artist, and that the promotion of peace was a central concern of his art making, communicated most effectively through the visual techniques of persuasive allegory.[8]

The central figure of *Minerva Protects Pax from Mars* is a representation of peace, personified as Ceres, goddess of the earth, with her cornucopia, a symbol of abundance and nourishment. Depicted as a female nude, grasping her breast and moving to feed an adoring putto to her left, Ceres is accompanied by accessory figures, who reinforce the bounty that peace brings. The satyr and leopard placed at Ceres' feet are members of Bacchus' entourage, the god of wine, while two nymphs approach from the left hand side of the scene, one carrying riches and the other dancing with a tambourine. Behind Ceres, Minerva, goddess of wisdom, drives off Mars, the god of war, and the fury, Alecto. In the right foreground, three children are greeted by putti, who hold an olive wreath, symbol of peace and the caduceus of Mercury, symbol of diplomacy and negotiation. These children in contemporary dress are a tangible reminder of the reality of peace and its value to the future of the family and the state. While the personifications and symbols can be decoded and read as a narrative of wealth and prosperity brought through the elimination of war, it is the richness of color, painterly brushwork, and dynamic movement of the figures that persuade the viewer of the pleasures of peace, which revolve, quite literally, around the exposed breast of Ceres. Peace is made seductive through its embodiment in the form of a female nude.

PEACE AND SOVEREIGNTY

During the seventeenth century, European monarchs found it desirable to represent themselves as rulers who pursued peace. Allegorical language conveyed these meanings, with symbols generously deployed in public images that reinforced the notion of the benevolent ruler. Rubens, once again, was an innovator with this genre, developing techniques and conventions that would inform official royal portraiture and images of rulers within decorative cycles across the courts of Europe for the next two centuries. In 1622 Rubens began the cycle of twenty-four paintings that would document the life of Marie de' Medici, dowager Queen of France and mother of Louis XIII, to decorate her newly-built private residence, the Luxembourg Palace. The commission had both personal and political purpose. According to the dictates of Salic law, a woman could not rule France in her own right. When Henri IV was assassinated, Marie de' Medici became regent until her son was old enough to rule on his own. Her regency was marked by political intrigue and revolt by the princes of blood and Nobles of the Sword. Her son eventually exiled the dowager queen to Blois, in an attempt to assert his authority and independence, early on in his majority. The central point of conflict was her support of the Spanish Habsburgs, an abandonment of the traditional anti-Habsburg foreign policy of the French. To secure this alliance between France and Spain, she arranged the marriages of her children, Louis XIII to Anne of Austria and Elisabeth to the future Philip IV. This exchange of the princesses was a cornerstone of Marie de' Medici's self image, as she wanted to see her children seated on all the thrones of Europe. It was also a significant effort to secure the prospect of peace, by brokering alliances through marriage, which she achieved again with the marriage of her daughter Henrietta Maria to Charles I of Spain. It was an explicitly female approach to the objectives of diplomacy, good government and statecraft, which would be followed by other powerful women who ruled during the eighteenth century, namely Maria Theresa, Empress of Austria.[9]

Rubens was thus presented with a difficult task. He was commissioned, as his contract stated, to paint the "highly illustrious life and heroic deeds" of a woman who was a disgraced regent in need of repairing her relationship with the king (as quoted in Millen and Wolf 1989: 5). Straightforward vindication was an impossibility. There was a sensitivity between mother and son that had to be carefully negotiated, as did the difficulty of assigning the more masculine associations of illustriousness and heroism to a woman. The extraordinary interpretive complexities of the Medici cycle are part of Rubens' solution to the specific challenges of the commission, aided by his characteristic bravura brushstrokes and seductive use of color. The artist's powers of visual persuasion were mobilized not only to restore the reputation of Marie de' Medici in the present, but also to secure the legacy of her queenship for posterity. At the same time, as the consummate diplomat artist, Rubens sought to advance his own agenda in promoting peace.

In what has now become a definition of Baroque artistic qualities, Rubens blurred the boundaries of different genres. He combined the depiction of recent historical events with conventions of portraiture. Moreover, he adapted his extensive knowledge of the imagery of Classical antiquity to the task, employing a wide range of mythological themes, allegorical symbols, personifications and emblematics. Together these pictorial techniques and interpretive devices convey an image of Marie de' Medici as an ideal ruler, wife and mother who was, above all else, an exemplar of the motto PAX OPTIMA RERUM (Peace is the highest good).[10] This approach was part of Rubens' contribution to the representation of peace during this period, by understanding the task of the commission as one connected to Classical values that promoted the image of the ruler as moral example.[11] The cycle represents Marie de' Medici as a model of good government and statecraft because she pursued peace as a personal and political goal.

While peace was perpetually present as an underlying theme connecting the twenty-four paintings in the Luxembourg gallery, it was even more overtly asserted within the architectural space surrounding the Hall of Mirrors in the palace of Versailles. Designed by Jules Hardouin-Mansart in 1678 and decorated by a team of artists working under the direction of Charles Le Brun over the next decade, the intention was to glorify the reign of Louis XIV. An impressive cycle of Grand Manner painting covers the coving of the vault, with large and small panels depicting recent historic events from the accession of Louis XIV to the Treaty of Nijmegen. At either end of the gallery, the Salon of War and the Salon of Peace frame the thematic veneration of Louis XIV's reign and communicate the crux of the ceiling's meaning in regards to the king's sovereignty. War and peace exist in balance during the reign of Louis XIV, with the entire palace of Versailles demonstrating to its inhabitants and visitors the pleasures afforded by the authority and power of the king. On the one hand, the implications of the sequence of rooms appears to be a warning

FIGURE 5.5: The Salon of Peace, Versailles. Todd Strand. Alamy Stock Photo.

directed at foreign ambassadors, who walked the length of the gallery, after passing through the Salon of War, to meet the king enthroned at the end. It is equally likely, on the other hand, that the message was directed at the French nobility, who witnessed the daily ceremonial movements of the king in this space.

The central canvas entitled "The King Governs by Himself, 1661" reinforces this more domestic message to an audience who had challenged the authority of the king during the Fronde, a civil war between 1648 and 1653. The painting blends elements of allegory, mythology, classical references, and portraiture to convey its meanings. Louis XIV is dressed in Classical armor and an ermine-lined robe, seated on a throne and holding the tiller of state. He is surrounded by gods and goddesses: the three Graces symbolize his talents granted by Heaven; Minerva and Mars together represent the king's glory that is obtained through wisdom and courage. Numerous putti are arranged at the king's feet, enjoying the pleasures of the arts and other amusements that his kingship secures for Frenchmen, including gambling, a favored distraction of his courtiers. Peace, in this context, projects itself as only one side of Louis XIV's reign, existing in balance with the threat of war and his past victories.

By the early eighteenth century, the use of complex allegories was critiqued as excessive and impenetrable. In his influential *Réflexions critiques sur la poésie et sur la peinture* (1719), the Abbé Dubos complained that the "ingenious fictions" designed by Rubens and Le Brun respectively for the galleries of Luxembourg and Versailles produced enigmas "even more obscure than those of the Sphinx" (Dubos 1719: 1, 188–92). He went on to note that neither individuals who knew a great deal about the life of Marie de' Medici, nor scholars well versed in mythology and emblematics, could comprehend half of Rubens' thoughts

FIGURE 5.6: Charles Le Brun, *The King Governs by Himself*, 1661 (1680s). Heritage Image Partnership. Alamy Stock Photo.

within the Marie de' Medici cycle. Dubos proclaimed the subjects that were "purely historic" to be the most pleasing because they appeared more truthful (Dubos 1719: 1, 193).

Eighteenth-century monarchs, however, continued to draw on the visual traditions of allegory and metaphor to picture their authority and divine right to rule, particularly in portraiture. Female rulers were attracted to the mythological figure of Minerva, whose primary attribute of wisdom, status as protector of the arts, and ability to vanquish Mars (or mindless warfare) appealed in relation to the image that these powerful women hoped to project, not only at home, or in foreign courts, but also for posterity. Symbols of peace were ever-present in these portrayals of the benevolent female ruler.

Stefano Torelli's portrait of *Catherine the Great in the Guise of Minerva, Patroness of Art* (1770; Tretyakov Gallery, Moscow), for example, depicts the empress of Russia wearing a plumed helmet and Classical garb, striding through a picturesque landscape, attended by female courtiers in contemporary dress and surrounded by clusters of putti. The blending of nature and artifice is typical of the period, simplifying and updating the more complicated allegorical references of the seventeenth century by integrating them into a natural setting to signal the truthfulness of the painting's more metaphorical claims. Palm trees and olive branches became ubiquitous references to peace within these types of ruler portraits because they could be naturalized within the landscape, while still functioning as a generic symbol of exemplary rule. More individualized were the narrative paintings that combined elements of portraiture and allegory to depict recent historic events. Torelli's *Allegory on the Victory of Catherine the Great over Turks and Tatars* (1772) is one such image that attempts to modify the conventions of Western battlefield processions to communicate a more personalized biography of Catherine II and the territorial ambitions of the Russian empire under her rule.

Like Frederick II of Prussia who fashioned himself as a philosopher-king, Catherine presented herself as an enlightened autocrat. She corresponded with major figures of the Enlightenment, such as Voltaire, Grimm and Diderot, and developed a reputation

FIGURE 5.7: Stefano Torelli, *Catherine the Great in the Guise of Minerva, Patroness of Art* (1770). Reproduced with the kind permission of the Tretyakov Gallery, Moscow, Russia.

FIGURE 5.8: Stefano Torelli, *Allegory on the Victory of Catherine the Great over Turks and Tatars* (1772). Heritage Image Partnership. Alamy Stock Photo.

throughout Europe as a learned patron of the arts. She was also a woman with considerable political and military ambitions for the Russian state, and was staunchly authoritarian in her approach to rule. Catherine continued the Westernization reforms initiated by Peter I, which had substantially strengthened Russia at the turn of the eighteenth century, when it emerged as a major European power with the ability to challenge the Ottoman empire. Catherine achieved a number of strategic victories over the Ottomans in the late 1760s and early 1770s, in her attempt to take control of the Black Sea and expand her south eastern frontier. In spite of her numerous aggressions directed at the expansion of Russian political power, and the value she placed on her own sovereignty, she regularly projected an image of herself as an enlightened ruler bringing peace to the world. In Torelli's composition, Catherine's entourage is made up of figures in both Turkish and European dress. Several Russian generals appear in the scene, but Catherine's authority over them is conveyed through her positioning. The empress sits just off the center of the composition, but she is clearly a figure of enviable authority, aided by, but superior to, the men over whom she rules. Once again, Catherine wears the Ostrich-plumed helmet of Minerva, while above, Peace, Fame, and Victory personify her glorification.

While Catherine used conventional Baroque visual imagery when she anticipated an elite audience for a painting by an Italian court artist, she also sought to commemorate her victories with the people, touted as celebrations of peace. One such celebration was held on the Khodynka field, a large open space in the northwest of Moscow. The Russian nobleman and intellectual A. T. Bolotov described this event in the following way: "Several small vessels were built and they were distributed in different parts of the valley depicting the sea. They were meant to look like they were floating. I kept thinking that they should have ploughed the fields and removed the grass to make it look like sea even more."[12] To reach an even wider audience than those who were able to witness the celebrations, Catherine had the event commemorated as the subject for a lubok.

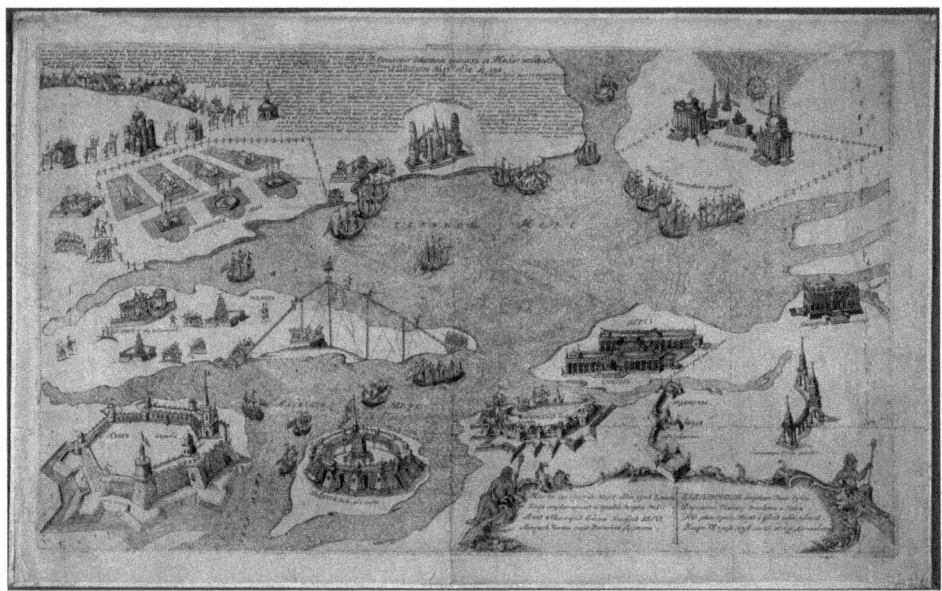

FIGURE 5.9: Matvey Fedorovich Kazakov, *Public Celebration that was Held on the Khodynka Field on 19 July 1775* (1775). Reproduced with the kind permission of the Rossiiskii Gosudarstvennyi Arkhiv Drevnikh Aktov (*RGADA*: Russian State Archive of Early Acts).

Created at the Akhmetev factory in Moscow, this type of Russian popular print is a rare example of an image made for common people that is dedicated to contemporary events. A vernacular art form, Lubki traditionally were used to decorate houses and inns, taking their subjects from popular tales and religious stories, and employing simple graphics to convey meanings. Like the allegorical paintings that draw on European Baroque conventions of representation adapted to the specifics of Catherine's history, the prints have a persuasive purpose tied to the image of Catherine II as an enlightened ruler who brings peace to Russia through victory in battle and imperial annexation. The text at the top was taken from the Moscow *Vedomosty* newspaper, creating a direct link to contemporary reports of the events:

> Places where Mars shed the streams of blood when the sharp knife raged in the battlefields in Azov, Taganrog, Enikol, Kinburn, Kerch are celebrating becoming a part of Russia. They are covered by the hand of Catherine and taste the quiet, satisfaction and peace that are created by the rivers of Black Pont and fleet. These are the benefits of peace.[13]

As the inscription makes clear, there is a stated relationship between imperial aggression and the pleasures peace affords, which Catherine wanted to communicate to the Russian people, promoting an image of herself as a benevolent ruler. The metaphorical association between Mars and Catherine, secured through the dual reference to the "sharp knife" that "raged" and the "hand" of the empress, are perhaps unique to textual references, as to picture a female ruler in the guise of Mars would have been too much of a contravention of gender roles within the conventions of allegorical imagery.

PEACE AND PORTRAITURE

Gender conventions proved particularly challenging for powerful female sovereigns attempting to negotiate the dictates of femininity and the expectations of their rule, which was often directed by the particular biography that they were constructing for themselves in terms of protectors of peace. Maria Theresa, empress of Austria and rival of Catherine II, took a less aggressive approach that has been far more kind to her reputation in posterity. She developed and promoted an image of herself as a dowager queen, using maternal influence to guide her son, Joseph II, towards peaceful rule. Like Marie de' Medici, she understood the diplomatic significance of motherhood, producing sixteen children with the intention that many of them would sit on the thrones of Europe, securing peace for the Habsburg empire through marriage. Regardless of the visual imagery and rhetoric that pictured Maria Theresa as a retiring widow, she clearly valued her authority and power as sovereign of the Holy Roman Empire. She did not pass the Habsburg throne on to her son when her husband died in 1765, but instead appointed him co-regent, refusing to relinquish her personal authority until she died in 1780.

Maria Theresa's succession to the throne was marked by controversy. Her father, Charles VI, reformed Salic Law in the Holy Roman Empire by issuing the Pragmatic Sanction, which would allow Maria Theresa to rule in her own right, in spite of the fact that she was a woman. When she succeeded to the throne in 1740, her authority was challenged by other European powers, led by Frederick II of Prussia, who used the Pragmatic Sanction as an opportunity to claim Hapsburg territories for his kingdom. The rulers of France and Bavaria launched similar invasions of Habsburg lands, resulting first in the War of Austrian Succession (1740–48), followed by the Seven Years' War (1756–63), and then the War of Bavarian Succession (1778–79). Maria Theresa's reign was thus punctuated by alternating periods of war and peace. As her ability to hold off aggressive military action launched by other European powers was obviously limited, the promotion of peace as a primary attribute of her rule became an important value to be linked to her image. In addition, the title "*Kaiserinwitwe*", or empress-widow, which she assumed in order to share, rather than to relinquish power to her son required an even more radical revision to the Baroque conventions of ruler portraiture.

For the most part, the conventions of kingship were redefined in the late seventeenth and early eighteenth century by Louis XIV.[14] The model of kingship in absolutist terms, Hyacinthe Rigaud's *Portrait of Louis XIV* (1701; Musée du Louvre, Paris) became the model for official court portraiture well into the next century and beyond. It incorporates the grandeur of Louis XIV's court, the magnificence of his rule as embodied in his person, and his absolute power, not through allegorical metaphors and mythological personifications that refer to military triumph and the rewards of peace, but through the idealization of Louis XIV himself—in pose, gesture, dress, and demeanor, as a model to be emulated but never equaled.[15] His military power is suggested by his sword at his side, but it is his physical presence that conveys to the viewer his personal power and political authority. Allegorical references to war and peace are effectively irrelevant, as the painting projects a sacrosanct image of the king that defies challenge. Peace, as a justification for warfare, is replaced by the visual language of absolutism, whereby the king's will is the only justification required for any action taken.

In spite of the fact that she was a Habsburg and an empress, Maria Theresa was in no position to make parallel claims in relation to her personal power and political authority. Her portraits, therefore, had to make a virtue out of her personal limitations, which

FIGURE 5.10: Anton von Maron, *Portrait of Empress Maria Theresa as a Widow* (1773), KHM-Museumsverband. Reproduced with the kind permission of the Kunsthistorisches Museum, Vienna, Austria.

included her status as a woman and the weakening of the Habsburg empire under her rule in the face of military challenges led by other heads of states. In relation to these limitations, peace became a virtue to be promoted in connection with Maria Theresa's widowed monarchical identity.[16] Anton Maron's *Portrait of Empress Maria Theresa as a Widow* employs some stock attributes of Baroque court portraiture—the column behind the sitter, the ornate furniture, the Classical sculptural group, and the gesture towards an architectural plan of the imperial residence. It is the more personal features of the image that make the portrait distinctive in relation to the representation of peace. Her widow's dress is both a marker of her faithful duty to a husband, as a woman, and a claim to power reframed through her authority as a *Kaiserinwitwe*, theoretically sharing the position of leader of the Holy Roman Empire with her son. Motherhood is equally present in this reference to her position. The main foreground diagonal extends from the lower left hand corner of the painting, across the lower half of Maria Theresa's body, and up to her face. This is balanced by the primary diagonal of the composition that extends from the lower right hand corner into the background where the viewer takes in the well-lit sculptural group depicting the figure of Peace accompanied by two putti. One putto floats above holding a single olive branch, while the other embraces a cornucopia filled with several branches. Abundance is more than a traditional reference to the prosperity here. It takes on more personal meaning in connection with the body of Maria Theresa, specifically in relation to her fertility and role as a producer of heirs. Significantly, the only crown present within the portrait is made of olive branches, held by Peace over the head of Maria Theresa, reinforcing the notion that the pursuit of peace is the guiding feature of her governance and ultimate source of her power and authority.

ACTS, ACTIONS, AND ACTORS OF PEACE

Peace personified was ultimately female. As Maria Theresa's portrait suggests visually, the long-standing iconographic connections among fertility, abundance, peace, and prosperity were embodied, not solely in the form of a Classical ideal personified, but also in the flesh and in the present, through the policies and actions of a benevolent female ruler. This is an entirely different approach to personification, one that acts in the present, rather than in an ideal past. Consequently, the embodiment of peace becomes transferred to the acts of real women, who personify the values of peace, not simply its attributes. As the depiction of current events began to emerge as the subject matter of modern history painting, peace was visualized, not through allegory, but in the actions of men.

In the same year that von Maron painted his portrait of Maria Theresa and Torelli completed his *Allegory on the Victory of Catherine the Great over Turks and Tatars* (1772), the American artist Benjamin West completed *William Penn's Treaty with the Indians* (1771–72), a groundbreaking portrayal of a legendary event in the English colonies, depicted as contemporary history in the making. Thomas Penn commissioned West to paint his father's encounter in 1683 with the Lenni Lenape, or "Delaware Indians" as they were called by the colonists, reportedly under the shade of an elm tree at Shackamaxon. The painting depicts William Penn, the founder of the Pennsylvania colony, standing just left of center in the composition, arms extended in an open gesture of welcome, with the Delaware River in the background. The main character of the scene, Penn stands with other recently arrived Quakers, who are shown trading goods with the Lenape. At the far left are two Swedes, who were already in the area and may have acted as translators. Set in a landscape to reinforce the naturalism of the scene, European buildings are going up in the background and English ships are seen at the far left. While themes of economy and the progress of civilization are present in the image, interpretive focus is directed towards the overriding theme of peace, represented in terms of the New World.[17] A native man in the foreground holds a lowered peace pipe. Next to him lie a discarded bow and quiver of arrows. To the right, a native woman is breast feeding an infant, a traditional sign of charity and maternal abundance. One child to her left gestures towards the trading activity that denotes the context for the treaty, while another boy, wearing a quiver of arrows and holding a bow, walks away towards the group of Lenape under a tree who gather by more primitive shelters.

While there is an attempt to enhance the naturalism of the scene by depicting identifiable features of the landscape (the elm tree and the river), as well as by relaxing the composition through an asymmetrical arrangement of figural groups, the scene is carefully constructed and idealized through the use of dramatic gestures and emblematic details.

FIGURE 5.11: Benjamin West, *The Treaty of William Penn with the Indians* (1771–72). Reproduced with the kind permission of the Pennyslvania Academy of Fine Arts, Philadelphia, USA.

The treaty is handled allegorically, extending beyond the depiction of a moment at the actual event to stand in for the essential role of peace in the progress of mankind. In Enlightenment terms, the right hand side of the scene represents an earlier stage of human development, while the left hand side represents the promise and achievement of European civilization. At the center, in what is a specifically New World take on this philosophical understanding of historical time, the colonists represent the future. The Old World Swedes in idealized poses adapted from Classical sculpture are as much a part of the past as the native mother and children on the right. The theme of peace, rather than warfare (note the absence of guns amongst the Quakers, known for their peaceful beliefs, and the discarded weapons of the Native Americans), is at the crux of progress, further distinguishing this modern allegory of peace from the allegorical representations of the past that emphasized conquest.

European art at the very end of the eighteenth century was no less influenced by a shift in the reception of allegory related to the theme of peace, no doubt in response to the violence and warfare of the French Revolution of 1789, which overturned the established order and meanings of the Old Regime. While the use of personifications of peace, such as in the works by Batoni and Vigée-Lebrun were increasingly read in terms of real, rather than idealized bodies, which undermined their effectiveness as emblems, Neo-Classical artists like Jacques-Louis David turned to the actions of individuals at turning points in history as a way of engaging with themes of peace, love and the fate of civilization.[18] Personifications of Peace were undermined by a new interest in human actors in history who were exemplary through their unique actions, no longer represented as generic examples of a universal attribute.

FIGURE 5.12: Jacques-Louis David, *Intervention of the Sabine Women* (1799). Peter Horree, Alamy Stock Photo.

David's *Intervention of the Sabine Women*, as Dorothy Johnson has argued, takes as one of its central themes the "primordial and essential role" of women in the establishment of civilization.[19] The scene depicts a legendary event from Rome's beginning in the eighth century BCE. Some years after the abduction of the Sabine women by the Romans, the Sabine men attacked, in an attempt to get their women back. Rather than rejoicing at their potential rescue, the Sabine women intervene to stop the battle raging outside the ramparts of Rome. For they are now not only Sabine daughters; they are also Roman wives and the mothers of children who are both Sabine and Roman. Herselia, the woman with outstretched arms striding into the foreground, positions herself between her father Tatius, king of the Sabines, and her husband Romulus, king of the Romans. Next to her, another Sabine woman gestures towards her children, who are about to be trampled, innocent victims of the unfolding violence, while a third woman grasps the leg of Tatius to halt his action. Women play a crucial role here. Drawing on the allegorical associations of women with personifications of Peace, David reinterprets the metaphors of prosperity, fertility and the promise of abundance by depicting real women as actors in history, changing the course of events and bringing about peace through personal action.

Antoine-Jean Gros, David's student, was appointed Napoleon's official battle painter in 1793. Together, patron and artist developed a distinctive approach to the representation of peace that ironically revolved around the imagery of warfare. Gros interpreted Napoleon's campaigns through a program of idealization. He created large-scale contemporary history paintings that successfully communicated propaganda, largely by transforming Napoleon from battlefield commander into a compassionate leader and by shifting attention away from the actual battle. One of his last works of this type, *Napoleon on the Battlefield of Eylau* (1807), was commissioned to convey an idea of the ruler as a

FIGURE 5.13: Antoine Jean Gros, *Napoleon on the Battlefield of Eylau* (1807). Reproduced with the kind permission of the Toledo Museum of Art, Toledo, Ohio, USA.

Prince of Peace, rather than a heroic warrior. Under Napoleon, the French empire was built through nearly a decade of continuous military action, which followed on from the Revolution of 1789 and the Terror. The French people began to wonder if they would ever be at peace. Gros' image was intended to respond to these concerns and growing negative public opinion. To achieve the aims of this commission, Gros created an image that focused on Napoleon's actions the day after the battle. Napoleon has possession of the field, and is consequently the victor, but in that moment he is there to bring comfort to those who fought.[20] The horrors of war are immediately evident in the bodies of dead and dying soldiers who sprawl across the foreground of the images. In the middle ground, to the left of center, Napoleon rides in on his horse, a figure of composure and concern, his hand raised in a gesture of benediction. Behind him, the city burns and endless lines of soldiers extend in the far distance on the right hand side. The chaos of war is evident, and while Napoleon led the campaign, the image deflects his responsibility through his representation as a compassionate leader.

Peace is thus represented idealistically at the turn of the nineteenth century, but in more naturalistic terms than earlier images, which had used personifications and the visual language of mythological allegory to convey its benefits. Gros' scene, in contrast, is convincing because it conveys the horrific consequences of war: death, destruction, and insanity. Viewers are not persuaded by the pleasures of peace, but instead by its opposite. In turn, the visual pleasures of peace personified in the form of the female nude had been replaced by a highly original form of propaganda that stimulated the emotions of fear and repulsion through scenes of dramatic action based around the biography of the ruler as an individual actor on the stage of history.

CHAPTER SIX

Peace Movements

STEPHEN CONWAY

Anyone who knows about post-1815 developments in the history of pacifism would be forgiven for thinking that they are about to read a chapter in search of a subject. If by "peace movements" we mean organized and broadly based opposition to war, as distinct from the irenical efforts of individuals, then the period between the establishment of a new European order in the Peace of Westphalia in 1648 and the forging of a fresh international settlement at Vienna in 1815 seems remarkable, from a modern perspective, for the lack of such movements. Many historians see the end of the long and bloody Napoleonic Wars as the start of an era of peace movements in North America and Europe. The formation of peace societies at New York and Massachusetts in 1815, followed the next year by the London-based Society for the Promotion of Permanent and Universal Peace, usually known as the British or London Peace Society, began a trend. Further peace societies emerged in France in 1821, the United States in 1828, Geneva in 1830, and the Netherlands in 1831–32 (Van der Linden 1987: chs. 1–7). In the succeeding decades, the different peace societies, together with free-trade enthusiasts, played a major part in promoting international agitation against war. A general peace convention, with delegates from many different countries, assembled in London in 1843. International peace congresses then met in various European cities between 1848 and 1853. The Crimean War dealt a serious blow to these international efforts, but not a fatal one. From the 1870s, the London Peace Society worked with the new International Workman's Peace Association, later renamed the International Arbitration League. In 1873, Henry Richard, the secretary of the London Peace Society, persuaded the House of Commons to approve the principle of arbitration to solve international disputes; in 1880, he secured parliamentary support for a motion urging European arms reductions. Richard's success owed much to the popularity of anti-war sentiments amongst the radical grassroots activists of the Victorian Liberal Party, for whom hostility to international armed conflict, if not pure pacifism, remained a defining characteristic into the twentieth century.

Yet peace movements existed long before 1815. Protestant religious groups, such as the German and Dutch Mennonites, adopted a pacifist stance, in accord, as they saw it, with the teachings and practice of the early Christians (Brock 1972: esp. chs. 3–6). But if we can find collective irenical activity in various parts of continental Europe, perhaps Britain and its North American colonies provided more examples of organized hostility to war than anywhere else. The reasons for this prominence are unclear, though the existence of a relatively free press and robust parliamentary debates on foreign and imperial policy may well have encouraged criticism of war in the wider public sphere. In any event, the years from the Peace of Westphalia to the Congress of Vienna saw many different attempts to promote peace in Britain and its overseas extensions. Few, admittedly, took the form of pure and uncompromising pacifism, which disapproved of all forms of violence. Many more argued against the legitimacy of a particular conflict, and can be considered, following Martin Ceadel's terminology, as "pacificist" rather than pacifist, by which he means opposed to certain types of war only, and willing to accept wars of self-defense (Ceadel 1989: 5). Even so, as we will see, the case made to oppose a specific war could easily be applied to other wars, or even to all wars. Indeed, the points favored by irenic generalists during the post-1815 heyday of the international peace movement often drew on arguments first articulated in the eighteenth century.

The chapter begins by considering the pioneering work of the Quakers and other religious groups committed to a pacifist stance, placing them in the context of more broadly accepted views on war, both providential and enlightened. It then proceeds to consider the development of practical arguments against war, commonly advanced by both religiously inspired and more secular enthusiasts for peace. Special attention is paid to the emergence of the first large-scale peace campaigns in Britain during the conflict against the American colonies (1775–83), and the still more important British agitation for peace during the wars against revolutionary and Napoleonic France (1793–1815). A concluding section attempts to draw out the key points.

*

The Quakers, or Society of Friends, formed perhaps the most important pacifist group in the English-speaking world. The Quakers emerged in the great turmoil of the mid-seventeenth-century English Revolution, when established ideas in church and state faced serious challenges from radicals determined to return to first principles (Ceadel 1996: 145–51). To extreme Protestants like the Quakers, the true path lay in recovering the purity of the early Christian church, which the Quakers, and other groups that thought in a similar way, believed had been committed to non-violence in all circumstances. With few exceptions, Quakers came quickly to embrace absolute pacifism. They retained their faith in non-violent methods throughout the period that we are considering (and continue to do so in our own times). As the Quaker Joseph Besse wrote during the War of the Austrian Succession (1740–48), "*Wars* and fighting, are neither consonant to the *Laws of Nature*, nor to the *Doctrine of* Christianity" (Besse 1747: 13). Quakers' willingness to argue the case for pure pacifism and non-violence put them at the forefront of many attempts to promote peace or avoid war. Both William Penn's proposal in the late seventeenth century for a European diet or parliament to settle international disputes (Penn 1693) and John Bellers' similar irenic scheme at the beginning of the eighteenth century (Bellers 1710)—while being responses to ongoing armed conflicts in which England and Britain were involved—drew inspiration from the Quakerism of their authors (see Brock 1972: 276–77 and, by contrast, Hinsley 1967: 38–40).

Some Quakers, admittedly, compromised their beliefs. Information circulated during the 1745–46 uprising that Quaker merchants had sided with the government against the Jacobite rebels, who supported a restoration of the exiled Stuart monarch. Some Quakers reportedly supplied the royal army that fought against the Jacobites (Hughes 1956: 49). In the War of American Independence, at least some British Quakers again inclined to support the government and to look with disfavor on the colonial insurgents. But any temptation to interpret these incidents as a sign that Quakers had abandoned their radical beliefs, and had become conservative supporters of the established order, must be resisted; special circumstances explain what should be seen as departures from the Quakers' generally hard-line pacifist stance. In the first instance, the threat of a restoration of the Catholic Stuart dynasty brought out the Quakers' fundamental Protestantism; at least some of them found it impossible to remain strictly neutral in a contest that could end up with a Catholic back on the throne. In the second case, historical Quaker animosity to the Puritans of New England, who had persecuted Quakers in the seventeenth century, seems to provide the rationale for a willingness, on the part of at least a few Quakers, to celebrate British victories over the Americans, whom they described as "the enemy" (Winchester 1994: 340, 351–52, 358, 363, 392).

What is striking, however, is not the occasional deviation of some Quakers from their strict pacifist beliefs, but their general consistency in upholding them, often in the most trying of circumstances. As Jacob Price has observed, as time went on, the Quakers tended to become more, not less, doctrinaire in their views about non-violence in war. In a study of Atlantic maritime trade, he notes the harder pacifist line adopted by Quaker merchants from the 1740s (Price 1996: 64–86). At about the same time, in 1745, the governor of New Jersey complained that Quakers in the colony's assembly blocked his attempts to raise a body of troops to fight the French and their native allies (Sheridan 1993: 347). At the beginning of the Seven Years' War (1756–63), similar charges were leveled against the Pennsylvanian Quaker legislators, who would not sanction the raising of military forces in the province to combat the enemy who ravaged its borders ("Letter from Pennsylvania," *Public Advertiser*, January 19, 1756). Quakers in London who refused to put lights in the windows of their homes to celebrate the victory of the British and allied forces over the French at Minden in Germany in the summer of 1759 had their windows broken by drunken crowds (London Metropolitan Archives, Eliot and Howard Family Papers, Acc. 1017/983, Philip Eliot to John Eliot III, August 9, 1759).

A further contextual point is in order. The Quakers, and other less well-known Christian pacifist groups, formed a small minority amongst the religiously committed in seventeenth- and eighteenth-century Britain and its colonies. Even at their most popular, the Quakers comprised but a small sect: in the 1680s, when their membership was perhaps as high as 60,000, the English population, the vast bulk of it Protestant, probably numbered some five millions. By the 1730s, Quaker strength had diminished to about 50,000, and that at a time when the population of England and Wales had grown to just over six millions. The Quakers, in other words, not only represented a tiny part of the total Protestant whole, they were also a numerically dwindling force (Ceadel 1996: 151). The same was true of British North America. Quakers had founded Pennsylvania in the 1680s, but even there they formed a minority of the settler population from the outset. By the middle of the eighteenth century, they had become a proportionately much smaller presence, with Presbyterians from Scotland or Ulster, and Lutherans and other German Protestant groups, easily outnumbering them.

More importantly, the Quakers' views were far from representative of the mainstream. John Conybear, dean of Christ Church, Oxford, believed that "War, in every view of it, is a terrible Calamity"; yet he had no doubt that Britain's participation in the recently concluded War of the Austrian Succession had been both right and necessary ([Conybear] 1749: 37). As a clergyman of the established (that is, state-supported) church, delivering a sermon to celebrate the end of that particular conflict, Conybear might be expected to express such sentiments. But it was not just members of the Anglican establishment who regarded defensive war, or war in a "good cause" (however defined), as perfectly legitimate. The congregation of the Independent Church in Bedford celebrated enthusiastically at the end of April 1746 news of "the complete victory over the rebels" by the Duke of Cumberland at Culloden (Tibbutt 1976: 174). Most Protestant Dissenters seem to have thought in much the same way. Catholics could hardly be expected to rejoice at the defeat of the Catholic Stuart claimant, but they generally had no more qualms than Anglicans or most Protestant Dissenters about the use of force in what they regarded as a worthy cause.

War, like harvest failure, or plague, featured in the cosmology of most Christians as a divine instrument. At the height of the 1745–46 rebellion, when the Jacobites looked poised to overthrow the Hanoverian regime and the Protestant Succession in England, a British officer hoped that "after it has pleas'd God to chastise us wch we deserve he will have mercy & put a stop to our growing Calamities" (Staffordshire Record Office, Congreve Papers, D 1057/M/12/3). "National Corruption and Depravity," as the title of one Seven Years' War sermon explained, were "the Principal Cause of National Disappointments" (Dupont [1757]). Even a government minister, reflecting in the same war on the failure of allied arms in a battle against the French, concluded that "There is no commanding Events, Victory is in the Hand of God" (British Library, Holland House Papers, Add. MS 51,380, fo. 352, Earl of Holderness, 1760). From this perspective, armed conflict, though involving human suffering and human actions that caused that suffering, was a reflection of God's will and could not ultimately be understood in terms of human agency. For as long as such providential views of war dominated, the opportunities for the emergence of broad-based pacific, or even pacificist, sentiment remained distinctly limited.

Writers on political economy, it must be said, increasingly pointed out from the middle of the eighteenth century that war caused disruption and loss and so, in the words of Sir James Steuart, was "inconsistent with the prosperity of a modern state" (Steuart 1767: I. 448). But it would be a mistake to assume from the political economists, or the irenic schemes of philosophers, such as Immanuel Kant ([1795] 1983), that enlightened opinion was necessarily pacific, or even pacificist. Enlightened enquiry often confirmed, rather than challenged, general acceptance of war as part of life. William Robertson, the great Scottish historian, believed that the character of war had changed, making it far more acceptable than in past ages. Limitations on the use of violence, and the protection of non-combatants from many of the horrors of armed conflict, Robertson claimed, meant that "Civilized nations" now fought their wars with remarkably "little rancour, or animosity," with the result that "war amongst them is disarmed of half its terrors" (Robertson 1769: I. 9). Adam Ferguson, another key figure of the Scottish Enlightenment, argued in a work of social analysis published at about the same time that human beings naturally inclined to violence, and were addicted to armed conflict. To try to prevent war was therefore a fruitless endeavor (Ferguson [1767] 1966: 201–05, 98). His fellow Scot Lord Kames claimed that war, despite its suffering, should not always be counted as a misfortune. Perpetual war would be highly undesirable, he conceded, but perpetual peace would perhaps be even more damaging. War, he maintained, acted as "a school for improving every manly virtue," while peace promoted selfishness and turned men into "beasts of burden" (Kames 1774: I. 426–38). Writers of the period frequently invoked peace in this unflattering way. The "luxury" associated with uninterrupted commerce appears in many texts not as the cause for celebration but as the reason for national degeneracy and effeminacy. Military service, on the other hand, especially in formations independent of central government control, such as the militia or volunteers, tended to be viewed as the means by which liberty and virtue may be promoted (Wilson 1995: 187).

The War of American Independence did not mark the end of this kind of thinking. Clergymen of the established church and Protestant dissenting denominations, as well as the religiously committed laity, continued to regard the conflict, especially when it broadened to include the French, Spanish, and Dutch as British enemies, as a divine punishment for national sins. Beilby Porteus, the bishop of Chester, told the House of Lords in 1779 that the Seven Years' War had produced such wealth for Britain that had led to "wanton extravagance and wild excess, which loudly called for some signal check; and that check it has now received" (Porteus 1779: 12). An Irish Quaker, alarmed by the prospect of French invasion, similarly invoked Isaiah 26:9 to explain the crisis: "the judgments of the Lord are upon this land, that the inhabitants thereof may learn righteousness" (National Library of Ireland, MS 4242, Diary of a Cork Quaker, June 7, 1778). The war's outcome may even have persuaded some Britons that the time had come to tackle the issue of slavery, which they saw as one of the causes of God's displeasure and so Britain's loss of the thirteen colonies (Brown 2006).

The idea that war and certain kinds of military service promoted liberty also surfaced regularly. The Irish volunteers, formed when Franco-Spanish invasion seemed a real possibility, made much of their role as "citizen soldiers," prepared to put their commitment to defending their communities above personal comfort and safety. They appeared in many accounts as the embodiment of "republican virtue" (McBride 1998: 123–33). John Cartwright, the English reformer, hoped to see similar bodies emerging in his own country, and making a similar contribution "to the cause of freedom" (National Library of Ireland, Dobbs Papers, MS 2251, Cartwright to Francis Dobbs, 12 Jan. 1780). Those British volunteer units that did form between 1779 and 1783—in all parts of the country, not only those most exposed to the threat of invasion (Conway 2004)—earned lavish praise from many contemporaries, impressed by "this Military Spirit," which provided an antidote to prevailing "Effeminacy of Manners" (Wiltshire and Swindon History Centre, Wansey Papers, 314/4/2, George Wansey to Richard Laurence, October 1, 1779 and Henry Wansey to the same, October 1, 1779).

But alongside providential interpretations of the war and a continuing emphasis on the need for moral regeneration through military service, came a willingness to argue against the legitimacy of armed conflict—a willingness that extended far beyond the Quakers and other religiously inspired pacifist groups. The War of American Independence differed significantly from earlier eighteenth-century wars. It divided the transatlantic British nation, with Americans entering the war in defense of their British rights and asserting their continued loyalty to the British crown. Independence in 1776 changed the perspective of many of the former colonists, but many Britons, whether they viewed the Americans as fellow subjects nobly defending liberty, or as rebels against legitimate authority, still saw them as part of the extended British nation. For many of the British, the Americans' alliance of 1778 with the French proved a turning point; fellow subjects had, by associating with the hereditary enemy, become themselves foreigners. Even so, the sense that the Americans, despite their conduct, remained in important ways British, or even English, lingered in British imaginations (Conway 2002).

The internecine character of the conflict meant, almost inevitably, that the British government came in for much domestic criticism for its coercion of fellow subjects, especially in the first stage of the war, when a permanent separation looked unlikely. The months preceding the outbreak of hostilities between the British armed forces and the colonial rebels, and the first months of the conflict itself, brought forth a great many conciliatory petitions, from counties and boroughs across Britain, calling on Lord North's government not to fight the Americans. The work of James Bradley, who studied the petitioning movement in detail, suggests that the number of signatories on anti-war petitions exceeded the number on pro-coercion loyal addresses submitted in the same period (Bradley 1986: 65–69, 137; Bradley 1990: ch. 9). While signatures constitute only a crude measure of public sentiment, they provide us with an indication of the strength and breadth of opposition to the war against the colonists.

Even so, historians generally downplay the significance of the anti-war sentiment expressed in the American conflict. In part this is a result of the general perception, based on contemporary testimony, that the war was widely supported in Britain, at least in its first years. The retrospective judgment of one witness that "There does not perhaps occur in the annals of Britain a single instance of a war more popular at its commencement than that which took place between Britain and her colonies" seems to accord with many pessimistic observations by opponents of the conflict (Somerville 1996: 187). Those MPs who criticized government policy had no doubt that they were in a minority, not just in Parliament, but in the country at large. "We are not only *patriots out of place*," Sir George Savile wrote plaintively to the Marquis of Rockingham, "but patriots out *of the opinion of the public*" (Albemarle 1852: II. 305).

More importantly, those expressions of opposition to the war that can be found were decidedly conditional. Joshua Toulmin, a dissenting clergyman, attacked the American war in a sermon, claiming that the struggle was "pregnant with peculiar evils." The only gainers, he asserted, would be the French, Britain's true foe. To Toulmin, in other words, this was the wrong kind of war—a war against our American brethren. A war against "our natural enemies," the French, on the other hand, he implied, would be unobjectionable (Toulmin 1776: 3, 8–11). Similar sentiments encouraged the Independent congregation at Isleham, Cambridgeshire, to ask God to "put an end to this bloody and unnatural war" against the Americans. But once the French entered the conflict in 1778, the same congregation prayed that He would intervene on their side "against the French" (Parson 1984: 97–98, 102, 111, 120). The Newtonards volunteers in County Down put the matter succinctly in one of their toasts at a dinner in July of that year: "Speedy peace with America, and war with France" (*Belfast News-letter*, July 3–7, 1778). Unsurprisingly, then, to Paul Langford, the American war did not see a movement dedicated to opposing armed conflict as such (Langford 1989: 626–67). Martin Ceadel, the leading authority on British peace movements, is inclined to the same view. He accords the War of Independence some importance to the extent that it involved an "embryonic *pacifism*"; but he does not see the struggle with America as bringing forth a genuine peace movement, committed to opposing war in all its forms (Ceadel 1996: 164–65).

Yet, as Ceadel suggests, the war against America provided an opportunity for arguments to be deployed that would be applied more generally in the future. The case against the conflict with the colonists created material that could be turned into a critique of war in general—even if those who articulated their opposition to the American war directed their fire at this particular armed contest only, and often became enthusiastic supporters of war against the French and then from 1779 against the Spanish. Opponents of the coercion of the colonists, admittedly, drew in part on established arguments, particularly the earlier criticisms of war voiced by political economists such as Steuart. But the emergence of a concerted campaign against the American war gave these arguments much more exposure—in petitions, pamphlets, newspapers, and parliamentary debates—and therefore much more force than they possessed in the pages of little-read treatises.

Joshua Toulmin, as we have seen, opposed the war against the Americans, yet had few qualms about fighting the French. But when, in the course of his sermon denouncing the American war, he referred to the "calamities common to the devastating sword," he was making a point about suffering that could be applied to war in general, not just the particular war that he was criticizing (Toulmin 1776: 3, 8). Likewise, when the Presbyterian Synod of Ulster rejoiced in June 1782 that "Brother will no more rise up against Brother," the delegates probably had in mind simply the struggle between Britain and its former North American colonies (in which a good many Presbyterians of Scots-Irish descent had settled). Again, however, the language they used could be deployed to criticize wars of all kinds, which inevitably divided mankind, pitting brother against brother and sister against sister (Synod of Ulster 1890–98: III. 46). To Matthew Robinson Morris, an anti-American war pamphleteer, it was self-evident that the struggle disrupted commerce and so reduced national wealth. But when he argued that "Commerce is the offspring of peace and war is her irreconcilable enemy," he advanced a proposition relevant to all wars, not just the war to which he objected (Morris 1777: 9). The opposition pamphleteer who wrote *The Letters of Valens* (almost certainly William Burke), also made a point of wider applicability when in his objections to the war against the rebellious colonies he claimed that "The influence of the Crown, considerable in peace, in war is boundless" ([Burke] 1777: iii). In all wars of the eighteenth and early nineteenth centuries, after all, the expansion of the armed forces and the revenue services gave government new opportunities to secure support through the politically astute distribution of patronage, either in the form of posts or supply contracts. The same point about wider applicability can be made of David Hartley's insistence that high and general taxation was an inevitable consequence of the conflict with the Americans: it was equally true of every large-scale war (Wyvill 1774–1802: III. 184). These arguments, we should note, became the mainstay of the case against war in general for later generations of peace campaigners, whose stock in trade was that armed conflict caused great and intolerable suffering, undermined the economy, expanded government power, and increased taxation.

*

Jeremy Bentham, the utilitarian philosopher, in the course of his criticism in 1789 of William Pitt the Younger's foreign policy, recommended the establishment of a "Pacific or Philharmonic society," which would promote peace and amity between nations (University College London, Bentham MSS, Box cix. 2). Exactly what Bentham had in mind is unclear; but we can surmise that he envisaged a body rather like the London Peace Society that he joined in the 1820s, which acted as the proselytizing core of the emerging post-1815 British peace movement (London Peace Society Papers, Minute-book 1816–36: 139; London Peace Society 1823: 33; London Peace Society 1824: 29; London Peace Society 1825: 44). Bentham's campaign against Pitt failed to resonate, however, and his proposed peace society remained a dream for more than a quarter of a century. It was to be the coming of the French Revolutionary War in 1793 and the succeeding conflict against Napoleon that lasted to 1815, rather than Bentham's writings, that laid the foundations for the London Peace Society.

The outbreak of war with revolutionary France did not at first seem to promise a great surge of irenical sentiment. France, as Britain's long-standing and traditional enemy—the nation against which the British habitually defined themselves—unsurprisingly elicited less open sympathy than the Americans had done in 1775–76 (Colley 2009). While the new regime in Paris perhaps had certain features in common with the former colonists—both became associated with republican forms of government—many pro-ministerial writers and politicians in 1793 emphasized the similarities between the new order and the old; the revolutionary government seemed as determined as the aggrandizing Bourbon monarchs to expand France's frontiers. As William Black, one of these ministerial apologists, put it: "The vast and mischievous schemes of Louis XIV are now acted out again, only under a different disguise" (Black 1793: 32–33). France declared war on Britain, but even before this formal beginning of hostilities, Pitt's government was preparing to enter the conflict in pursuit of a very traditional British foreign policy objective—the defense of the Low Countries. Pitt and his colleagues sent troops to Flanders to protect the Austrian Netherlands and the Dutch Republic (regarded as Britain's outer defenses) from French invasion, just as ministers in London had done in the War of the League of Augsburg at the end of the seventeenth century, the War of the Spanish Succession at the beginning of the eighteenth century, and the War of the Austrian Succession in the 1740s (Conway 2011: 64–66).

But if some pro-government commentators emphasized continuity with previous wars against the French, others stressed the peculiar dangers posed by the new regime in Paris. The French Revolution, Edmund Burke famously argued in his *Reflections on the Revolution in France* (1790), should not be viewed complacently by Britons, some of whom mistakenly saw parallels with Britain's own Glorious Revolution of a hundred years before. The events in France should be seen as a major challenge to established institutions in Britain itself. The French Revolution threatened, furthermore, not just the very fabric of British society, but the social order in all the European states. Burke lamented the undermining of what he called "the system of Europe, taking in laws, manners, religion and politics, in which I delighted so much" (Copeland 1958–78: IX. 307, Burke to French Laurence, April 11, 1797). The Revolution's challenge to the Catholic Church in France, and the willingness of its leaders to overthrow all forms of established order and replace them with systems invented from scratch, alarmed not just Burke, but, thanks in part to his overheated rhetoric, property owners in general. Most British politicians came to believe that the Revolution in France could easily be exported to Britain if appropriate measures were not taken to contain the contagion. The war therefore took on an ideological flavor, with French democratic principles opposed by British commitment to a balanced constitution. Fear of unrestrained democracy, and of the expropriation that many of the propertied classes saw as its inevitable corollary, gave British elites cause to view the French Revolutionary War as a particularly dangerous conflict, against a particularly dangerous enemy, and so created an atmosphere in which pacific ideas struggled to be heard (Macleod 1998: esp. chs. 1–3).

This is not to say that the British political nation accepted the war without demur. In Parliament, the opposition Whigs continued to fear government power more than they feared the French Revolution. Charles James Fox, who emerged as the leader of those Whigs who were unwilling to rally behind Pitt's ministry, criticized the war against France as a threat to British liberty. Already concerned at what he saw as the excessive influence of government, which he claimed had increased under Pitt, Fox argued that war inevitably made matters worse, by giving ministers still greater patronage to dispense, enabling them to buy support in the legislature (Mitchell 1992). The parliamentary opposition, however, found itself in an even weaker position than the Rockingham Whigs in the early years of the American war. In 1775–76, the Rockinghams had at least been united in opposing the war; in 1793–94, the Whigs split, with many conservative Whigs reckoning that the existential threat to European civilization posed by atheistic republicanism in France required them to support Pitt and put aside their traditional opposition concerns about growing government power (Mori 2000: esp. ch. 1).

Much more significant than the Foxite parliamentary opposition was wider public hostility, which grew as the war dragged on. Even in 1793–94, peace tracts sought to encourage the creation of a peace movement. The tracts were largely penned by rational Christians—some of them Anglicans, but most Protestant dissenters—who fervently believed in the capacity of man to change the world for the better (Clark 1985: esp. 389–92). These rational Christians, rather than the Quakers, formed the intellectual leadership of the peace campaigns that emerged during the war years. Less helpful, perhaps, were those political radicals whose opposition to the war was influenced by their sympathy for the democratic principles espoused by the French revolutionaries. Enthusiasts for reform in Britain itself often found themselves accused of supporting the French, and those accusations appeared credible because some radicals adopted the language and even the organization of the revolutionaries in Paris. The supposed disloyalty of such radicals made it easy for government apologists to portray all opponents of the war as closet Jacobins who wished not for peace but for the victory of the enemy.

Even so, an identifiable peace movement emerged in 1795. Fourteen peace petitions arrived in Parliament that January and February. The disruption of trade caused by the conflict and rising food prices created an anti-war mood in various parts of the country. A demonstration at the opening of Parliament in the autumn called for "No War" as well as "Bread." The government's heavy-handed response—the Treasonable Practices Act and the Seditious Meetings Act—provoked still more criticism, with more than a hundred peace petitions, bearing in excess of 130,000 signatures, condemning Pitt's "war system," flooding into Parliament in November and December (Cookson 1982: 190). Some of these petitions may well have been orchestrated by the Foxites, who sought to take control of extra-parliamentary opposition to the government, much as the Rockinghamites had done at the time of the American war. But J. E. Cookson, the leading authority on popular anti-war sentiment between 1793 and 1815, argues that most of the petitions should be seen as genuine expressions of grassroots concern about the strains caused by the war and growing impatience with a government that seemed impervious to the case put by the parliamentary opposition (Cookson 1982: 123, 152, 279–80). French success in conquering not only the Austrian Netherlands but also in 1795 the Dutch Republic led to the withdrawal of most British forces from the Continent, further increasing pressure on Pitt's ministry.

In 1797, conditions deteriorated again. At home, financial crisis obliged the Bank of England to suspend cash payments in February. The government had little choice but to reduce borrowing and try to squeeze more money out of taxpayers. The British system of war finance, which had proved so successful in previous eighteenth-century conflicts, now appeared to be on the verge of collapse, or at least was placing unprecedented burdens on large swathes of the British public. The war situation also grew worse. The Austrians, Britain's chief ally, pulled out of the conflict, making a separate peace with the French. The Foxites succeeded in stimulating a fresh wave of petitions calling for an end to hostilities from boroughs and counties in which they had influence. The following year, French invasion seemed a real possibility, and French troops actually landed in Ireland. But these developments in 1798, though providing further ammunition for the parliamentary opposition in their criticism of Pitt and his ministers, made the task of peace campaigners more not less difficult. The threat of invasion turned a war of aggression (as many peace activists saw it) into a defensive war, so many of those disposed to peace, but not pure and absolute pacifists, pressed their case less insistently, or even dropped their opposition to the war altogether. Amongst the wider population, patriotic fervor abounded. It, together perhaps with social ambition and civic pride, brought forth a great surge in volunteering, which made the volunteer activity in Britain during the preceding American war seem very small scale (Gee 2003; Cookson 1997: esp. ch. 3).

The failure of the French landing in Ireland and the general improvement in the war situation, reduced the inhibitions of those who wanted to see peace. They received a boost with the introduction of the new income tax in 1799. Criticism of the war now emphasized its financial costs—particularly for the industrious middle-classes—and the redistribution of wealth to those who benefited from government contracts. The case for peace was also furthered by fresh food crises that began in 1799 and went on until 1801, and by the government's bringing in further repressive measures, notably the legislation directed against unlawful combinations of 1799 and 1800. Now, to a greater extent than ever before, condemnation of the ministry and criticism of the war became inextricably connected. In 1801, petitions from the major manufacturing districts, particularly the textile-producing areas of the West Riding of Yorkshire, put the case for peace. These petitions, Cookson argues, had nothing to do with the parliamentary opposition or local Whig influence, but represented "the mobilization of an interest group," inspired by rational dissenting manufacturers (Cookson 1982: 202).

The Peace of Amiens, signed in March 1802, brought Britain's conflict with revolutionary France to an end and provided some justification for the efforts of the peace campaigners. Pitt's resignation, and the formation of a new government, had seemingly been the necessary preliminary to any settlement with the French. But any boost given to the peace cause was short-lived (see Grainger 2004). Hostilities resumed in May 1803, when Napoleon's ambitions for territorial expansion persuaded ministers in London that they had no choice but to commit British forces to war again. Worse still, from an irenical point of view, the threat of French invasion, with a powerful army assembled at Boulogne, rallied public opinion behind the government and made the task of peace campaigners much more difficult. Pacifists faced strong criticism, including from churchmen determined to show that Christian doctrine accepted the legitimate use of violence, especially in cases of self-defense. Not until the danger of invasion receded—in the minds of many British contemporaries, after Nelson's victory at the battle of Trafalgar in October 1805, though in reality some months earlier—did the environment become more conducive to peace campaigning.

The abandonment of the French invasion plans encouraged Napoleon, now emperor, to turn to economic warfare to drive Britain out of the conflict. The introduction of the "Continental system" in 1806–07, designed to close markets throughout Europe to British goods, led to British retaliation in the form of orders in council that sought to stop neutral commerce with Britain's enemies. The consequent stagnation of overseas trade stimulated major peace petitions from the industrial areas of the north of England in 1808, bearing a total of some 150,000 signatures (Cookson 1982: 190). On this occasion, though the inspiration was economic, arguments against the destruction and loss of life caused by war circulated alongside criticisms of the government's orders in council, with William Roscoe, a Liverpool merchant, contributing a strong and multi-dimensional attack on the war ([Roscoe] 1808). The main message of the peace campaigners at this point, however, was that war benefited a narrow elite that gained power and wealth at the expense of the rest of society. The critique, though meant to be applied specifically to the conditions of the time, implicitly condemned international armed conflict in general.

The message of the peace campaigners perhaps made greater inroads as a result of wartime developments. A scandal involving the Duke of York, the commander-in-chief of the army, gave credence to the long-standing criticism that promotion in the military rested on connection rather than merit, and so exposed the workings of an apparently corrupt system. Military failure, first in South America, where an expedition to capture Buenos Aires ended in disaster in July 1807, and then nearer home at Walcheren Island, in the Low Countries, where a major British force experienced appalling losses from disease before ignominiously withdrawing in the closing months of 1809, reinforced discontent with the existing dispensation. The cause of peace, as well as political radicalism, benefited from these embarrassments. Even so, the orders in council continued to act as the main focus for criticism of the government, especially as relations with the United States deteriorated as a result of British interference with neutral shipping.

High food prices in Britain, a severe depression in exports, and widespread destruction of new machinery by workers who feared for their jobs, created a combustible situation. But to the manufacturers in places like the north of Staffordshire and West Yorkshire, the principal grievance was the damage being done by the orders in council. Lord Liverpool's government withdrew the orders in June, but too late to prevent a war with the United States. The impression that the ministry had given way to public pressure provided campaigners against the orders with the appearance of success. Emboldened, peace activists renewed their efforts. That August, a meeting of "the Friends of Peace" of the East Midlands counties at Loughborough led to a peace petition "founded on the broad basis of Christianity and humanity" (Ceadel 1996: 199). The petition, and others like it in that year and the next, seem largely to have been the work of the rational dissenting middle classes, such as William Strutt, a Unitarian manufacturer from Derby, who ensured that the Loughborough petition received national publicity. The petitions of this period increasingly emphasized the human suffering as well as the material damage done by war. Perhaps this stress on death and injury was a natural consequence of the mounting casualty rate in a long and demanding war. From 1808, British forces had been committed to the Iberian Peninsula, fighting in increasingly large numbers in Portugal and Spain against the French. British money subsidized allies and auxiliaries, as it had done before, but now many more Britons were dying or suffering debilitating wounds.

Calls for peace continued to be heard in the early months of 1813, with the east Midlands again leading the way. Nottingham, where dissenters exerted great influence on the corporation, submitted a well-supported peace petition at this time. But as Napoleon's fortunes declined, and the allies started to defeat his armies in Germany and Spain, the prospect of outright victory over the French emperor seems to have reduced an enthusiasm for peace that had been nourished by war-weariness. Though in 1813 peace campaigners discussed amongst themselves the idea of establishing a peace society to promote the irenical cause, no progress was made in this direction until Napoleon's eventual defeat in March 1814, when Prussian, Russian, and Austrian troops entered Paris. Even then, Napoleon's brief return from exile in February 1815, together with disagreement amongst peace activists about whether a British peace society should be open only to pure pacifists, or welcome pacificists, appears to have delayed the formation of the London Peace Society (Ceadel 1996: 207–08). Napoleon's final defeat at Waterloo in June 1815 removed the immediate cause for caution, but the dispute about the form of the projected society remained unresolved. The eventual compromise, with membership of the Peace Society's committee confined to out-and-out pacifists, but subscriptions for ordinary membership open to those who accepted defensive war, allowed the organization to play an influential part in peace campaigning in the post-Napoleonic War era.

*

What general conclusions can we draw from this survey of British peace movements? The first and most obvious is perhaps that it took a particularly long and demanding war against revolutionary and Napoleonic France to bring forth a true peace movement. The arguments used by peace campaigners after 1793 had, of course, been anticipated by Quaker testimony in the seventeenth century, and in pamphlets, tracts, and sermons decrying various aspects of war earlier in the eighteenth century. They had been deployed, furthermore, in concentrated form in the peculiar circumstances of the War of American Independence to criticize an "unnatural" conflict against fellow Britons. But it was not until the French Revolutionary War that these arguments come to be applied more generally against armed conflict by a significant number of people acting in concert.

Yet our second conclusion must surely be that if it took the protracted, expensive, disruptive, and bloody struggle against the French Revolution and Napoleon—the "Great War," as it came to be known to nineteenth-century Britons—to create a genuine peace movement in Britain, that same struggle produced conditions that made peace activity very difficult and its success almost impossible. As in earlier eighteenth-century wars, both providential religion and enlightened thinking suggested not that war was wrong, but that it was a divine test of virtue, or a necessary preservative of freedom. Both traditional and modern ideas, in other words, worked against the efforts of peace campaigners. Irenical enthusiasts also had to contend with the patriotic feelings engendered during all international conflicts, especially when the country faced the danger of invasion. That had been true in the War of the Austrian Succession, the Seven Years' War, and the War of American Independence. But it was perhaps particularly true in the French Revolutionary and Napoleonic Wars. In this conflict, anxiety amongst property owners about the export of the democracy from Paris increased the tendency to see opponents of war as dangerous subversives, acting against the interests of the state. In the end, the London Peace Society, and other peace societies in North America that anticipated it, came into being only when the fighting had stopped. Perhaps ironically, peace campaigners found it easier to mobilize to preserve peace than to halt war.

CHAPTER SEVEN

Peace, Security, and Deterrence

DOOHWAN AHN AND RICHARD WHATMORE

Shortly after the outbreak of the War of the Spanish Succession in July 1702, François Fénelon, archbishop of Cambrai, decided to add a short supplement to a book of political maxims that he just completed for his royal student Duc de Bourgogne, grandson of the Sun King and second heir to the French throne (Fénelon 1747: 76–91).[1] The reopening of hostilities between France and three key members of the Grand Alliance, Britain, Austria, and the Dutch Republic, after five short years of peace since the Treaty of Ryswick in September 1697, brought home to Fénelon the urgent need to remind the young Duc that the maintenance of international peace and security was central to patriot kingship (Blom, Laursen and Simonutti 2007). However, unlike earlier Christian humanist thinkers, Fénelon did not stop at pointing out the horrors and devastations of war (Hinsley 1967: 13–80; Howard 2008: 5–21). He went much further and delineated the following four types of international system. Although, due to this additional discussion, the book only came out posthumously in 1734, nearly twenty years after the author's death, it nonetheless prefigured and encapsulated a prevalent strand of the Enlightenment discourse on war and peace.[2]

The first system Fénelon examined was uni-polarity with a single dominant power, "absolutely superior to all other powers even when united" (Fénelon 1747: 85). He noted that this system was "most apt to dazzle," but disapproved it outright because it "cannot be obtained without committing great wrongs and violences of all sorts" (Fénelon 1747: 86–87). Worse yet, "universal monarchy," in contemporary parlance, caused more suffering by its fall, as was evidenced by that of the Roman Empire.[3] The second system was "of a power superior to all others singly, but as near as may be equal to them when united" (Fénelon 1747: 87). Fénelon judged this to be the worst of all four kinds of international system on the grounds that "it can never tend, in its most prosperous condition, but to pass into the former system" (Fénelon 1747: 88). His next system referred to a situation when "a power inferior to another, but so that the inferior, united with the rest of Europe, constitutes the equilibrium against the superior, and the security of all the other lesser states" (Fénelon 1747: 88). This, according to Fénelon, was more preferable than the previous one as there was a higher chance of subduing the pretender to universal monarchy with less cost. Last but not least, the royal preceptor set forth to his beloved prince what he believed to be the ideal international system. To be in this condition of "a power very nearly equal to another, with which it forms the equilibrium for the publick security," "without inclination to depart from it," Fénelon declared, "is the wisest and happiest state" (Fénelon 1747: 89–90).

It is not difficult to see why the French ministry was determined to suppress this entire work. The archbishop was not merely criticizing his master Louis XIV, but, far more seriously, he was championing his archenemy William III of England, who had passed away earlier in the year. Europe at the turn of the century, in Fénelon's opinion, was precariously oscillating between the second and third systems. In 1686, William, together with Emperor Leopold I, organized a defensive coalition named the League of Augsburg and succeeded, with great difficulty, in rescuing Europe from Fénelon's second system, forestalling Louis' first major attempt to become another Charlemagne. Five years later, Louis was again dragging Europe into the second system by trying to put his second grandson Philippe Duc d'Anjou (the future Felipe V) on the Spanish throne which was left empty by the demise of Carlos II in November 1700. In point of fact, Fénelon devoted much of his supplementary analysis to justifying the rights of lesser powers to form a defensive alliance against a would-be hegemon. "To hinder a neighbour from growing too powerful," he emphatically argued, "is not to do evil; it is to secure ourselves from slavery, and our neighbours also; it is to stand up in the cause of liberty, tranquillity and the public safety" (Fénelon 1747: 78).

The Enlightenment era opened and ended with wars. The eighteenth century began across Europe with the ongoing wars of the Sun King, and closed with those of the French Revolution and Napoleon Bonaparte. An age that aspired to bring a permanent stop to violence, disorder, and war ended with unprecedented chaos and bloodshed. Why was an era associated with reform, progress, and improvement so scarred by continuous battle? The answer to this question may be found in Fénelon's above remark. For him and many of his contemporaries, what mattered was not so much simply ending war as establishing a perfect balance of power. They believed that the future of European civilization hinged ultimately on the latter. Fortunately, in 1713, after eleven years of heavy fighting and casualties, Fénelon's third system of multi-polarity was established by the Treaty of Utrecht between Britain and France, actually ushering in a new era of prosperity through peaceful economic competition (Fénelon 1747: 82; Schuurman 2012, 179–99). Such was its importance that the renowned intellectual historian John Pocock has recently coined the term "Utrecht Enlightenment" to characterize the central role of the balance of power in Europe's eventual escape from barbarism and religion (Pocock 1997: 23; 1999a: 106–14). The eighteenth-century obsession with the balance of power was linked to "the optimism and belief in the ability of man to control his own fate" (Anderson 1970: 198). The balance of power, in short, was an enlightenment concept, rather than one instantiated with the treaties of Westphalia (1648) and the Pyrenees (1659). After all, the age of Enlightenment was the "Golden Age" of the balance of power both in theory and practice.[4]

Strictly speaking, however, there is no deterrence against possible aggression in the system of balance of power. "Every nation," as Fénelon himself cautioned in the same place, "is desirous of prevailing over all the others that lie round it. Every nation, therefore, is obliged, for its own security, to be continually upon its guard, to prevent the excessive growth of power in every neighbour" (Fénelon 1747: 77). Put differently, the basic aim of the balance of power is not peace in the sense of the absence of war but insurance against aspirations to universal monarchy, both secular and theocratic. It is essentially a system of constant checks and balances, whether militarily or diplomatically (Ghervas 2017: 404–25).

This chapter revisits the balance of power as a concept and in practice in the eighteenth century. Although much has been written about this subject, little attention has been paid to growing concerns through the eighteenth century about the stability of the balance of power system and its ultimate failure by the early years of the French Revolution (Haslam 2002: 89–127; Sheehan 1996; Luard 1992; Maurseth 1964: 120–36; Dehio 1962). However, as the century progressed, apocalyptic predictions of the imminent collapse of state across Europe by barbarians from the east, civil war, or general bankruptcy, were increasingly prominent (Hont 2005a: 1–158). Concomitantly, it became abundantly clear that maintaining security and stability through the balance of power was a near impossibility. In this regard, it is more than a coincidence that Immanuel Kant endeavored to rehabilitate the Abbé de Saint-Pierre's plan for a European union in the wake of the French Revolutionary Wars (1792–1802) and the 1793 Second Partition of Poland, as an alternative to the balance of power (Kant 1991a: 47–49; 1991b: 87–92; 1991c: 93–130). Less than a decade later, the Napoleonic Wars (1803–15) brutally confirmed Saint-Pierre's dismal diagnosis, made on the eve of the Treaty of Utrecht, that the European states, at least in their relationship with one another, were in the position of "the Heads of Families among savages," or of "the petty Kings of Africa, of the miserable Caciques, or petty Sovereigns of America" (Saint-Pierre 1714: 3). Whether the Concert of Europe, established by the 1815 Congress of Vienna, was a restoration of the balance of power or a new system of order is still very much contested, but there can be no doubt that the balance of power mechanism failed miserably to thwart Napoleon and his Grand Armée from marching freely across the European continent (Schroeder 1994; Mitzen 2013; Vick 2014; Ghervas 2019: 95–113). This chapter charts the failure of the balance of power, and the parallel loss of any sense of security or deterrence in a world of war rather than peace. The eighteenth century, so heralded as an era of reform, progress, and improvement, was rather one of war, fear, and failure from the perspective of international relations.

II

Enlightenment acceptance of the balance of power as a principal instrument for regulating international relations had its origin in a Europe-wide reaction to the ascendancy of France after the Thirty Years' War (1618–48) and the Franco–Spanish War (1635–59). Many contemporaries noted that it was part and parcel of the experience of Louis XIV, who effectively took power in 1661 after the death of Cardinal Jules Mazarin and launched his first war of aggression into the Spanish Netherlands in 1667, a year after the death of his overbearing mother, Queen Anne of Austria. Most notably, Samuel Pufendorf, in his remarkable *An Introduction to the History of the Principal Kingdoms and States of Europe* (1682), based on lectures he had given as Professor of Natural Law at the University of Lund between 1668 and 1676, pointed to a possible disruption of the hard-won Westphalian order by Louis' France. Written against the background of the War of Devolution (1667–68) and the Franco–Dutch War (1672–78), Pufendorf's book was an urgent call for an alliance against the rising France. Every central chapter concluded with a detailed assessment of the nature and scale of the threat posed by the French in relation to the particular circumstances of each country. Taken together, Pufendorf was putting forward arguably the first systematic plan for European peace through the balance of power.

To start with, Pufendorf counseled that Sweden, which had formerly been on friendly terms with France in order to limit "the overgrown Greatness of the House of Austria," must redirect its foreign policy (Pufendorf 2013: 602). The situation of Europe's states had changed dramatically since the conclusion of the Thirty Years' War. As Pufendorf put it, "The King of France now pretends to play the Master over Princes," and went on to advise that "Sweden ought not to assist France in those Designs which overturn the Westphalian Treaty" (Pufendorf 2013: 602). More specifically, Pufendorf urged Sweden to ally itself with the Dutch Republic. The latter in its turn ought to "keep fair with the Princes of Germany, who else would permit the French to march through their Territories, or else perhaps join with them" (Pufendorf 2013: 311). Pufendorf, in addition, exhorted the Dutch Republic to "endeavour the Preservation of the Spanish Netherlands, which they ought to consider as their Frontier, and such a Frontier as obliges Spain always to Side with Holland against France" (Pufendorf 2013: 311). Pufendorf envisaged both the German Empire and Spain also joining an anti-Bourbon coalition for their own security, in the hope of balancing the power of the super-state. The German Empire was held by Pufendorf to be potentially as powerful militarily as France, but at a great disadvantage in terms of its political structure, "being neither one entire Kingdom, neither properly a Confederacy, but participating of both kinds" (Pufendorf 2013: 350; 2007). Pufendorf's biggest worry was the political disunity of Germany. "If Germany be divided within itself," especially in the face of the French threat, Pufendorf predicted, "nothing but fatal Consequences can attend it" (Pufendorf 2013: 358).

In Pufendorf's view, Spain was the state that would lose the most through the ascent of France. Louis XIV "not only longs to devour the rest of the Netherlands, but also aims at the Conquest of other parts of Spain," he noted (Pufendorf 2013: 95). Making matters worse, Spain was suffering from the problem of royal succession. King Felipe IV had fathered five sons in two marriages, but only one child had survived: this was Carlos II, who was born with physical and mental disabilities. Furthermore, being a minor, Carlos II had been placed under the regency of his mother, Mariana of Austria, until 1675, but more significantly, Carlos II died in 1700 without an heir. Clearly anticipating the resulting War of the Spanish Succession, Pufendorf deplored, "what Revolution may happen in Spain if the present Royal Family, which has no Heirs yet, should fail, is beyond Human Understanding to determine or foresee" (Pufendorf 2013: 95–96). To put it differently, there was a high possibility that the entire Spanish Empire might disintegrate, in which case France would certainly take the lion's share and become a universal monarchy on mainland Europe. The only way to ensure that "the Liberty and Possessions of all the States in Europe may not depend on the Pleasure and Will of one single person," Pufendorf advised, was to form a balance-of-power alliance for the purpose of preserving Spain (Pufendorf 2013: 95). Last but not least, Pufendorf assigned the role of the balancer to England. England was described as "a powerfull and considerable Kingdom, which is able to keep up the Balance betwixt the Christian Princes in Europe; and which depending on its own Strength, is powerfull enough to defend it self" (Pufendorf 2013: 187). In particular, Pufendorf strongly asserted that "the chiefest Interest of England" was "to keep up the Balance betwixt France and Spain, and to take a special care that the King of France do not become Master of all the Netherlands," because then he "would be superiour in Power to any in Europe" (Pufendorf 2013: 189). In this respect, the three Anglo–Dutch naval wars, fought in 1652–54, 1665–67, and 1672–74, according to Pufendorf, were at root distractions from the real issue of the day (Pufendorf 2013: 189, 310–12).

Forming a defensive alliance against France, however, was easier said than done, and Pufendorf was very much aware of this. In the long term, as Pufendorf made clear in meticulous detail, it served the interests of all the neighboring states. But it was quite another thing for them to enter into a coalition with one another, especially when it involved sacrificing their immediate interests to the longer-term goal of security and peace. The so-called Secret Treaty of Dover of 1670 between Louis and Charles II of England is a case in point. To break Dutch dominance in overseas trade, Charles betrayed the Triple Alliance with the Dutch Republic and Sweden, which two years before had successfully forced Louis to sign the Treaty of Aix-la-Chapelle with Spain, terminating the War of Devolution. As Pufendorf put it, "whilst one of them is engag'd in a War against France, it seems to be the Interest of the other to stand Nuter [neutral], and to promote its own Trade and Navigation with the other's demise" (Pufendorf 2013: 270). Nor, Pufendorf added, were "the Princes of Germany, especially those of the Protestant Religion . . . willing to see France fall before the House of Austria; since both their Power and Religion would stand upon slippery Ground, if not supported by a Foreign Power" (Pufendorf 2013: 271). The sheer difficulty of organizing a balance-of-power alliance against France led Pufendorf to a conclusion similar to one expounded by Montesquieu in his *Considérations sur les causes de la grandeur des Romains et de leur décadence* (1734), underlining the seemingly inexorable growth of Roman power (Montesquieu 1999). "By extending its Conquests too far," Pufendorf conjectured, France "would be weaken'd within" as Rome had been. This mattered little because, as Pufendorf added in a dejected tone, "In the meantime, those lesser States bordering upon France are in great danger to be devour'd by so flourishing a Kingdom" (Pufendorf 2013: 271).

Understandably, much of the ensuing discussion of the balance of power centered around the question of identifying the right moment to counteract the hegemony seeker. Nowhere was this issue more extensively and heatedly debated than in England (Black 2004, 2011). For, as Pufendorf pointed out, England was uniquely placed geographically to play the role of balancer state. England's ability to play such a role was bolstered by the Revolution of 1688 (Gibbs 1969: 59–79; Thompson 2011: 267–82). Upon taking over the English throne from his Catholic father-in-law James II, the Dutch Stadtholder William III of Orange-Nassau put his new kingdom at the forefront of the anti-Bourbon League of Augsburg, which he himself had created two years before, in 1686, together with Emperor Leopold I. As the renowned Huguenot historian, Rapin de Thoyras, who had accompanied William to Torbay in Devon, related in his multi-volume *History of England* (1724–27), the Glorious Revolution was conceived first and foremost as "the only means to check the overgrown power of France" (Thoyras 1744: 29).

The following Nine Years' War (1688–97) accordingly was justified in the main as a much belated attempt to restore a power equilibrium across Europe. For example, Charles Davenant, a Tory pamphleteer who later became Inspector General of the Imports and Exports and helped the ministry of Robert Harley, Earl of Oxford, in the preparation of the Treaty of Utrecht, opened his widely read commentary on English foreign policy, *Essays upon I. The Ballance of Power. II. The Right of Making War, Peace, and Alliances. III. Universal Monarchy* (1701), by confessing that "For many Years we have pretended to hold the Ballance of Europe, and the Body of the People will neither think it consistent with our Honour nor our Safety to quit that Post" (Davenant 1701: 7). Davenant, too, condemned Charles II's decision to abandon the Triple Alliance, but he went further back and accused Oliver Cromwell of laying "the first Stone of that mighty Building which France has since Erected" (Davenant 1701: 15). By taking over the strategic port of Dunkirk from Spain in 1658, Cromwell, in Davenant's view, had tilted the European balance firmly in favor of France. In other words, Cromwell had missed a perfect opportunity to reduce French power, leaving Charles II and his brother and successor James II with little option but to jump onto Louis XIV's bandwagon. As Davenant put it, this was altogether explicable, because weaker nations were drawn to the powerful, hoping to dominate their own neighbors, and seeking commerce and wealth from the master's table:

> Power is a Plant that from a small Seed, will grow to a Prodigious height, 'twill draw to its own Roots all the Nourishment, and it will so spread itself as to overshadow whatever is round about it; 'tis not difficult to interrupt its beginnings, but when it has attain'd to its full Strength, 'tis hardly to be Shaken; we should contemplate *Primas Dominandi Spes in arduo; ubi sis ingressus adesse Studia et Ministros*. Before a Prince has fully establish'd his ominion [sic] common Interest may unite his Neighbours in a common danger, but if he be suffered to fix himself strongly, Fear, Interest, and Flattery, will intervene. Nations will Crowd in, and beg they may be admitted to receive his Yoke; some will want his Protection, some will request his Aid, in order to oppress others, some States will perhaps submit, as being careless who, has the Dominion so they may have the Trade and Riches.
>
> —Davenant 1701: 284, 289

Half a century of siding with the strongest power had taken an extremely heavy toll on England. To check overgrown French power, England had to fight for nine years, spending unprecedented amounts of public money in the process (Jones 1988). Davenant bemoaned the consequence that in order to rectify previous mistakes in foreign policy, England had to endure a perpetual public debt, high domestic taxes, and a large standing army, each of which endangered the Revolution Settlement (Dickson 1967; Brewer 1989; Schwoerer 1974; Pocock 1975: 423–61).

A similar account to Davenant's was provided by Henry St. John, Viscount Bolingbroke, in his brilliant *Letters on the Study and Use of History* (1752), which was initially composed in about 1735 for the education of Henry Hyde, Viscount Cornbury, the great-grandson of Edward Hyde, 1st Earl of Clarendon. Bolingbroke was a vociferous Tory leader who had served as Secretary of State during the last phase of the War of the Spanish Succession. Like Davenant, Bolingbroke criticized Cromwell for allying with Mazarin's rapidly ascending France. He agreed with Davenant that had it not been for Cromwell's league with France, the Treaty of the Pyrenees of 1659, which served as a stepping stone for France's intrusion into the Spanish Netherlands by arranging marriage between the Dauphin and the Infanta, as well as by securing France's western border, would not have been possible (St. John 1932: 32).

Davenant, writing in the aftermath of the Nine Years' War, put considerable emphasis on taking early preventive action against the rising power of France; Bolingbroke, by contrast, wanted to vindicate his controversial decision to bring to an early end the War of the Spanish Succession that resulted in the Treaty of Utrecht (MacLachlan 1969: 197–215). To put it more simply, it was equally important, if not more important, to know when to break up an anti-hegemonic coalition, especially if, as in post-Westphalian Europe, there were two great powers competing for supremacy, France and the Austrian Empire. In this respect, as Bolingbroke went on to explain, Cromwell's pro-French policy was a serious but commonplace mistake, because of uncertainty about the state of the balance at different times:

> The precise point at which the scales of power turn like that of the solstice in either tropic, is imperceptible to common observation: and, in one case as in the other, some

progress must be made in the new direction, before the change is perceived. They who are in the sinking scale, for in the political balance of power, unlike to all others, the scale that is empty sinks, and that which is full rises; they who are in the sinking scale do not easily come off the habitual prejudices of superior wealth, or power, or skill, or courage, nor from the confidence that these prejudices or courage, nor from the confidence that these prejudices inspire. They who are in the rising scale do not immediately feel their strength, nor assume the confidence in it which successful experience gives them afterwards. They who are the most concerned to watch the variations of this balance, mis-judge often in the same manner, and from the same prejudices.

—St. John 1932: 32–33

As Cromwell had rallied to France's side by overestimating Spanish power, the Whig party, which persisted with the pro-Habsburg policy of "No Peace without Spain," did so, according to Bolingbroke, by overestimating French strength (Hare 1711a, 1711b; Swift 1916). Before the sudden demise of the Holy Roman Emperor Joseph I in April 1711, which made his younger brother and successor Karl VI claimant to the Spanish crown in addition to being Holy Roman Emperor, the Whig party had every reason to exaggerate the French threat (Anon. 1714). To continue to fight, however, to present Emperor Karl VI with the entire Spanish Empire, as Bolingbroke's close associate Jonathan Swift thundered, was "in direct Violation of a fundamental Maxim, the Ballance of Power" (Swift 1712). Swift's literary rival Daniel Defoe shared the view that Britain, after the Union with Scotland in 1707, "now holds the Ballance, and will turn the Scale, and that which Side soever pushes to Extremity, must split upon this Rock, must have the British full in their Way" (Defoe 1712: 817). For Bolingbroke, it was evident that as the balancing state, Britain must concentrate on ensuring that "the deviations be not too great" (St. John 1932: 84). Maintaining the balance required above all the ability to anticipate and to respond swiftly to change, something incompatible with permanent allegiance to any continental power. Bolingbroke summarized the difficulties in operating the balance:

When they are little their increase may be easily prevented by early care and the precautions that good policy suggests. But when they become great for want of this care and these precautions, or by the force of unforeseen events, more vigour is to be exerted, and greater efforts to be made. But even in such cases, much reflection is necessary on all the circumstances that form the conjuncture; lest, by attacking with ill success, the deviation be confirmed, and the power that is deemed already exorbitant become more so; and lest, by attacking with good success, whilst one scale is pillaged, too much weight of power be thrown into the other.

—St. John 1932: 84

While in Britain economic concerns became a key factor in the debate about the European balance, the atmosphere on the other side of the Channel was somewhat different. It was in France that two notable attempts were made to rethink fundamentally the balance of power, one by the Abbé de Saint-Pierre, and the other by François Fénelon, archbishop of Cambrai.

III

The conclusion of the War of the Spanish Succession has been portrayed as a watershed in the evolution of thinking about the balance of power. There were, on the one hand, a few, like the Abbé de Saint-Pierre and the English Quakers William Penn and John Bellers, who, bringing up the inherent instability of the balance of power system, advocated a European league of states (Saint Pierre 1714; Penn 1693; Bellers 1710). The majority, however, were not so radical as to reject the balance of power principle. Quite the opposite, as noted at the start of this chapter. Instead they pondered how to make the hard-won European balance more stable without too much reliance on Britain's balancing acts. Many, especially in France, as the Sun King was entering his dotage, sought solutions in reforming France's absolute monarchy (Rothkrug 1965). Leading the discussion was none other than Fénelon, all the more so because his royal pupil Duc de Bourgogne became Dauphin of France in the same month as the death of the Holy Roman Emperor Joseph I.[5] Fénelon's reputation as arguably the most trenchant critic of Louis XIV began with the publication in 1699 of a Homeric political novel called *Les aventures de Télémaque, fils d'Ulysse* (Schmitt-Maaß, Stockhorst and Ahn 2014). In it, Fénelon laid out his vision of post-Louis XIV France, hoping that the young Duc would not follow in his grandfather's footsteps. At the heart of Fénelon's argument was the belief that tyranny and conquest were two sides of the same coin. "Of what advantage," Fénelon asserted, "is it to any people that their king brings other nations under their yoke, if, at the same time, they themselves are miserable under his reign" (Fénelon 1994: 69). Arguing that "the best bulwarks to a state are justice, moderation, good faith, and the confidence of your neighbours that you are incapable of usurping their territories" (Fénelon 1994: 134), the archbishop outlined the guiding principle of French foreign policy as maintaining peace as follows:

> Happy the king, who loves his people, and is beloved by them; who trusts his neighbours, and is trusted by them; who, far from making war upon them, prevents their going to war with one another, and who makes the happiness his subjects enjoy under his government, to be envied by all other nations.
> —Fénelon 1994: 148

Like Bolingbroke and many others in Britain, Fénelon proclaimed in his above-discussed supplement composed for his royal student that "Humanity ... lays the neighbouring nations under a mutual obligation to defend the common safety against a neighbouring state, which becomes too powerful," but he was not satisfied with the system of checks and balances (Fénelon 1747: 83). Fénelon clearly understood that the balance of power was ultimately inadequate as a solution to the security dilemma (Fénelon 1747: 82–83). Yet, unlike Saint-Pierre, who saw no hope at all in the balance of power, Fénelon was convinced that it was still possible to transform the balance of power into a durable system of peace, if France took the role of something like an "honest broker" (Fénelon 1747: 89–90). "Instead of carrying fire and sword," as had his grandfather, Fénelon instructed the Duc de Bourgogne to "avoid jealousy of your neighbours" at all costs and "assume the glorious character of judges and mediators" (Fénelon 1994: 134, 143). "Thereby," the archbishop explained, "you will acquire a more sure and solid glory than that of conquerors; you will gain the love and esteem of foreigners; they will court your friendship, and you will reign over them in consequence of the respect they have for you" (Fénelon 1994: 197). Central to his peace proposal was the idea that the nature of the balance of power ultimately depended upon the policy pursued by the dominant state (Fénelon 1747: 91).

More significantly, Fénelon argued that the states of Europe, in trying to preserve the balance of power, as well as through economic exchange, had come to constitute "a kind of society and general republick" (Fénelon 1747: 76). "This care to keep up a kind of equality and equilibrium amongst neighbouring nations," he averred, "is that which secures the common repose. In this respect, all the nations that are neighbours to each other, and united by commerce, make up a great body, and a kind of community" (Fénelon 1747: 82). In short, whereas Bolingbroke reflected on the European balance chiefly with the intention of exploiting it to Britain's commercial advantage, Fénelon was much more visionary in that he imagined Europe as a society of states bound by common interests and shared prosperity under the aegis of a reformed France.

The untimely death of the Duc de Bourgogne in early 1712 notwithstanding, Fénelon's solution gained wide currency across Europe. Not only did the Peace of Utrecht, completed by the Treaty of Baden between France and the Holy Roman Empire in September 1714, restore the European equilibrium, but it was effectively defended four years later in 1718 by the Quadruple Alliance between France, Britain, the Dutch Republic, and the Austrian Empire against the newly recalcitrant Spain. This change in mood was eloquently captured by the French diplomat and writer François de Callières in his hugely popular *De la manière de négociér avec les Souverains* (1716), where he emphasized the importance of keeping good faith in diplomacy (Callières 1716).[6] Besides, the regent Philippe II, Duc d'Orléans, who came to power in September 1715, implemented a series of reforms, including the Abbé de Saint-Pierre's polysynody or government by councils, which was also endorsed by Fénelon (Saint-Pierre 1719; Fénelon 1997: 1085–1105).

Perhaps the most enthusiastic portrayal of post-Utrecht Europe as a confederation of sovereign states was the one offered by David Hume in his short essay entitled "Of the Rise and Progress of the Arts and Sciences" (1742). Undeterred by the outbreak of the War of the Austrian Succession (1740–48), which brought an end to more than twenty-five years of peace between Britain and France, Hume proclaimed that "nothing is more favourable to the rise of politeness and learning, than a number of neighbouring and independent states, connected together by commerce and policy" (Hume 1994d: 64). Equally important, he put the French monarchy at the center of the civilizing process, appreciating the changes in domestic and foreign policy brought about by the Regent and then Cardinal André-Hercule de Fleury (Wilson 1936). At long last, as Fénelon had wished, France was transformed into a "civilised monarchy," and thereby the nature of European politics was changing (Hume 1994d: 67–70). Hume was certain that the balance of power had done its work and could be forgotten, being replaced by the spirit of competition and emulation, which had the capacity to propel Europe to world leadership, just as competition and emulation had done in previous centuries to the ancient Greek states:

> If we consider the face of the globe, Europe, of all the four parts of the world, is the most broken by seas, rivers, and mountains; and Greece of all countries of Europe. Hence these regions were naturally divided into several distinct governments. And hence the sciences arose in Greece; and Europe has been hitherto the most constant habitation of them.
>
> —Hume 1994d: 67

In his hugely influential *De l'esprit des lois*, appearing on the eve of the Treaty of Aix-la-Chapelle of 1748, Charles de Montesquieu took a more cautious stance on Europe's future. The Utrecht settlement, which the youthful Hume drew upon for his Greek analogy, was no longer in existence. Montesquieu concurred with Hume that France had become a "moderate monarchy" governed not by the arbitrary whims of rulers but by law, yet he insisted that "the spirit of monarchy is war and expansion" (Montesquieu 1989: 132). Although Montesquieu was no less critical of the Sun King's quest for glory than Fénelon, describing all his wars as invasions in violation of the law of nations, it was his underlying assumption that even a reformed France would remain as a potential threat to European stability (Montesquieu 1989: 136). Small republics, whose governing principle, in his opinion, was "peace and moderation," should, therefore, always be ready to form a defensive alliance and if necessary launch a pre-emptive attack on the great monarchies of France and of the Austrian Empire (Montesquieu 1989: 138–39).

It is true that Montesquieu, like Hume, postulated that "the natural effect of commerce is to lead to peace" (Montesquieu 1989: 338). Commerce, Montesquieu affirmed, had not only made European states dependent upon one another, but also increased mutual understanding and respectful tolerance. Nonetheless, in spite of his seeming advocacy of free trade, Montesquieu was skeptical about commercial sociability. Having witnessed the renewal of Anglo–French enmity, Montesquieu accepted the reality of European power politics, and, more especially, that it inhibited commerce from curing destructive prejudices. Every European state, he observed, had "made commercial interests give way to political interests" (Montesquieu 1989: 343). Britain was no exception. On the contrary, Montesquieu inferred from the Anglo–Spanish War of Jenkins' Ear of 1739 that "the spirit of commerce" was in serious jeopardy (Montesquieu 1989: 346–47).[7]

In fact, by the late 1730s, there was a growing realization in Britain that the Treaty of Utrecht had not provided peace but rather amounted to a temporary armistice. The belief that it provided France with much-needed time to resuscitate her war-stricken economy for another war against Britain was reflected in, and confirmed by, a resurgence of "mercantilist" ideas that equated national wealth with national strength (Wilson 1995: 137–205; Colley 2009: 55–100). In 1729, Joshua Gee, as Hume noted many years later, "struck the nation with an universal panic" with his *Trade and Navigation of Great-Britain considered*, where he demonstrated that the balance of trade had been heavily in France's favor (Gee 1738; Hume 1994c: 137). Nine years later, in 1738, Jean-François Melon's *Essai politique sur le commerce* (1734), which affirmed France's comparative advantage over Britain, was translated into English (Melon 1738). The implication was obvious. The European balance was again threatened by France, and Britain had to act at once before it was too late. In this regard, the War of 1739 was not so much about revenge for British humiliation at the hands of Spanish guarda costas, but rather it was essentially conceived as a pre-emptive war against a Bourbon universal monarchy. Early in the year, George Lyttelton, then secretary to Frederick, Prince of Wales, called for a naval war against Spain. For Lyttelton trade lay behind the balance of power, and maintaining trade beyond Europe was a key means to maintaining peace within Europe: "a due Balance of Trade in the West Indies, as settled by Treaties, has been long looked upon as one of the most effectual Means of preserving that just Circulation of Treasure, that is so necessary to the Preservation of the Balance of Power in Europe" (Lyttelton 1739: 1–2). A year later in 1740, upon hearing the news of the Marquis d'Antin's French squadron heading for the Caribbean Sea, another writer reiterated the point in even stronger terms, arguing that French desire for international trade was a prelude to war in Europe:

> His Most Christian Majesty [Louis XV], I am convinced, seems now to assume a Concern for the Balance of Power in the New World, in order to overturn the Balance of Power in the Old. This Design the French have long had in View, and they now think they have got an Opportunity of making a large Step towards it. In this Design,

they have always been hitherto defeated by the Riches, the Strength, and the Conduct of this Nation; and therefore, if they can by Degrees render us so poor and feeble, as not to be in a Capacity to give any effectual Assistance to our Neighbours upon the Continent, they hope to be at last to effectuate their long-mediated Design.

—Anon. 1740: 18–19

To both Britain and France, the War of the Austrian Succession was, in large part, a continuation of the war over Spanish America, and the War of Jenkins' Ear was fought on the premise that "the Ballance of Power (in the strict Sense of that Phrase) was created by Trade," as John Campbell succinctly put it in his lengthy diagnosis of European politics, *The Present State of Europe*, appeared in 1750 (Campbell 1750: 24). If a balance of trade had to exist in order to sustain the balance of power, because national wealth translated into military victory, it was more difficult than ever to maintain an equilibrium between the many states of Europe. Furthermore, if states were reliant upon commerce to maintain the balance of power, the instability that was inherent in trade had to be reconsidered. Two problems were especially evident to contemporaries. The first was that commerce thrived best where markets were large and increasing, making the lust for new markets a rationale for empire-building. Second, commercial power was perceived by many to be far less stable than political power, because states that were successful could be undermined by those whose labor costs were lower, creating a cycle of fall and rise that Istvan Hont has perceptively termed "the rich country, poor country problem" (Hont 2005b: 267–324; 2007: 222–342). When Fénelon placed agriculture at the center of his economic reform plan submitted to the Duc de Bourgogne, he was clearly anticipating this situation (Cuche 2009: 103–18; Hont 2006: 397–418). Commercialization was incompatible with the operation of any balance, made every form of deterrence unstable, and fostered war (Kapossy, Nakhimovsky and Whatmore 2017).

IV

While Anglo-French commercial and colonial rivalry led the European balance to totter by the end of the 1730s, unresolved dynastic issues added to the instability. The Anglo–French Alliance of 1716–31, upon which the post-Utrecht status quo rested, had been made possible by two concurrent dynastic events, the establishment in 1715 of the French Regency and the Hanoverian Succession in the previous year. Having succeeded Queen Anne during the Great Northern War (1700–21), George I needed French help to protect his German duchy from Sweden, as well as to suppress any foreign-aided revolt in support of the exiled Stuart monarchy. The French Regent, as John Trenchard and Thomas Gordon noted in their celebrated *Cato's Letters* (1724, but published originally in *The London Journal* from 1720 to 1723), referring to the pro-Spanish Cellamare conspiracy of 1718, "can never conspire against us, without conspiring against himself" (Trenchard and Gordon 1995: 619).

In Germany some thirty years later, in October 1740, when Karl VI died without a male heir, things were very different, however. Craftily taking advantage not only of the disorder in Vienna, but also of the revival of Anglo–French animosity, as well as the death of the Empress Anne of Russia in the same month as that of the Holy Roman Emperor, Friedrich II the Great of Prussia invaded Austrian Silesia in December, disrupting the German unity and thereby the entire European order. He reneged on Karl's Pragmatic Sanction of 1713, to which the other European rulers, including his father Friedrich

Wilhelm I, had pledged their support, and audaciously questioned the principle of the indivisibility of the Habsburg hereditary possessions. In his *Histoire de mon temps* (1746), published in the midst of the War of the Austrian Succession, Friedrich justified his opportunistic action as follows.

> But where is the tribunal that can redress a monarch's wrongs, should another monarch forfeit his engagement? The word of an individual can only involve an individual in misfortune, while that of a sovereign may draw down calamities on nations. The question then will be reduced to this, must the people perish or must the prince infringe a treaty?
>
> —Frederick II the Great 1789: xviii–xix

By the time of the outbreak of the Seven Years' War (1757–63), which was officially sparked off again by the Prussian king's stealthy invasion of the Austrian Empire, it was accepted that the balance of power established at Utrecht had collapsed (Nakhimovsky 2017: 44–77). The change of mood was embraced by Jean-Jacques Rousseau who systematically refuted Saint-Pierre's criticism of the balance of power (Rousseau 1991: 53–100). Britain and France were engaged in a war that would either confirm Britain's commercial superiority or restore what the French perceived was a more natural European order, entailing French dominion across mainland Europe, sustained by an agricultural economy and natural resources far greater than any Britain could muster (Baugh 2011). Although Britain prevailed over France, the sense of imminent decline and a renewal of international war grew ever greater (Riley 2014). Hume's loss of optimism was a sure indication of the decline of faith in the balance of power system. In a short essay called "Of the Balance of Power," appearing in 1752, the Scottish political philosopher lamented that "We seem to have been more possessed with the ancient Greek spirit of jealous emulation, than actuated by the prudent views of modern politics" (Hume 1994b: 158). In "Of Public Credit," also published in 1752, four years after the Treaty of Aix-la-Chapelle, Hume confessed "when I see princes and states fighting and quarrelling, amidst their debts, funds, and public mortgages, it always brings to my mind a match of cudgel-playing fought in a China shop" (Hume 1994a: 175). Until his death in 1776, Hume remained convinced that either public credit had to be limited, or it would destroy the nations of Europe. Commentators over the next fifty years worryingly observed that national debts continued to spiral. For one, writing in 1793, the walls of the house of Europe had itself become China, while the cudgel-match continued, the likely result being general bankruptcy and war (Wilson 1793: 30).

In his *Le droit des gens; ou Principes de la loi naturelle* (1758), the great Swiss jurist Emer de Vattel called Europe "a kind of republic" on the grounds that all the states were "linked together by the ties of common interest" and united "for the maintenance of order and liberty" (Vattel 2008: 496). The resulting "famous scheme of the political balance, or the equilibrium of power," by which "no one potentate be able absolutely to predominate, and prescribe laws to the others" was the outcome of this shared interest (Vattel 2008: 496). In the aftermath of the wars of the 1740s, Vattel was sure that uneven economic development, coupled with the overweening power of France, was preventing Britain from playing the role of balancing power, inaugurating a period when war was likely and uncertainty about the future overwhelming (Vattel 2008: 496). Others blamed Britain for upsetting the natural balance of power across Europe. For Laurent Angliviel de La Beaumelle, the contemporary upheaval in international relations he perceived was due to the rise of England. "The last century was the age of France," but, La Beaumelle noted with despair, "the present is the age of England. Louis XIV was arrived at universal monarchy, that is, to such a degree of power as enabled him alone to make head against all. The English will acquire it in their turn" (Beaumelle 1753: 85). In Rousseau's view, the invasion of Europe by genuine tartars was more likely, as commerce destroyed public virtue, and the monarchies of Europe were increasingly divided, weak, and impoverished. In particular, the Genevan political philosopher was deeply concerned about the effects of the intensifying German dualism of Austria and Prussia (Scott 2001). In the second book of his *Du contrat social; ou Principes du droit politique*, published shortly after the signing of the Treaty of Saint Petersburg in May 1762 between Friedrich II and Pyotr III that fortuitously saved Prussia from ruin, Rousseau projected, "The Russian Empire will try to subjugate Europe, and will itself be subjugated. The Tartars, its subjects or neighbours, will become its masters and ours: This revolution seems to me inevitable. All the Kings of Europe are working in concert to hasten it" (Rousseau 1997b: 73).

Literatures of jeremiad and of apocalypse were commonplace between the end of the Seven Years' War and the French Revolution. To many, debt and war on such a scale seemed to be confirming the predictions of Fénelon about the dire consequences of growing commerce. For the poet Oliver Goldsmith, commerce was not only changing contemporary morals, it was leading to population decline, epitomized by the depiction of "The Deserted Village" (1770) (Price 1780: 17–30). Other commentators held that the lust for empire, and especially commercial empire, was leading to a rapid reduction in the numbers of states, especially in Europe. One author predicted that "in less than a century there will not be above seven or eight sovereignties in all Europe where formerly there were above a thousand" (Lloyd 1771: 70–71). The Scottish philosopher Adam Ferguson was equally concerned at the apparent decline of once-powerful states at the end of the Seven Years' War. While small states of every kind were under attack because of "the ruinous progress of empire," whereby "ambitious men, under the enlargement of territory, find a more plentiful harvest of power, and of wealth," it was especially noticeable that the republics of Europe were in a pitiful state (Ferguson 1995: 60–61). Ferguson likened their condition to "shrubs, under the shade of a taller wood, choked by the neighbourhood of more powerful states" (Ferguson 1995: 61–62). Contemporary international relations had altered and were in crisis. Nothing appeared to be able to impede the growth of the great commercial powers and the result was constant war, by economic or by military means, against fellow commercial giants, tearing themselves apart in their lust for land and markets. Security could not be found and the balance of power was altogether history. Traditional strategies of deterrence had failed, and civil and international war was evermore likely.

V

After the Seven Years' War, optimism about any strategy for preventing war was hard to find. The earlier Utrecht belief that the balance of power, once restored, would naturally give rise to a peaceful and prosperous Europe, bound together by commerce and the sense of community, was seriously shattered by "a pathological conjunction between politics and the economy" or, as Hume shrewdly described in one of his 1759 essays, "the jealousy of trade" (Hont 2005a: 1–156; Hume 1994e: 150–53). France and Britain were on a collision course and drawing other powers into the catastrophe. This process would only end when one or the other prevailed, most likely through an invasion that crippled future military capacity, effectively preventing a state from fighting war. Until the French

Revolution it seemed more likely that France would defeat Britain. Ironically, this gave grounds for a short period of optimism, not by the operation of a balance of power, but by a commercial union between the states, as each recognized the futility of war, and the need to dismantle the commercial monopolies that corrupted statesmen and persuaded them into war, as Britain was being defeated by the alliance of its former colonies in North America with France, Spain and the Dutch Republic (The American Revolutionary War of 1775–83). One of the advocates of commercial unions as means to deter war was William Petty, 2nd Earl of Shelburne, who served as First Lord of the Treasury from July 1782 to April 1783 and signed a provisional treaty of peace between Britain and the United States at Paris on 13 November 1782 and preliminary articles with France and with Spain on January 20, 1783. For Shelburne and his friends, the Treaty of Paris, in putting an end to a period of war that had lasted since the 1740s, underlined the negative effects of the lust for empire and the mercantile system of controlled trade (Kippis 1783: 5, 79–81). Shelburne ensured that a timetable for a commercial union between Britain and France was included in the clauses of the Treaty of Paris. Although he soon lost office, Shelburne heralded an "era of Protestantism in trade," when freedom of trade and freedom of religion would challenge monopolies and corruption, ensuring in the process that war became an irrational object of policy and always to be avoided (Shelburne 1783: 4). A treaty of "amity and commerce" was signed between Prussia and North America in 1785, and it was followed by that between Britain and France. William Eden and Gerard de Rayneval, at Paris on September 26, 1786, expressed the intention to "adopt a system of commerce on the basis of reciprocity and mutual convenience, which, by discontinuing the prohibitions and prohibitory duties which have existed for almost a century between the two nations, might procure the most solid advantages, on both sides, to the national productions and industry" (Eden and Rayneval 1786: 3).

Looking back in 1790, Shelburne stated that "the general system of the late peace" had for a time extinguished "all mistaken ideas of rival-ship" (Shelburne 1790: 7). By 1785, however, commerce again seemed to be making war more likely rather than maintaining peace, with the Holy Roman Emperor Joseph II of Austria demanding free passage through the River Scheldt controlled by the Dutch Republic. In September 1787 Prussia invaded Holland in support of the besieged Stadtholder, again threatening European war, and leading William Pitt to begin a process of rearmament in Britain (Rose 1909: 262–83). In the early years of the French Revolution once again there was optimism about the possibility of a general peace on the basis of a commercial union and political alliance between France and Britain. Thomas Paine was consistently of the view that war was a consequence of the need for revenue within monarchical polities, the consequence being that if states became republican they would also become pacific (Paine 1791: 169–70). It is significant that as Paine began to accept that Britain would not become a "sister republic" to North America and revolutionary France by popular rebellion, it was necessary to initiate a war to the death against Britain. Peace could never be concluded with a state whose history was "a perpetual system of war and expense," that "drains the country and defeats the general felicity of which civilization is capable" (Paine 1792: 79-84). Paine's former friend Edmund Burke was equally an advocate of ceaseless war, but against revolutionary France and in order to defend Britain. Burke came out of retirement at the end of his life to counter the possibility of a peace treaty between France and Britain. Burke depicted a French Republic addicted to conquest in the fraudulent name of liberty. Britain's war against France, he cried, was "just, necessary, manly, pious" a war "for all nations" (Burke 1991: 191–97, 238–42, 248–57). Although Burke was not confident that

Britain could defeat revolutionary France, he concluded that war was vital to defeat states like France, which he perceived to be seeking universal dominion, by eating up all of the small states that had hitherto constituted the continent of Europe. Meanwhile, despite Rousseau's erudite effort to prevent it, the moribund Polish–Lithuanian Commonwealth quietly disappeared from the map of Europe, gradually divided and absorbed by the three Eastern powers, Prussia, Austria, and Russia, in the name of peace and stability (1772, 1793, 1795) (Rousseau 1985; Whatmore 2012).

The long eighteenth century, commonly portrayed as the age of Reason, was fraught with war and conflict. Moreover, nearly every war from the Nine Years' War to the wars against Napoleon was considered necessary and even just. What was abhorred and dreaded throughout was not so much war as such, rather the establishment of universal monarchy. Underlying this aversion to the Roman imperial past was the Enlightenment idea that Europe was composed of diverse states with different political cultures and different political needs, and her historical progress, as Edward Gibbon, for one, expounded in his *History of the Rise and Fall of the Roman Empire* (1776), making a detailed analogy with the classical Greek world of city states, was fundamentally dependent on protecting it (Gibbon 1994: 287–97). The balance of power was conceived as the surest means to guarantee the "Liberties of Europe," as contemporaries used to call it. The problem was that any durable peace or stability based on the balance of power required, first and foremost, an unyielding commitment to it by every major actor. As one British MP put it in the middle of the century, "We are never to suppose that any Prince of Europe will engage against the Liberties of Europe," "unless he be very much blinded by some particular Interest of his own" (Parliamentary Debates 1742: 92). Many believed and hoped that commerce would inculcate European rulers with a sense of their shared interest and destiny, functioning as a powerful deterrent to any violent deviation from the balance of power. But, as Fénelon foresaw, it was repeatedly proven otherwise. As the century drew to a close, with yet another impending catastrophe, Kant arrived at a radically different solution with his gloomy concept of "unsocial sociability" (*ungesellige Geselligkeit*) (Kant 1991a: 41–53). It soon became woefully clear that Enlightenment Europe learned very little from the wars she had fought for the sake of the balance of power.

ACKNOWLEDGMENTS

For Doohwan Ahn: This work was supported by the Ministry of Education of the Republic of Korea and the National Research Foundation of Korea (NRF-2016S1A3A2924409).

CHAPTER EIGHT

Peace as Integration

MARTTI KOSKENNIEMI

A WORLD OF STATES

"Peace is not only the absence of war." This familiar cliché points to a wide, "sociological" understanding of conflict-avoidance. It also raises the question of what might be the conditions for peacefulness? Is democracy a recipe for peace or conflict? What about the role of international commerce—"*doux commerce*" or "jealousy of trade"? A densely integrated community may indeed be a peaceful community. But "dense integration" may also signify imperial control and the suppression of difference. Disagreement over the kind of community—integration—that best enhances peace has always provided fertile ground for political struggle at home and abroad.[1] It is easy to agree that a lasting peace can be attained only once humanity is united. But united under what conditions?

The period 1648–1815 was one of almost incessant conflict in Europe. Religious wars had torn the political order to pieces. The Peace of Westphalia (1648) provided temporary relief but strategy and geopolitics continued to throw the great powers against each other. The Ottoman Empire was knocking at the gates of Vienna and expansion in the colonies continued violently even at times of relative European peace. During the years usually addressed as the European "Enlightenment" political thinkers, lawyers and philosophers focused intensely on conditions under which societies would live in peace. Old authorities were no longer trustworthy; neither the Church nor the Holy Roman Empire functioned as credible peacemakers or ideological centers around which the rest of Europe could unite. Many believed that the government of Europe had to be founded on new ideas—especially those of science and law. Might the advances of natural science be enlisted for this purpose? One of the thinkers who thought so was the Dutchman Hugo Grotius (1583–1645) who suggested that it was possible to extract a quality in human nature that he called "sociability" (*appetitus societatis*) that would accord with "reason" and produce principles that would allow the peaceful internal and external government of societies. The truths offered by nature would be compelling because they were "manifest and self-evident, almost after the same Manner as those Things are that we perceive with our outward Senses" (Grotius [1625] 2005: 111).

Grotius' principal work, *De iure belli ac pacis* (1625/1632) sought peace through the discovery of true principles of human government, articulated as the law of nature and of nations. At the heart of this law lay the concept of the monarchic state.[2] Unlike the communist utopias by Thomas More or Tommaso Campanella, early modern natural lawyers took for granted the beneficial character of the early modern state with a strong sovereign at its head. By the mid-seventeenth century, European monarchs were understood as rulers of states, and natural law competed with different variants of

"Machiavellianism" in putting forward proposals about just how they should go about the business of ruling their states to attain the peace and, if possible, happiness of their subjects. Not all sovereigns were trustworthy in this respect, and ambitious monarchs—especially the French king—were often accused of harboring a desire for "universal monarchy" (Leibniz, 1988: 119–45). But natural lawyers agreed that a credible internal and external peace could only be realized within the frame of territorially confined statehood. Nor was this mere theory. The diplomats and politicians present at Utrecht (1713) and Vienna (1815) believed firmly that the great task of European politics henceforth would be to square the circle of protecting sovereign statehood while simultaneously integrating states in some "supra-national" system (typically the balance of power) that would eliminate the temptation of war.

The state was a historical and sociological datum and a political construct. But it was also a *legal* notion. The very concept of "sovereignty" that was supposed to characterize European statehood (as well as the power of the king) in the aftermath of 1648 emerged from a combination of Roman law and Aristotelian thinking about the independent *civitas*. Its scope and content had been the subject of intense debate since the early twelfth century and natural lawyers used that heritage to offer the principal alternative to purportedly immutable principles of *ragion di stato* as the frame within which external relations could be debated. Not everyone believed in natural "sociability", however. Political thinkers such as the Englishman Thomas Hobbes (1588–1679) had a much more skeptical view. But even he thought that peace ought to be looked for by the application of scientific methods, by observation and reasoning from true facts of human nature. Integration was necessary, he argued, but it would not arise naturally. It could only be attained if everyone gave up their dangerous liberty to the sovereign. Such contrasting views were reflected in different opinions about the possibility of international peace as well. Would Europeans be able to integrate by the force of their very sociability as Grotius had suggested? Or were "sovereign" monarchs and their states unavoidably "in continual jealousies, and [thus] in the state and posture of gladiators; having their weapons pointing and their eyes fixed on one another" (Hobbes [1651] 1996: 85). There was broad agreement among writers that even as Europe was divided into states with different histories and "jealousies," it was also united by a shared legal-political vocabulary through which European monarchs could address their differing ambitions. For centuries, this vocabulary had extended to rules on treaty-making, trade, war and formal diplomatic relations. As the high envoy of Louis IX, François de Callières (1645–1717) remarked in his much read analysis of diplomatic negotiations soon after the Utrecht peace, links had been formed between the states of Europe that entitled considering them "like members of one and the same republic" so that it was difficult to consider any major change in any of them without this troubling the peace of all (de Callières [1716] 2006, 17). He was groping towards a notion of a "system" of inter-state relations, at least in Europe, to be grounded in the interdependence of European states and their dynasties whose peaceful management would be the principal task of foreign policy. Many thought that finding and following the rules of operation of this system was an absolute political, economic (and perhaps moral) necessity.

This chapter will examine the use of law—legal rules and institutions—in the period 1648–1815 to give reality to the intuitive sense among the contemporaries that European states were integrated historically, culturally and politically in a community (often referred to as "Christendom") where conflicts were amenable to peaceful resolution through the values and techniques enshrined in law. Because political and legal thinkers drew their experience from what they had learned at home, their plans of "integration" often differed greatly. For example, they had learned to deal with religious strife sometimes by enforcing a strict religious uniformity, sometimes by providing for more or less regulated "tolerance." The exercise of public power had been organized in alternatively "conservative" and "liberal" ways, with more or less openness to commercial relations with the outside world. The struggle over extra-European resources made thinking about peace in simply European terms impossible and the gap between domestic absolutism and the rise of bourgeois civil society fomented revolutions that provided an alternative view on what "unity" and "peace" might mean in both domestic and international terms.

In the first three sections below I will examine how the legal cultures of Germany, France, and Britain developed different ways of understanding how the states of Europe could be seen as both "sovereign" and integrated within some peaceful system under law. A final section examines attitudes to peace outside Europe. Under what conditions might non-European territories be integrated in the world as Europeans imagined it? Unavoidably, European thinking would remain parochial if not solipsistic: debate on the "social" conditions for peace remained centered on how European states and their dynasties could perpetuate themselves.

PEACE UNDER THE LAW OF NATURE AND OF NATIONS: GERMANY 1648–1815

The territory of the Holy Roman Empire of the German Nation had been devastated in the Thirty Years' War. The Peace of Münster and Osnabrück (Westphalia) was designated to provide a constitution for the empire to guarantee the peace of Protestant and Catholic estates and balance of power among external actors. The war had undermined the debate among German jurists on the constitutional character of the empire. As the Saxon Samuel Pufendorf (1632–1694) showed, the old Aristotelian categories ("monarchy," "aristocracy," "polity") had proved themselves too abstract to fit a complex reality (Pufendorf [1667] 2007). A new start was sought from what came to be called the "law of nature and of nations" (*ius naturae et gentium*), a heavily academic and authoritarian approach to questions of order and justice in Europe. Having occupied the first chair in the new discipline at Heidelberg in 1661, Pufendorf constructed it on what he called a "geometric" method that embodied a view of human nature situated midway between the "sociability" of Hugo Grotius and the anthropological pessimism of Hobbes. Avoiding the extremes of innate sociability and innate enmity, and denying that the treaties between states were really binding, Pufendorf set up a powerful calculus to explain how Europeans were united by their shared need of self-protection. Humans were selfish but weak. Because, unlike other animals, they were also rational, they would understand that only by joining together they could protect themselves and work towards wealth and happiness (Pufendorf [1674] 1994: 148–57). *Reason* told humans to form states and elect powerful leaders to maintain peace and order. These rational rulers would then understand that peace and cooperation among nations were ultimately beneficial for themselves as well.

This view suited well the German princes hoping to consolidate their power over their small principalities. Natural law teaching soon encompassed most German Protestant and some Catholic universities. But it did not have that much to say about international progress. It supported comparative and historical studies as bases of finding "universal" norms but its practice was used to support enlightened absolutism. Only five chapters at the end of Pufendorf's main work dealt with such international matters as war and peace, leagues and treaties—and these mostly in the idiom of the *raison d'état*, a field to which also his later historical works were devoted. Because there was no sovereign above states, he assumed that states existed in a state of nature. The only laws between them were those that "reason" could derive from their situation so as to promote their search for security and happiness. But natural law had little to say about such derivations. It was soon replaced by such technical disciplines as policy-science and "*Staatskunst*," systems of expertise about how to run what popular metaphor increasingly often addressed as the "state-machine" (Stollberg-Rilinger 1986).

During the eighteenth century natural lawyers reflected on the conditions of peace from empirical and rationalist directions. Empirical thinkers such as Hieronymus Gundling (1671–1729) from Halle regarded "utility" as the foundation of a peaceful international order (Gundling 1734). But although it would be useful for states to engage in commerce and cooperation, in practice their leaders followed their short-term interests. They could not be trusted to keep their agreements, and so the only foundation for peace was the balance of power—including the right to strike first against potential aggressors (Gundling 1757: 4–6,19). By contrast, rationalists such as Christian Wolff (1679–1754) argued that the need of every state to perfect itself allowed the rational derivation of policies. Because all states shared this need, and as it could only be realized by cooperation, they were already joined in a world-wide "supreme state" (*Civitas maxima*) that enjoyed "a kind of sovereignty" over individual states (Wolff [1749] 1934: 13–17). Wolff encountered Gundling's pessimism with almost unbounded optimism: the only relevant questions about security and happiness were scientific and technological ones. Using some of Wolff's language, Emer de Vattel (1714–1767) from Neuchatel produced a widely translated textbook *Droit des Gens* (1758) that put in a condensed form the state-centered theories of the Germans and accepted that, out of their regard for their enlightened self-interest, a peaceful international order would emerge among states. As a man of the Enlightenment Vattel would write confidently of a single "society of the human race" (de Vattel [1758]: 72). But this society had no formal expression. By contrast, what did exist was a historically based community of diplomats and politicians, advisors and sovereigns, all parts of a "system of states" that overlay humankind's natural moral unity. States may not have joined in a republic amongst themselves but they did, as a matter of history and social relationships, form a "political system, an integral body closely connected by the relations and different interests of the nations inhabiting this part of the world" (de Vattel [1758]: 496). This "political system" was maintained above all by the balance of power—an eighteenth-century obsession and a metaphor that irresistibly invoked the Newtonian ambitions of men thinking of states as "machines" and government as "science."

Vattel was one of those whom Immanuel Kant (1724–1804) indicted as "sorry comforters"—men whose proposals for peace "cannot have the slightest legal force" (Kant [1795] 1991: 103). In the *Critique of Pure Reason* (1788) Kant had demonstrated that natural law both in its empirical and rationalist versions had failed. Empirical generalizations such as those made by Gundling and his associates could not grasp the categories through which the facts of the world formed meaningful wholes so as to inform human action. Rationalists such as Wolff built their abstractions on nothing more than further abstractions, failing to see to their moral grounding in history and politics. In *Perpetual Peace* (1795) Kant attacked wholesale the warlike diplomacy of the eighteenth century. Lasting peace could only be based on binding law to which reason committed all statesmen (or at least those Kant called "moral politicians"). First, he proposed that the constitution of every State should become "republican." Free citizens would never endorse war against each other. Second, there should be a "federation of free states" where the danger of an oppressive "world state" would be avoided and national communities would rule themselves freely under a jointly agreed federal constitution. And finally, there was to be "cosmopolitan law" that would entitle individuals to move about freely in the world under conditions of universal "hospitality" (Kant [1795] 1991). The proposal was drafted in a gradualist fashion and was accompanied by a series of preliminary actions that were to be carried out as preconditions for the realization of the rest. It also included proposals about the relations of politics and morality and on the role of philosophers in government. Finally, Kant assumed (optimistically), that history itself and the way humans learned from their mistakes would guarantee the realization of perpetual peace.

Although Kant's proposals were read with interest in Germany and France, the conditions of the revolutionary wars prevented them from being taken seriously. After Napoleon had wrought destruction on German soil, only revolutionaries were left speaking the language of natural law or natural rights. The most significant carrier of the German debates into the nineteenth century was Georg Friedrich von Martens from Göttingen whose *Précis du droit des gens moderne de l'Europe fondé sur les traités et l'usage* (1795, 1798, 1801, 1821) avoided all speculations about universal norms and took for granted the existence of a European diplomatic tradition that it proposed to read as a kind of legal system in operation.³ Napoleon's troops had twice occupied Göttingen and Martens himself had been compelled to quarter French troops in his home. As a representative of Hannover at Vienna in 1814–1815 he shared the conference's conservative spirit. In his published reaction to the revolutionary proposal of a *Declaration of the rights of nations*, drafted by the Abbé Grégoire in the French national assembly in 1795, he admitted that it might be desirable if European powers were to set up a detailed code of international law. But the proposal was devoid of any realism. It was just like proposals for eternal peace that must, as long as men remain men, holding their fate in their own hands, remain a pure chimera. To declare principles of morality was pointless: they can be realized only under conditions which, if they were present, would make their declaration unnecessary (von Martens 1796: viii–ix).

FROM "UNIVERSAL MONARCHY" TO A EUROPE OF NATIONS: FRANCE 1648–1815

Although the vocabulary of the law of nature and nations had become familiar in France, too, it never developed into a university discipline and even less a predominant political idiom.⁴ This may have been in part because of its association with Protestantism and Huguenot policy, in part owing to what the society of the salon viewed as its pedantic scholasticism. The image of natural law in France was that of a reactionary set of abstractions and part of the justifying rhetoric of the old regime.⁵ Nevertheless, literary invocations of a golden age were often expressed in the languages of "humanity," "reason" and "nature" to attack the ills of the old regime. Diderot, Montesquieu, and Rousseau all had a complex debt to the natural law tradition.

Nor was the most well-known of the early eighteenth-century European peace planners, Charles Irenée Castel, Abbé de Saint-Pierre (1658–1743), any friend of abstract natural law. He had devoted his early years to science, had become close to the court and was appointed to the *Académie française* from which, however, he was later expelled. An effectual policy of peace was to be based on "evidence" and *"esprit de raisonnement."* In the context of the negotiations to the Treaty of Utrecht, Saint-Pierre produced his famous

Mémoire pour rendre la paix perpetuelle en Europe followed up by successive editions of the much larger *Projet pour rendre la paix perpetuelle en Europe* (Saint-Pierre [1712] 1717) As a literary achievement, the *Projet* was unimpressive, consisting of three volumes of poorly organized, repetitive arguments in defense of a permanent organization to guarantee peace and security among European sovereigns. Perhaps for this reason, he produced an *Abregé* in 1729 that became a much-used focus for debates on the possibility of European peace throughout the eighteenth century (Saint-Pierre [1729]).

Saint-Pierre did not believe in universal integration. In due course he removed Turkey from his proposed peace union and even came to advocate war against it. Adopting the plan, Saint-Pierre wrote, Europe's monarchies could guarantee their safety from external and internal dangers; in fact, the plan was more concerned with domestic rebellion than inter-state war. Europe's ruling houses themselves would benefit from channeling their passion for glory to peaceful pursuits, especially the growth of trade and industry (Saint-Pierre [1712] 1717: 153). But this would require a fundamental overhaul of the present system. Mutual promises among sovereigns, truces, treaties, guarantees, and alliances were too easily overridden. They, like the balance of power, were dependent on the whims of princes and changes of national fortune (Saint-Pierre [1712] 1717: 73). The Abbé tried to tie his proposals, as Pufendorf had done, to a conception of "reason" under which self-loving actors would learn to move from the search for immediate gratification to the pursuit of long-terms goals that would ultimately be of much greater benefit for them. Accordingly, he proposed the establishment of a permanent institution, a *Union européenne* with 18 or 24 sovereign members (the number varied in different parts of the plan) all of which would be Christian, European States.[6] The plan contained five principal elements (Saint-Pierre [1712] 1717: 271–366).First, members would agree to preserve the European territorial and dynastic status quo. The Union was not to intervene in the affairs of its members for any other reason than for implementing the guarantees, including suppression of domestic dissent. Peaceful territorial changes were allowed, and disputes were to be resolved through arbitration. Second, a permanent institution of the "European Union" was to be set up in which the sovereigns would be represented in a Senate, each of them having one vote. Third, the Senate was to organize European commerce on the basis of a general most-favored nation treatment. It would set up a Chamber of Commerce in each major town that would have alternate jurisdiction to adjudicate trade disputes and members would see to the enforcement of judgments. Fourth, the Senate would also arbitrate between sovereigns. A member taking arms or refusing to execute a judgment would be declared the enemy of all. Fifth, there would be a joint military force to protect the Union from external dangers—particularly against the Turks—as well as rebellion and civil war. Costs of operations would be shared in accordance with members' relative wealth.

The *Projet* was widely circulated among French elites who tended to regard it as hopelessly contradictory. Voltaire thought it as likely that peace could be maintained among European sovereigns "as the peace between elephants and rhinoceros, wolves and dogs. Carnivorous animals will tear each other apart at the first occasion" (Bois 1999: 211). The most famous critiques were those by Jean-Jacques Rousseau (1712–1778), written respectively as *Extract of the Plan for Perpetual Peace* in 1756 and the *Judgment on Perpetual Peace*, from 1782. Rousseau agreed that in principle the proposal contained a rational response to Europe's problems. But it was undermined by its underlying analysis. The monarchs were not the kind of rational interest-maximizers the proposal assumed. They would never sign into a federation that would go beyond their momentary interests, however irrational or arbitrary (Rousseau 2008a: 112–13). The very logic of statehood—the constant jealousy and fear among nations, their limitless search for conquest and subduing each other—accounted for the plan's unreality. It was futile to refer to common goals—being "common" they had no reality to anybody (Rousseau 2008b: 120).

Rousseau reversed the traditional presumption about the state system as a peacemaking device: "one does not become a soldier until after one has become a citizen" (Rousseau 2008c: 74). All states constantly compared themselves jealously to each other, fearing their neighbors unless they could feel capable of overpowering them (Rousseau 2008c: 76–77). This was the fateful, warlike logic of statehood: the "general will" that founded the state saw no limit to its power.

> What, then, is it to make war against a sovereign? It is to attack the public convention and everything that results from it; for the state does not consist of more than this. If the social contract could be destroyed by one single blow there would be no more war; and with that blow it would be killed, without the death of one single human being.
> —Rousseau 2008c: 81

Saint-Pierre's proposals did not confront the political heart of the problem of war, according to Rousseau. As long as there were entities resembling contemporary states, peace could be no more than a temporary truce, creating a breathing space to allow the states to collect their forces to strike anew. Though the proposals constituted an advance, they did not abolish the political "state of war" that always existed between states. The conflict between the powers of a Union and the sovereignty of its members remained (Rousseau 2008a: 98–113).

If republican freedom did not bring about peace, perhaps other aspects in global modernity might help? Rousseau was a sharp critic of economic expansion and trade in "luxury" (Rousseau [1762] 1958: 112). Not everyone agreed. The most famous person representing the contrary view—the view that the commercial spirit, including "commerce of luxury," was a pacifying force, sharply opposed to the spirit of conquest—was the Baron de la Brède, Charles de Secondat de Montesquieu (1689–1755) whose main work, *L'Esprit des lois* (1748) offered a totalizing image of the political, cultural, and economic conditions of modern government. Montesquieu accepted that Europe was a "single nation composed of many." A ubiquitous commercial spirit had arisen with modernity that contrasted sharply with the ancients' desire for glory and conquest. As Montesquieu famously summarized it, "peace is the natural effect of trade"(Montesquieu [1748] 1949: 316 [XX.2]). Commerce created a dependency among nations that was inimical to war. It also cultivated "agreeable manners" that were incompatible with ideas of military conquest. Especially important was "economical commerce" in which a large bourgeoisie engages in exchanges on domestic and global markets (Montesquieu [1748] 1949: 316–19 [XX.1–5]). Overall, many virtues accompanied the commercial spirit—"frugality, economy, moderation, labor, prudence, tranquillity, order and rule" (Montesquieu [1748] 1949: 46 [V, 6]).[7]

The Physiocratic movement took over many of these ideas. Their economic naturalism developed increasingly technical propositions about how society ought to be organized so that the productive cycle would create optimal wealth. Free trade was an essential aspect of this. Once domestic self-sufficiency in "necessities" had been guaranteed, free trade in "luxuries" and the surplus agricultural product would unite nations in a world of intensifying commercial exchanges. This view was radicalized by early revolutionaries such as Paul-Henri d'Holbach (1723–1789) for whom only scientific and technical questions remained about how to reach peace and happiness, interpreted as always also compatible with enlightened state interests (D'Holbach 1822: 310–11). Sovereigns did not exist in a state of war; all humans were joined in a moral community. War was an expression of the vain search for glory, the avarice of tyrants. But history showed that conquests were rarely useful, that large military forces were economically destructive and wars always ended in injustice (D'Holbach 1820: II 2–21).[8]

In the revolutionary assembly in Paris, deputies on the "left" condemned the public law of Europe as part of the old regime. It was to be replaced by, in the words of the Deputy Constantin Volney, "une politique vraie et généreuse, fondée sur les intérêts des nations" (Belissa 1998: 170).[9] The early debates peaked in the famous decree of May 22, 1790 where the assembly renounced all wars of conquest (Godechot 1983: 65–67).[10] But a revolution, if such it was, could not remain a simply French affair. To make the Declaration of War of April 20, 1792 on the Habsburg monarchy seem compatible with the decree of 1790, the "enthusiasts" argued that a war to bring liberty to peoples oppressed by tyrants was defensive and not at all a war for conquest. It was waged against princes, on behalf of their peoples.[11] And in no time at all, the revolutionaries had set up sister republics and annexed Belgium. With the Thermidorean turn, such actions (and words) were replaced by the more traditional effort to establish natural boundaries up to (and sometimes beyond) the Rhine (Godechot 1983: 71–74, 79–87).

In a more or less desperate effort to salvage revolutionary pacifism, in April 1795 the Abbé Grégoire (1750–1831), the initiator of the abolition of slavery in the French colonies, submitted to the French *National Convention* a proposal for a *Déclaration du droit des gens*. In 21 Articles, the declaration sought to do to the world what the *déclaration des droits de l'homme et du citoyen* had done to the old regime at home. The basis of the new order would be the right of "independence and sovereignty" of every European nation (Article 2). Every nation was to treat every other nation as it would wish itself to be treated (Article 3). It would have an obligation to peace, and if at war, it was to harm its adversary as little as possible (Article 4). There would be no distinction between representatives of nations, and ambassadors would enjoy immunity only inasmuch as that would be necessary for the accomplishment of their mission (Articles 19 and 20).[12] The Convention never adopted the draft declaration. It was this proposal that gave reason for Martens to reproduce the conservative critique of the ideas underlying it. National self-determination could not be a workable basis of peace and order in Europe. The ruling states would always want to maintain their freedom of maneuver. They would neither bind their hands in a *"Union européenne"* nor by declaring principles of national self-determination and peace.

COMMERCE AND INTEGRATION: ENGLAND

The one principle left alive from the French debates was that of *"doux commerce"*—the view of trade as an instrument of integrating the otherwise "jealous" nations into a system of peace. The period 1648–1815 can also be seen as the rise of England into a world power and that rise, more than any philosophical arguments, seemed to speak in favor of Montesquieu's thesis. From the English side, this thesis was always connected with a *raison d'état* view about the country's relative position with respect to its European rivals. The writings of the early political economists, Gerard Malynes, Edward Misselden, and Thomas Mun were committed to demonstrating that the power of the English state was inextricable from the prosperity of Englishmen so that "of the six members of all the governments of monarchies and common-weales, [the merchants] are the principal instruments to increase or decrease the wealth thereof" (Malynes [1629]: 62).

In the period between the mid seventeenth and the late eighteenth century, British jurists and political thinkers rarely used the idiom of natural law and the law of nations to address the question of international peace. The views of Thomas Hobbes were unavailable for any such speculation and even if John Locke's (1632–1704) work did apply to international relations—especially as a justification of colonization—his brief discussion of international affairs took the perspective of British constitution ("federative power") (Locke [1690] 1984: 191). The idiom of natural law played a very limited role in the writings of the common lawyers for obvious reasons. The reach of the common law was limited to the territory of England. In the late sixteenth and early seventeenth centuries, however, civil lawyers dominated law teaching at the universities and ruled institutions operating under the royal prerogative; their jurisdiction extended into England's commercial and other relations with the external world. Civil lawyers were known for their cosmopolitan orientations and had no qualms about applying the law of nature and nations to England's external relations. But perhaps it was their intense professional rivalry with the common lawyers that made them refrain from abstract speculations about international peace and order. Even Charles Molloy's (1646–1690) *De jure maritimo et navali* (first edition 1676), the first full-scale English treatment of its subject-matter since Selden's (very different) response to Grotius refrained from deducing the laws of commerce from natural law and instead invoked "the Law of Will, or Common Consent [that] yet appears every where observed [and thus part of] that which is called the *Law of Nations*" (Molloy [1676] 1722: xv). Molloy singled out Holland, Venice, Genoa and Lübeck as worthy of emulation and celebrated English explorations around the world, observing that "among all nations, there [was] a Common Law which govern the mighty Thing of Navigation and Commerce" (Molloy [1676] 1722: xii). His view of international cooperation was strictly tied to domestic concerns, growth and the protection of property:

> It is Foreign Trade that renders us rich, honourable and great, that gives us a name and Esteem of the World and makes us masters of the treasures of other Nations and Countries and begets and maintains our Ships and Seamen, the Walls and Bulwarks of our Country.
> —Molloy [1676] 1722: 456–57

But even as Molloy stressed that foreign trade made England great, he also understood it as a useful instrument for the pacification of the international world. Perhaps his admiration of Grotius led Molloy to adopt a providential view where the intensification of trade would ultimately be to everyone's benefit. Considerations of balance of power did not enter his legal world.

No doubt it was John Locke's deliberations about property and labor that constituted the most significant thinking about the conditions of peace in Britain at the turn of the eighteenth century. Natural law for Locke was universal, providing for the right of property—for which Locke understood both "life, liberty and estate" and the more narrow category of "lands and goods," the topic of the famous Chapter 5 of the *Second Treatise of Government* (1689/90).[13] Under Locke's universal natural law, all men would agree, for example, on "the free passage of envoys, free trade, and other things of that kind." They would also fix boundaries and organize diplomacy and international trade.

But there was nothing natural about these arrangements, based as they were on "common expediency" and not necessarily applicable "by other peoples of Asia and America" (Locke [1664] 1997: 108). In this, they contrasted with the natural *right* of property that *was* applicable everywhere, including the colonies, and under which even the Indians rightfully possess what they had occupied (though of course their labor only entitled them to a fraction of the lands they claimed) (Locke [1690] 1984: 129).

In Locke's famous view, "the great and chief end . . . of men uniting into commonwealths, and putting themselves under government is the preservation of their property" (Locke [1690] 1984: 108). This reduced statehood to an instrument of the civil society that continued to be ruled by a system of (pre-political) right to property that also provided the standard to assess political government. Unlike Hobbes, Locke did not think that the state of nature was a state of perpetual fear; it was possible for the individuals to enjoy rights, to labor, and contract even without a state. Locke even assumed that the turn to a monetary economy—an extremely important moment—took place before the establishment of the commonwealth (Locke [1690] 1984: 139–40).[14] A state was needed only to get rid of the "inconveniences" that property-holders otherwise experienced.[15] But it did not *create* their rights. This reconstructed the *international* realm in two superimposed levels. On the one hand, there was natural law that joined all property-holders of the world in a "great and natural community" (Locke [1690] 1984: 181). On the other hand, there was the law of nations, the positive laws of treaty and custom upheld and regulated by professional diplomacy and statecraft that in Britain were administered under the "federative power" of the royal prerogative (Locke [1690] 1984: 191).

Eighteenth-century English jurists faced the formidable task of integrating the British legal system to the conditions of global trade that formed the foundation of their empire. Little in this literature dealt with the conditions of general peace. The connection that Montesquieu and others had made between commerce and peacefulness was undermined by English victory in the Seven Years' War (1756–63) that resulted, it was agreed, from its astonishing ability to wage war while intensifying its commercial dealings across the oceans. As the former governor of Massachusetts, one of the most influential commentators of Britain's' policy, Thomas Pownall (1722–1805) wrote in 1766, speculating on the character of the period that was beginning:

> . . . the spirit of *commerce* will become that predominant power, which will form the general policy, and rule the powers of Europe; and hence a grand commercial interest, the basis of a great commercial dominion, under the present scite and circumstances of the world, will be formed and arise.
> —Pownall 1774: I, 5 [original italics]

British commentators were astonishingly deaf to the concerns of others about the growing British commercial power.[16] Even such an astute observer as the philosopher and historian David Hume (1711–1776) argued that if everybody only traded openly with their neighbors, there was no reason to fear that the richer countries would be gradually overtaken by poorer ones—the great fear in British public debates at the time. The diversification of the economy of the rich countries would allow them to move to more profitable production while the poor countries would benefit from their goods penetrating into the rich country's market. Instead of being a zero-sum game, free trading actually benefited everyone (Hume [1752] 1994: 150). The same view was of course held by Hume's friend, Adam Smith (1723–1790), who believed that because the economic realm could always be expressed in terms of calculable interests, it would gradually come to offer a general algorithm that would turn government away from irrational short-term objectives. The natural law of economics would become a universal standard of state policy.[17] When Smith's four-stage theory peaked in commercial society—the one attained in late eighteenth century Britain—it was *highest* because passions there had been translated into economic interests whose free operation was guaranteed by law. This pacifying logic, he assumed, was fully applicable in the relations between nations as well (Smith [1776] 1999: 67).

A couple of lesser known British students of natural law contemplated the conditions of international peace at the end of the eighteenth century in a way that reflected the country's imperial ambitions. In his lectures at Lincoln's Inn in 1796 the Whig jurist and politician Sir James Mackintosh (1765–1832) suggested that humankind was united by two types of natural law, one covering the relations of individuals across the world and another organizing the intercourse of Christian nations (Mackintosh 1828: 9–11). This view was shared by Robert Plumer Ward (1765–1846), the author of the first English-language history of the law of nations (1795) (Armitage 2013: 184). Ward opened his massive work with a touching admission that once he had collected all the treaties, cases and other historical materials, he was at a loss about how to answer the question about their binding force (Ward 1795). Although he could see how the practices of Christian nations might become binding to Christians, he found no basis to regard them as binding everywhere. Because "natural law" meant different things to different people, it was futile and misleading to treat it as universal law. Only religion could provide certainty; where religions differed, unity was impossible. Accordingly, there must be "a different law of nations for different parts of the globe" (Ward 1795: xiv, xii–xv).

At the turn of the nineteenth century, the law of nations in Britain equaled laws of neutrality and maritime capture—technical questions important for the ruler of the seas but empty as reflections on the larger questions of international peace. The Scottish lawyer James Reddie (1773–1852) was not wrong when he noted that to write a treatise on the matter in Britain, one could not do better than avail oneself of the German sources—"the great and parental cultivatrix of the science of international law" (Reddie 1851: II, 88).The space for engaging with the conditions of peace in Europe and the world was largely occupied by the prolific writings of Jeremy Bentham (1748–1832), whose utilitarianism knew no jurisdictional boundaries. All human beings not only look for happiness but have an equal desire and capacity for it. Even as his views vacillated in reaction to the French revolution, he came in 1809 to set himself firmly in favor of democratic reform.[18] Nations did not enjoy any special historical legitimacy. Nor was their claim to political obedience based on any past contract. States were nothing but facts of habitual obedience that a group of people paid to a government (Bentham [1776] 1998: 40–41). Why and to what extent they should obey was a fact about the expectations they had about the government's ability to realize their happiness. Obedience as well as eventual rebellion were governed by the principle of utility (Bentham [1776] 1998: 56, 99, 105). The search for happiness was not limited within the boundaries of one's nation. As Bentham wrote in the essay on "A Plan for an Universal and Perpetual Peace" (1789):

> . . . there is no nation that has any points to gain to the prejudice of any other. Between the interests of nations, there is nowhere any real conflict: if they appear repugnant anywhere, it is only in proportion as they are misunderstood.
> —Bentham 1843c: 559

Bentham believed that the principles informing this critique could be applied everywhere. In a late work on a "complete code of laws" he came to conclude that any project for international legislation with binding tribunals was unrealistic (Bentham 1843a: 200). But he continued to advocate an international "code" as well as the establishment of an international tribunal. His many essays on peace and war, colonialism, and trade likewise supported treaty-based legal cooperation even in the absence of genuine enforcement. "If a citizen of the world had to prepare an international code," he once wrote, "what would he propose as his object? It would be the common and equal utility of all nations" (Bentham 1843b: 537). An international code would thus be no different from any other code of law. It would call upon the government to legislate for the "happiness of the individuals, of whom a community is composed" (Bentham [1781/89] 1988: 24).

THE NON-EUROPEAN WORLD: THE GREAT ABSENCE

Perhaps the most striking fact about the way European jurists and philosophers imagined the conditions of peace in 1648–1815 lies in the almost complete absence of serious deliberation on the role of the non-European world. Thinking about peace was obsessively about integrating *European* states and monarchs into a some kind of a peace system while the new genre of *ius naturae et gentium* concentrated on developing an ethical code (largely in the form of a "good" *raison d'état*) for European princes.[19] The overseas world appeared only as an occasional sideshow in the form of a question about what to do with the Ottoman empire (whether one could ally with the "infidel," typically),[20] how to open trade routes in the "Indies" or a concern about the "barbarians" who make war "without apparent reason or motive" and were therefore "enemies of humankind" that all nations had the right to "exterminate," to borrow Vattel's language (Vattel [1758]: 487).

Natural lawyers had learned to reason about peace and integration by taking their starting-point from a hypothesized "state of nature" in which all humans were free and equal. This predisposed them to include non-European peoples as part of "humanity" united by its search for security and happiness. The Spanish theologians of the sixteenth century had argued that God had endowed "Indians" with the same rights of property and political sovereignty that Europeans enjoyed.[21] Although they were critical of the way the "conquest" was being carried out, they had no doubt about the need to "integrate" the pagans of the New World by converting them into Christianity. Indeed, any contrary suggestion could only have seemed a wholly insensitive abandonment of the native inhabitants to the devil. But integrating them under a Christian natural law meant that they could also be disciplined by the "masters" of Christianity—the Spaniards themselves—who would now see themselves justified in eradicating their habits and teaching them (like "children") to the ways of the Christians. Whichever way the argument went, the native inhabitants would see themselves subordinated to the Christians.[22] By the end of the seventeenth century, the "right of conquest" based on the mere infidelity of a non-European community had been largely (though not wholly) abandoned—although one wonders to what extent native populations were able to appreciate the fine distinction Europeans made between the prohibition of forcible conversion and the right to make war in case the pagans obstructed preaching. Just war was nevertheless advocated to eradicate "unnatural" practices such as cannibalism and human sacrifice. A distinction was made in the legal debate about the non-European world between the great Asian empires (China, Japan, Siam, the Ottoman and Moghul empires) as well as the rulers of the "Spice Islands" with whom extensive treaty relations in the field of commerce had been conducted and the more or less temporary alliances Europeans made with the native communities of America and Africa, sometimes for commercial, sometimes for defensive purposes. With the growth of the relative power of Europeans towards indigenous partners, treaty-making with the latter became increasingly often just a smokescreen for colonization, if the treaty formality was followed at all.[23]

Whether the non-European world was left out from European peacemaking under the doctrine "no peace beyond the line" has been subject to some historiographic polemic. The Wars of Spanish Succession (1701–14) already saw the Great Powers, Spain, France and Britain clash in the colonies, and the Seven Years' War (1756–63) has been called the "first world war" owing to extensive Franco–British warfare in America and the Indian peninsula. But it is doubtful that any general doctrine would have excluded non-European territory from European peace.[24] Limited conflict under letters of marque and reprisal was an everyday occurrence and all Great Powers had recourse to privateers to disturb each others' commerce around the world. In theory, this was formalized as the law of prize under which cases of capture were adjudicated in domestic courts of admiralty. Perhaps ironically, global integration took first place under the rules of prize law that domestic courts extended to naval captures everywhere.

The "barbarian" communities subject to European land-grab were never depicted as equal partners in a joint project. For example, the early charters of English colonization authorized the appropriation of land "not belonging to any Christian prince or people" without the question of the rights of native populations being even posed. Such lands were seen initially as "vacant" and therefore amenable for European settlement. If anything was said about the native populations, this was to propagate conversion as one motive of colonization.[25] The idea of "vacant space" was extended in the eighteenth century by the Lockean argument about labor as the basis of property rights on land. When Vattel explained that enjoyment of such rights depended on the cultivation of the soil, he was expressing merely one variant of the ideology of "improvement" as part of the civilizing rhetoric that was gradually replacing theological ways to think about the Europeans' relations with others (Vattel [1758]: 216).[26] It was also available for waging war against the native Americans whose defense of their hunting grounds was read as making unnatural claims over exorbitant stretches of land.

Natural law did provide a way to "integrate" the barbarian communities in thinking about the government of international affairs. Protestant naturalists regularly referred to the "*Leyenda negra*" of the Spanish conquest and on that basis advocated their own commitment to humane treatment of the pagans. Vattel, for example, praised the "laudable example ... followed by William Penn and the colony of quakers." But apart from some of Diderot's famous passages in Abbé Raynal's *Histoire des deux Indes* (3rd edn. 1780) the men of the Enlightenment did not seriously doubt the justice and beneficial nature of colonization. Perhaps typical in this respect was one of the more famous late natural lawyers in Germany, Gottfried Achenwall (1719–1772), whose textbook Kant used in his pre-critical period. At the end of his career Achenwall became increasingly interested in deepening his view of civil society and using for that purpose the reports of the "savages" that were pouring to Europe. In a short essay on North America from 1767 that he composed after having been visited by Benjamin Franklin in Göttingen he discussed the European presence on the American continent, as well as the ways of life of its original inhabitants (Achenwall 1769). Achenwall admired the colonists—including what he believed to be their relative "liberal" slave laws—and assumed that their relations with Indian tribes were conducted under principles of natural law that were also recognized by the latter. He appreciated the spontaneity and peacefulness of the natives who did not at all seem to need organized statehood to live in peace. The tragedy was that once they had received knowledge of civilization they could no longer continue leading their old lives and, not quite civilized themselves, fell in between the two. Achenwall did not believe in stories about the greatness of the Aztec empire: without agriculture and arts they could not have possibly constructed such a great city (Achenwall 1769: 8, 25). His use of ethnographic data had the same purpose as Rousseau's, namely to develop a genetic type of natural law that would view the lives of "savage" peoples as incidents of early stages of humanity on the basis of which projections could be made about the laws of human development everywhere. The debate in which he was participating would lead into the kinds of ethnographic studies of which Johann Friedrich Blumenbach's work is an example that defended the unity of the human race (against polygenesis) and saw non-European cultures and "races" as degraded variants—to be countered by the more charitable view of them as earlier versions of present Europeans.[27]

For all their talk against "slavery," the men of the French Enlightenment were usually thinking about their own submission to the tyranny of absolutist rulers. Their political horizon was limited within Europe. Rousseau wrote admiringly of noble savages and critiqued the superficiality with which European travelers had discussed them.[28] Yet nowhere did he address the actuality of European colonization. The famous critique of slavery in Chapter I of the *Social Contract*, for example, was intended to work as a conceptual basis for making a distinction "between subduing a multitude and ruling a society" (Rousseau [1762]: 58). But the problem in the Caribbean at the time was not about subduing a multitude of free savages—there were none any longer. It was about the operation of a system of plantation slavery with an African workforce that was vital for France's foreign trade. Rousseau had nothing to say in the whole of his career about the half-million slaves in the French Antilles that were the source of the tea he enjoyed with his conversation partners in Europe (Buck-Morss 2009: 29-34). Montesquieu's intellectual sweep was somewhat wider. Although *Persian Letters* (1721) was predominantly about the state of Europe, it provided a reasonably positive and nuanced (though of course "Orientalist") view of the non-European world. *The Spirit of the Laws* made profuse reference to Chinese and Japanese laws and was strongly poised against ideas of uniformity that, Montesquieu wrote, "infallibly make an impression on little souls" (Montesquieu [1748] 1949: 169). The book was nothing if not a statement of a relativist approach to the study of laws as reflective of the differences between human societies, flowing from the varying environmental, psychological, and historical conditions. Montesquieu pleaded for religious toleration between Christians, Jews and Islamic countries, looking for a world where everyone would be ruled and adjudged by laws under which they were born.[29] He also undertook a sharp attack on the "scientific" justifications that had been made to defend the enslavement of Africans (Montesquieu [1748] 1949: 238–39). These arguments co-existed however, with Montesquieu's acceptance of many of the prejudices and stereotypes that were the common stock of European racialism. The physical, mental, and moral properties of African "savages" compared in all respects unfavorably to those of whites. Life in warm climates, he wrote, produced "weakness," "despondency" and "total incapacity" and "[t]he inhabitants of warm countries [were], like old men, timorous [while] the people in cold countries are like young men, brave." Moreover, because the "inclinations" of the inhabitants of warm climates were all "passive," it also remained the case that slavery there was "more supportable" (Montesquieu [1748] 1949: 223–24).

CONCLUSION: INTEGRATION UNDER WHICH CONDITIONS?

By 1815, statehood had come to stay as the basic principle of European peace. The international law treatises that came out from Germany first, and then gradually from Britain and the United States were clear that the new order (invariably presented as a continuation of the old one) was to be based on the statehood of a limited number of European entities whose relations were to be regulated under a specifically "European" law of nations. The treatises narrated the emergence of this order by giving rapid overviews of the history of the relations of European states, the influence that Christianity and diplomatic culture had had on the formation of a shared normative framework, addressing special sections to the rise of the United States, the problematic presence of the Ottoman empire at Europe's gates and the myriad of "half-sovereign" states that were under the tutelage of greater European powers. Little or no attention at all was given to the colonial world. One of the principal ideological architects of this post-revolutionary order, the publicist and secretary to the Vienna negotiations, Friedrich von Gentz (1764–1832) often described the new order as a kind of peace utopia where the law of nations would play an important, albeit limited role. To the untrustworthy principle of the balance of power, he wrote, "there has succeeded a principle of general union, uniting all states with a federal bond, under the guidance of the five principal Powers" (Gentz quoted in Stråth 2016: 54). In Gentz's federation states of the "second, third and fourth order" had tacitly agreed to be subordinated by the directorate while those of the "fifth" would still lack the sovereignty the others would enjoy. The role of law in this system was inscribed in the Declaration of Aix-la-Chapelle of November 1818 in which the (short-lived) directory of great powers aimed to consolidate the achievements of Vienna:

> Les Souverains, en formant cette union auguste, ont regardé comme la base fondamentale, leur invariable résolution de ne jamais s'écarter ni entre eux, ni dans leurs relations avec d'autres états, de l'observation la plus stricte des principes du droit des gens, principes qui dans leur application à un état de paix permanent, peuvent seuls garantir efficacement l'indépendance de chaque gouvernement et la stabilité de l'association Générale.
> —Declaration of Aix-la-Chapelle, November 18, 1818, de Martens 1820: 560–61

The declaration spoke of peace and a new "political system" that was based on the "intimate union of the monarchs associated with that system." Gentz himself was perfectly clear on the utter fragility of the idea and stressed the need for wise diplomacy and calculations of balance to keep it alive. Like the international jurists of the post-revolutionary era, Gentz had to tie himself in knots to explain how the states could be both sovereign and independent and simultaneously bound by a system of law enforced by a directorate of superior powers. But the hubris of Aix-la-Chapelle disappeared almost as soon as it had arisen. In the third edition of his leading textbook on European international law, published in 1821, Martens observed that even as nothing prevents one from *imagining* the formation of a federal union in Europe, nothing of the kind had been agreed in Westphalia, Utrecht, Vienna, or Aix-la-Chapelle. Outside specific treaty arrangements, European states were not united by any general law of nations; nor was it likely for such legal federation to ever exist (*"probablement il existera jamais"*) (de Martens [1821]: 9).

When European jurists like Martens wrote of peace and "system" around 1815, they did this by confining full-bodied statehood only to European and Christian nations, plus the United States. As Europeans nevertheless carried out diplomatic and commercial contacts with China, Japan, and the Ottoman empire, they did this behind treaty-based regimes of extraterritoriality that isolated the legal relations involving Europeans from the jurisdiction of local laws.[30] No deep "integration" in any universal peace system was desired or expected. Whether or not the—again treaty-based—relations that European colonizers had set up with non-European communities across the world had once been based on reciprocity, early nineteenth-century jurists and diplomats refrained from speculating about their role in any large peace utopia. Nations that came sweepingly to be labelled the "Orient" were always regarded by Europeans as outsiders. While commercial and territorial exchanges could be concluded with them, a debate about their status as possibly "members" of a legal community of nations—a peaceful "federation"—would begin only in the last decades of the nineteenth century.[31] That this attitude was not restricted to conservatives is shown by the length of time it took for the revolutionaries in the French national assembly to take notice of the slave rebellion in *Saint Domingue*.[32] From 1804 as general Dessalines had purged the island of practically all remaining Europeans and declared it independent as Haiti, it took more than a century before legal recognition was given to it by France.[33]

"Peace is not only the absence of war." The years 1648–1815 were formative to the emergence in Europe of a "modern" consciousness of "society" that had its own intrinsic laws that it was necessary to know how to operate so as to eradicate the causes of war. The knowledge of those social laws took the character of science, including when it was articulated in the vocabulary of the "law of nature and of nations." To realize the requirements of that law was not a matter of choice, it was a necessity so that human communities could live peaceful and happy lives. Although there were many versions of natural law, most of them projected an optimistic trajectory that saw the shared religious and cultural heritage eventually integrate European nations into some kind of peaceful federation. Apart from the brief revolutionary interlude, most natural lawyers had an authoritarian image of society where the largest part of the population would be scarcely more than objects of monarchic management through the skillful operation of the "state-machine." Non-European peoples had no role in this image; they provided resources for European expansion, but no intellectual or cultural contribution was expected of them to the inevitable spread of what Europeans by the beginning of the nineteenth century were learning to call "civilization."

NOTES

Introduction

1. Opening quotation, "Beati pacifici. Cedant arma togae", in Penn 1693, Section II "Fruit of Government, as Government, is from Society, and Society from Consent," citing Matthew 5:9 and Cicero, *De officiis*, I. 77 ("cedant arma togae, concedat laurea laudi").
2. There is a rich literature on this subject. Among recent publications, see e.g. Croxton (1999); Schröder (1999); Bély (2000); Malettke (2001); Blin (2006).
3. For detailed accounts of this period, see Ghervas (2008); Dallas (2011); Jarrett (2013); Vick (2014); Gruner (2014); Stauber (2014).
4. See also, for example, Corrado Giaquinto, "Allegory of Justice and Peace" (1753–54): https://www.museodelprado.es/en/the-collection/art-work/allegory-of-justice-and-peace/1e7c0108-b36f-4ff1-91d0-4bb49d6e99da.
5. See particularly Croxton (1999); Osiander (2001); Teschke (2003); Piirimäe (2010).
6. "Treaty of Peace between the Holy Roman Empire and Sweden and the Treaty of Peace between France and the Holy Roman Empire" (signed and entered into force 24 October 1648) (1648-49) 1 CTS 198, 319; "Treaty of Peace between Spain and the Netherlands" (signed and entered into force 30 January 1648) 1 CTS 1.
7. "When we ask, Are we now living in an enlightened age? the answer is, No, but we live in an age of enlightenment."
8. The expression was coined at the time of the Revolutionary Wars.
9. Assemblée constituante, "Décret du 22 mai 1790 concernant le droit de faire la paix et la guerre."

Chapter 1

1. This was written in response to the Comte de Hauterive's *L'État de la France à la fin de l'An VIII*, a defense of Napoleon's coup d'état of 18th Brumaire. See Nakhimovsky (2011) and Holbraad (1970: 18–19).
2. For a more nuanced account of Hobbes' views see Christov (2015: 104–40).
3. See Cavallar (2002: 211). Wolff was not the first, and he was certainly not the last, to point out that all contractual explanations for the origins of civil society presumed a knowledge of the very thing they were supposedly creating.
4. On Wolff's conception of the consensual "will of nations," see Koskenniemi (2005: 108–12).
5. For a more detailed, if somewhat different, account see Cavallar (2002: 208–15) and Schiffer (1954).
6. For selections from some of these see Aksu (2008).
7. See Hont (2005) and, for a somewhat darker view, Terjanian (2013).
8. On Constant's often ambiguous and shifting views on commerce, see Holmes (1984: 212–21). As Rosenblatt (2003) and others have pointed out, in the latter years of his life, as

he became more concerned with the civilizing potential of religion, Constant became less confident in the virtues of utilitarianism.
9. For Kant's influence, in particular on Alfred Zimmern, see Mazower (2009: 72–73), and in general for a useful account of subsequent interpretations of "Perpetual peace" see Easely (2004).
10. And see Yovel (1980, 151–54) and Hassner (1961).
11. On this see Ypi (2014).
12. As a number of scholars have pointed out, Kant's account of "republicanism" is, in its key essentials, very close to the modern notion of "liberal democracy." See Doyle (1983).
13. See Russett (1993) and Höffe (2006: 177–81). Kant, however, is not claiming that republics do not wage war on other republics; he is claiming that a properly constituted republic will not make war upon any state no matter what its constitution, unless no other option is available.
14. On Kant's shifting view of the form his "cosmopolitan whole" would finally take, see Hurrell (1990) and Mori (2004).
15. It of course depends on what kind of "empire" you have in mind. For the suggestion that the Carolingian empire might offer a possible model for the EU see Zielonka (2007, 2014).
16. This, however, would seem be a direct contradiction of Kant's general condemnation of all revolutions (including the American). But on his highly tendentious understanding, of the events that led up to the declaration of the Republic in 1792, it had been Louis XVI himself who, by calling the Estates-General in an attempt to resolve a financial crisis, had voluntarily, if inadvertently, surrendered the "supreme authority" within the French state to the people, and "the consequence was that the monarch's sovereignty wholly disappeared (it was not merely suspended) and passed to the people." Once anything like this has happened a situation is created in which "the united people does not merely represent the sovereign: it is itself the sovereign" (*Metaphysics of Morals*, Kant 1999b: 48–41). In other words the Revolution had been no revolution at all, but only a legal transfer of power.
17. For the idea that the period from 1918 until 1945 was a prolonged civil war within Europe, see Armitage (2017: 226–28).

Chapter 2

1. For a different account, where the modern state provided the best example of the kind of agent assumed by liberalism, see Tuck (1999).
2. For more on the role of skepticism in humanist thought, see Tuck (1993: 154–201).
3. This argument could be further extended to make the claim that the transformation from the natural to the civil state did not necessarily entail a dramatic change in property relations.
4. The meaning of *ius gladii* in this context should be regarded as "chastisement" or "vengeance" rather than the intentional infliction of malicious force.

Chapter 3

1. This "plan" was confected after his death by Bentham's editor, John Bowring, out of other MSS: see Hoogensen (2005, pp. 40–54).
2. For instance, Anna Colbjørnsdatter Arneberg (1667–1736); Maria Ursula d'Abreu e Lencastro (168–fl. 1714); Anna Maria Jansdotter Engsten (1762–fl. 1790); Jeanie Cameron (1695?–1773?); Céleste Bulkeley (1759–1832), Suzanne Bélair (1781–1805); Ketevan Andronikashvili (1754 –1782); Mary Anne Talbot (1778–1808). See also Watanabe-O'Kelly (2010).

NOTES

3. These two theorists frame the long eighteenth century; while both English, they drew from and were engaged with European intellectual movements and are therefore not as unrepresentative of their times as their place of birth might lead one to assume. A longer study might include such writers as Madame de Staël, who, like Benjamin Constant, became highly critical of Napoleonic wars of conquest, seeing them as regressive. See Fontana (2016: 201–02).
4. See for instance, Warner (1983).
5. See Nussbaum (1984).
6. Thus, Madame de Pompadour was painted as the Goddess of hunting, at least twice, once by François Boucher (1703–1770) in 1742, "Diana Resting after her Bath," one of his greatest works, and also by Jean-Marc Nattier (1685–1766) in 1746. See, Pierre Mignard's (1612–1695) portrait of Olympia Mancini (1638–1708), countess of Soissons depicted as Athena; likewise, Henri Gascard's (c. 1635–1701) portrait of Frances Teresa Stewart, Duchess of Richmond and Lennox (1647–1702); Jean-Baptiste Santerre's (French artist, 1658–1717) Philippe II d'Orleans 1674–1723 the Regent of France and Madame de Parabere as Minerva; that of Elżbieta Sieniawska née Lubomirska as Minerva by an unknown Polish artist c. 1700; John Fayram's portrait of the Bluestocking Elizabeth Carter (1717–1806) from c. 1735–41, shows her with helmet, armor and shield but holding a work by Plato rather than a spear; or the 1765 Louis-Michel van Loo's (1707–1771) portrait of Marie Leszczyńska, Queen of France and her daughter in law Maria Josepha of Saxony, Dauphine of France.
7. See Tomaselli (2001).
8. See Tomaselli (2006: 36–38); Jimack (2015).
9. See Tomaselli (2012); Tomaselli (2016).
10. For Ferguson's reluctance to use the term "civilization," see Forbes (1966: xix–xx).

Chapter 5

1. G. Claretta, *I Reali di Savoia* (Turin, 1893), 229–30, as quoted in Gedo (2002: 601–05).
2. Sheriff (1996: 76–78).
3. "Loterie pittoresque pour le Salon de 1783" in the Collection Deloynes, Paris, Bibliothèque Nationale, Cabinet des Estampes, XIII, No. 291: 22–23.
4. Kettering (1998: 605–14).
5. Gudlaugsson (1959–60: I, 64). Cited in Kettering (1998: 1).
6. Rubens' diplomatic skills were recognized by his first patron, Vincenzo I Gonzaga, who sent the artist to the Spanish court in 1603 as his personal representative. See Saward (1982: 185–86).
7. Martin (2011). See also Donovan (2004).
8. Rosenthal (2005).
9. Yonan (2011).
10. As Millen and Wolf discovered in a manuscript collection entitled "Impresas, Emblems, Crests, Reverses of Medals, and Other Symbols Used on Various Occasions by Personages of the Most Serene House of Medici in Tuscany," this was the motto of a caduceus found under the name of Maria de' Medici. See Millen and Wolf (1989: 7).
11. Saward (1982: 186).
12. Iovleva (1997: 95).
13. Ibid.
14. Burke (1994).
15. Marin (1988).

16. Yonan (2011: 52–53).
17. Abrams (1985: 192–95); and Abrams (1982: 61–68).
18. Johnson (1993: ch. 3); and Vidal (2000: 702–29).
19. Johnson (1993: 124).
20. Welch (2005: 42–50); O'Brien (2006: 155–61); and Gimblett (2011).

Chapter 7

1. Fénelon was appointed as tutor to the Dauphin's eldest son in 1689. For a general introduction to Fénelon's life and works, see Riley (1994: xiii–xxxi).
2. It was officially published in Amsterdam in 1734 under the title *Éducation royale ou Examen de conscience pour un grand prince*, and the English translation, which is used here, appeared in 1747. But the supplement under discussion was published in English in 1720 under the title *Two Essays on the Ballance of Power* (Fénelon 1720). The identity of the translator is unknown. For more on this translation and the reception of Fénelon's theory of international relations in general, see Ahn (2014).
3. For more on the concept, see Bosbach (1988); Pagden (1995).
4. It is generally agreed that the period between the Treaty of Utrecht and the First Partition of Poland of 1772 was the "Golden Age" of balance of power thinking, see Hassall (1896); Morgenthau (1961: 9, 189); Rosecrance (1963: 26); Butterfield (1966: 138–39); Wolf (1970); Anderson (1993: 163–89).
5. Louis, Grand Dauphin, died on 14 April 1711, three days earlier than the Emperor.
6. It is worth noting that Louis XIV, especially during the War of the Spanish Succession, was widely viewed as a tyrant who took pride and pleasure in breaking his promises, see Onnekink (2016: 69–91); (Schröder 2017: 154–76); Ahn (2017: 125–49).
7. In particular, Montesquieu reproached the British government's decision to punish anyone trading with Spain and her American colonies by execution.

Chapter 8

1. The use of the word "integration" involves an obvious anachronism. In the period under discussion, reference was often made to the "unity" of "Christendom" or "humanity"—without the necessary implication of a continuous process (as in "integration"), however.
2. Timing of the emergence of statehood is a classical *topos* in the history of political thought. Whatever one sees as the pertinent moment, and whoever as the relevant thinkers, by the early eighteenth century, the "state" was clearly the center of European political life and reflection.
3. See further Koskenniemi (2008):189–207.
4. See e.g. Heilbron (1995): 42–46, 67–68.
5. See e.g. Edelstein (2011): 58–59, and Heilbron (1995): 96–100.
6. Saint-Pierre wrote that he was following the examples of the constitution of the German-Roman Empire and the plan of the foreign minister of Henry IV, the Duke of Sully. Both claims were dubious. Saint Pierre believed—wrongly—that the German estates had entered the empire as sovereigns and that Sully's plan had been made *bona fide*. In fact, the German estates had never been sovereign and the hegemonic purposes of Sully's design were well-known. See Riley (1974):187–89.
7. See further MacGilvray (2011): 99–100, 104–05.
8. On this point among the philosophes generally, see Belissa (1998): 79–84.

9. On Volney's proposed Draft declaration of the Rights and Duties of Nations, see further Mirkine-Guetzévitch (1928): II: 308–09.
10. For the content of the decree of May 22, 1790, see http://fr.wikipedia.org/wiki/Décret_de_Déclaration_de_paix_au_monde
11. For a good overview, see Belissa (1998): 268–88, and Mirkine-Guetzévitch (1928): II, 305–16.
12. For the proposal, originally presented in 1793, see Mirkine-Guetzévitch (1928): II 309–16, and Belissa (1998): 365–66, 419–20.
13. See Locke ([1690] 1984): 179–80, 129–41.
14. See also Macpherson (1962) 2011: 209–10.
15. See Locke ([1690] 1984): 180–81.
16. For some of the concerns, see Muthu (2012): 205–20.
17. On Smith's effort to remove "politics" from government, see e.g. Winch (1996): 94–97.
18. On Bentham's early democratic views expressed in the context of the French revolution, and his later espousal of democratic parliamentary reform, see Schofield (2009): 78–94, 137–40.
19. The reasons for overlooking the non-European world by the natural lawyers of the eighteenth century are discussed in Tourme-Jouannet ([2013] 2014): 656–61.
20. Many such agreements had been made since the Franco–Ottoman alliance of 1536—at the time the target of widespread criticism. But Vattel, for example, believed that such alliances were binding because treaties were based on natural law that treated humans as humans "and not under the character of Christians or Mahommedans" Vattel (1758): 342. For the treaty relations with the Ottoman empire, see Ziegler ([2004] 2008): 235–46. Prejudice against the Ottomans lay deep and Saint-Pierre was hardly being eccentric when, as a condition of "perpetual peace" he was gradually moved to propose common war against them.
21. See Vitoria (1991): 239–52.
22. Out of a wealth of literature, see e.g. Todorov (1984); Anghie (2004).
23. The most extensive study of European colonial treaty-making is Hébié (2015). According to Hébié, until late in the nineteenth century, the Europeans took the colonial treaty relationship with local political entities seriously and as binding on both parties. The way that settlers in North American colonization began with treaty-making and, as European power grew, changed into conquest and occupation is well treated in Banner (2005).
24. See Fisch (1986).
25. A good overview of the British patents is Macmillan (2006): 79–120.
26. See further Anghie (2011): 244–49.
27. See especially Blumenbach (1806), 140 ff.
28. "In the two or three centuries since the inhabitants of Europe have been flooding to other parts of the world, endlessly publishing collections of voyages and travel, I am persuaded that we have come to know no other men except Europeans": Rousseau ([1755] 1984): 159. See also Curran (2011): 70–73.
29. See also Tomaselli (2006): 28–31.
30. See e.g. Kayaoglu (2010).
31. See Koskenniemi (2001), ch. 2.
32. The rebellion in Haiti of slaves and "*gens du couleur*" had began in 1791. Despite some effort by revolutionaries such as Abbé Grégoire to grant at least the "colored" population the rights listed in the 1789 Declaration, it was only in 1794, and even then as an outcome of the effort to enlist the slaves in war against the English, that the Assembly passed its famous abolition act (Decree of 16 pluviôse [4 February] 1794).
33. See Wesley (1917): 369–83.

BIBLIOGRAPHY

Abrams, Ann Uhry (1982), "Benjamin West's Documentation of Colonial History: *William Penn's Treaty with the Indians*," The Art Bulletin, 64: 59–75.
Abrams, Ann Uhry (1985), *The Valiant Hero: Benjamin West and Grand Style History Painting*, Washington DC: Smithsonian Institution Press.
Achenwall, Gottfried (1769), *Herrn Gottfried Achenwalls Anmerkungen über Nordamerika und über dasige Grossbritannische Colonien, aus mündlichen Nachrichten des Herrn Dr. Franklins*, Frankfurt and Leipzig.
Ahmed, Shahab (2016), *What Is Islam? On the Importance of Being Islamic*. Princeton, NJ: Princeton University Press.
Ahn, Doohwan (2014), "From Idomeneus to Protesilaus: Fénelon in Early Hanoverian Britain," in *Fénelon in the Enlightenment: Traditions, Adaptations, and Variations*, ed. Christoph Schmitt-Maaß, Stefanie Stockhorst, and Doohwan Ahn, Amsterdam: Brill.
Ahn, Doohwan (2017), "The Anglo-French Treaty of Utrecht of 1713 Revisited: The Politics of Rivalry and Alliance," in *The Politics of Commercial Treaties in the Eighteenth Century: Balance of Power, Balance of Trade*, ed. Antonella Alimento and Koen Stapelbroek, New York: Palgrave Macmillan.
Aksu, Eşref (2008), *Early Notions of Global Governance: Selected Eighteenth-Century Proposals for "Perpetual Peace."* Cardiff: University of Wales Press.
Albemarle, George Thomas Keppel, Earl of (1852), ed., *Memoirs of the Marquis of Rockingham*, 2 vols., London: Richard Bentley.
Anderson, M. S. (1970), "Eighteenth-Century Theories of the Balance of Power," in *Studies in Diplomatic History: Essays in Memory of David Bayne Horn*, ed. Ragnhild Hatton and M. S. Anderson, London: Longman.
Anderson, M. S. (1993), *The Rise of Modern Diplomacy, 1450–1919*, London: Longman.
Angell, Stephen W. and Pink Dandelion, eds. (2013), *The Oxford Handbook of Quaker Studies*. Oxford: Oxford University Press.
Anghie, Antony (2004), *Imperialism, Sovereignty and the Making of International Law*, Cambridge University Press.
Anghie, Antony (2011), "Vattel and Colonialism: Some Preliminary Observations", in *Vattel's International law in a XXIst Century Perspective*, ed. Vincent Chetail and Peter Haggenmacher, Leiden: Nijhoff.
Anon. (1714), *The Ballance of Power: Or, a Comparison of the Strength of the Emperor and the French King*, London: A. Baldwin.
Anon. (1740), *French Influence upon English Counsels demonstrated from an Impartial Examination of Our Measures for Twenty Years Past*, London: T. Cooper.
Anon, (1811), *The Female Instructor; Or, Young Woman's Companion*, Liverpool: Nuttall, Fisher, and Dixon.
Arcidiacono, Bruno (2011). *Cinq types de paix: une histoire des plans de pacification perpétuelle (XVIIe-XXe siècles)*. Paris: PUF.

Armitage, David (2013), *Foundations of Modern International Thought*. Cambridge: Cambridge University Press.

Armitage, David (2017), *Civil Wars: A History in Ideas*, New York: Alfred A. Knopf.

Asch, Ronald G. (2004), "The 'ius foederis' Re-examined: The Peace of Westphalia and the Constitution of the Holy Roman Empire", in ed. Randall Lesaffer, *Peace Treaties and International Law in European History: From the Late Middle Ages to World War One*, 319–37, Cambridge: Cambridge University Press.

Atwood, Craig (2009), *The Theology of the Czech Brethren from Hus to Comenius*. University Park, PA: Pennsylvania State University Press.

Aydin, Cemil (2017), *The Idea of the Muslim World*. Cambridge, MA: Harvard University Press.

Bachaumont, Louis Petit de. (1780–89), *Mémoires secrets pour server à l'histoire de la république de lettres en France depuis MDCCLXII jusqu'à nos jours, our Journal d'un observateur*, 36 vols., London: J. Adamson.

Banner, Stuart (2005), *How the Indians Lost their Land: Law and Power on the Frontier*, Cambridge, MA: Harvard University Press.

Barclay, Robert (1676), *An apology for the true Christian divinity, as the same is held forth, and preached by the people, called, in scorn, Quakers . . .* [London].

Baugh, Daniel A. (2011), *The Global Seven Years' War 1754–1763: Britain and France in a Great Power Contest*, London: Routledge.

Beales A. C. F. (1931), *The History of Peace: A Short Account of the Organized Movements for International Peace*. New York: The Dial Press.

Beaumelle, Laurent Angliviel de la (1753), *Reflections of ***** being a Series of Political Maxims, Illustrated by General History, as well as by Variety of Authentic Anecdotes (Never Published Before)*, London: D. Wilson, and T. Durham.

Belissa, Marc (1998), *Fraternité universelle et intérêt national (1713–1795). Les cosmopolitiques du droit des gens*, Paris: Kimé.

Bell, David (2007), *The First Total War: Napoleon's Europe and the Birth of Warfare As We Know It*, Boston: Houghton Mifflin Company.

Bell, Erin (2011), "The Early Quakers, the Peace Testimony and Masculinity in England, 1660–1720". *Gender & History* 23:2. 283–300.

Bellers, John (1710), *Some Reasons for an European State, Proposed to the Powers of Europe, by the Universal Guarantee, and Annual Congress, Senate, Dyet, or Parliament, to Settle any Disputes about the Bounds and Rights of Princes and States Hereafter*, London: s. n.

Bély, Lucien, ed. (2000), *L'Europe des traités de Westphalie: Esprit de la diplomatie et diplomatie de l'esprit*, Paris, PUF.

Bély, Lucien (2007), *L'art de la paix en Europe: Naissance de la diplomatie moderne XVIe-XVIIIe siècle*, Paris: PUF.

Bentham, Jeremy ([1776] 1988), *A Fragment on Government*, ed. Ross Harrison, Cambridge: Cambridge University Press.

Bentham, Jeremy ([1781/89] 1988), *Introduction to the Principles of Morals and Legislation*, Buffalo, NY: Prometheus.

Bentham, Jeremy (1843), "General View of a Complete Code of Laws", in John Bowring, *The Works of Jeremy Bentham*, Edinburgh; William Tait.

Bentham, Jeremy (1843), "Principles of International law", in John Bowring, *The Works of Jeremy Bentham*, Edinburgh; William Tait.

Bentham, Jeremy (1843), "A Plan for an Universal and Perpetual Peace", in John Bowring, *The Works of Jeremy Bentham*, Edinburgh; William Tait.

Besse, Joseph (1747), *An Enquiry into the Validity of a Late Discourse, Intituled The Nature and Duty of Self-Defence*, London: T. Sowle Raylton and Luke Hinde.

Black, Jeremy (2004), *Parliament and Foreign Policy in the Eighteenth-Century*, Cambridge: Cambridge University Press.

Black, Jeremy (2011), *Debating Foreign Policy in Eighteenth-Century Britain*, Farnham: Ashgate.

Black, William (1793), *Reasons for Preventing the French, Under the Mask of Liberty, from Trampling Upon Europe*, 2nd edn., London: J. Debrett.

Blin, Arnaud (2006), *1648: La Paix de Westphalie ou la naissance de l'Europe politique*, Brussels, Editions Complexe Bruxelles.

Blom, Hans, John Christian Laursen, and Luisa Simonutti, eds. (2007), *Monarchisms in the Age of Enlightenment: Liberty, Patriotism, and the Common Good*, Toronto: University of Toronto Press.

Blumenbach, Johann Friedrich (1806), *De l'unité du genre humain et de ses variétés*, trad. De 3ème éd., Paris: Allut.

Bois, Jean-Pierre (1999), *L'Europe à l'époque moderne: origines, utopies et réalités de l'idée d'Europe*, Paris: Colin.

Bosbach, Franz (1988), *Monarchia universalis: ein politischer Leitbegriff der Frühen Neuzeit*, Gottingen: Vandenhoeck & Ruprecht.

Bradley, James E. (1986), *Popular Politics and the American Revolution in England: Petitions, the Crown, and Public Opinion*, Macon, GA: Mercer University Press.

Bradley, James E. (1990), *Religion, Revolution, and English Radicalism*, Cambridge: Cambridge University Press.

Brewer, John (1989), *The Sinews of Power: War, Money and the English State, 1688–1783*, New York: Alfred A. Knopf.

Broad, Jacqueline, and Karen Green, (2009), *A History of Women's Political Thought in Europe, 1400–1700*, Cambridge: Cambridge University Press.

Brock, Peter (1957), *The Political and Social Doctrines of the Unity of Czech Brethren in the Fifteenth and Early Sixteenth Centuries*. Gravenhage: Mouton.

Brock, Peter (1968), *Radical Pacifists in Antebellum America*. Princeton, NJ: Princeton University Press.

Brock, Peter (1972), *Pacifism in Europe to 1914*, Princeton, NJ: Princeton University Press.

Brown, Christopher Leslie (2006), *Moral Capital: Foundations of British Abolitionism*, Chapel Hill, NC: University of North Carolina Press.

Buck-Morss, Susan (2009), *Hegel, Haiti and Universal History*, Pittsburgh: University of Pittsburgh Press.

Bull, Hedley (1981), "Hobbes and the International Anarchy". *Social Research* 48, no. 4: 717–38.

Burke, Edmund (1991), "First Letter on a Regicide Peace," in *The Writings and Speeches of Edmund Burke. Vol. IX: I. The Revolutionary War, 1794–1797. II. Ireland*, Oxford: Oxford University Press.

Burke, Peter (1994), *The Fabrication of Louis XIV*, New Haven, CT: Yale University Press.

[Burke, William] (1777), *The Letters of Valens*, London: J. Almon.

Butterfield, Herbert (1966), "The Balance of Power," in *Diplomatic Investigations: Essays in the Theory of International Politics*, ed. Herbert Butterfield and Martin Wight, Cambridge, MA: Harvard University Press.

Callières, François de (1716), *De la manière de négociér avec les Souverains*, Amsterdam: La Compagnie.

Callières, François de ([1716] 2006), *L'art de négocier sous Louis XIV*, Paris: Nouveau Monde.

Campbell, John (1750), *The Present State of Europe; Explaining the Interests, Connections, Political and Commercial Views of Its Several Powers*, Dublin: George Faulkner.

Cavazzocca Mazzanti, Vittorio (1923), "Rossini a Verona durante il Congresso del 1822," *Atti e Memorie Dell'Accademia di Agricultura Scienze e Lettere di Verona*, IV/24: 53–112.

Cavallar, Georg (2002), *The Rights of Strangers: Theories of International Hospitality, the Global Community, and Political Justice Since Vitoria*, Aldershot: Ashgate.

Cavendish, Margaret ([1662] 2003), "ORATIONS of DIVERS SORTS, accommodated to DIVERS PLACES. Written by the thrice Noble, Illustrious and excellent Princess, the Lady Marchioness OF NEW CASTLE", in Margaret Cavendish: *Political Writings*, 111–292, ed. Susan James, Cambridge: Cambridge University Press.

Ceadel, Martin (1989), *Thinking about Peace and War*, Oxford: Clarendon Press.

Ceadel, Martin (1996), *The Origins of War Prevention: The British Peace Movement and International Relations, 1730–1854*, Oxford: Clarendon Press.

Christov, Theodore (2015), *Before Anarchy. Hobbes and his Critics in Modern International Thought*, Cambridge: Cambridge University Press.

Clark, J. C. D. (1985), *English Society, 1688–1832: Ideology, Social Structure, and Political Practice during the Ancien Regime*, Cambridge: Cambridge University Press.

Cockburn, Cynthia (2012), *Anti-Militarism: Political and Gender Dynamics of Peace Movements*. New York: Palgrave Macmillan.

Coke, Roger (1662), *A Survey of the Politicks of Mr. Thomas White, Thomas Hobbs, and Hugo Grotius: Also, Elements of Power & Subjection, Or, the Causes of Humane, Christian, and Legal Society*, London: Printed for G. Bedell and T. Collins.

Colley, Linda (2009), *Britons: Forging the Nation, 1707–1837*, 3rd revised edn., New Haven, CT: Yale University Press.

Comenius, John Amos ([1667] 1945), *The Angel of Peace*, ed. Milos Safranek, trans. W. A. Morison, New York: Pantheon Books.

Conrad, Sebastian (2012), "Enlightenment in Global History: A Historiographical Critique," *American Historical Review*, 117: 999–1027.

Constant, Benjamin (1988), *Political Writings*, ed. Biancamaria Fontana, Cambridge: Cambridge University Press.

Constant, Benjamin (1998), *Écrits de jeunesse (1774–1799)*, ed. L. Omacini and J.-D. Candaux, Tübingen: Max Niemeyer Verlag.

Conway, Stephen (2002), "From Fellow-Nationals to Foreigners: British Perceptions of the Americans, c.1739–1783," *William & Mary Quarterly*, 3rd series, 59: 143–69.

Conway, Stephen (2004), "'Like the Irish'? Volunteer Corps and Volunteering during the American War," in *Britain and America Go To War: The Impact of War and Warfare in Anglo-America, 1754–1815*, ed. Julie Flavell and Stephen Conway, Gainesville, FL: University Press of Florida.

Conway, Stephen (2011), *Britain, Ireland, and Continental Europe in the Eighteenth Century: Similarities, Connections, Identities*, Oxford: Oxford University Press.

Conybear, John (1749), *True Patriotism: A Sermon Preach'd Before the Honourable House of Commons, at St. Margaret's Westminster, on Tuesday, April 25th, 1749. Being the Day of Thanksgiving for the General Peace*, London.

Cookson J. E. (1982), *The Friends of Peace: Anti-War Liberalism in England 1793–1815*. New York: Cambridge University Press.

Cookson, J. E. (1997), *The British Armed Nation, 1793–1815*, Oxford: Clarendon Press.

Copeland, Thomas W. et al. (1958–78), eds., *The Correspondence of Edmund Burke*, 10 vols., Cambridge: Cambridge University Press.

Cortright, David (2008), *Peace: A History of Movements and Ideas*. Cambridge: Cambridge University Press.
Cox, Jeffrey N. (1998), *Poetry and Politics in the Cockney School: Keats, Shelley, Hunt and Their Circle*. Cambridge: Cambridge University Press.
Croxton, Derek (1999), "The Peace of Westphalia of 1648 and the Origins of Sovereignty," *International History Review*, 21: 3, 569–91.
Croxton, Derek (2013), *Westphalia: The Last Christian Peace*, London: Palgrave Macmillan.
Cuche, François-Xavier (2009), "L'économie du Télémaque, l'économie dans le Télémaque," *Littératures classiques*, 70: 3, 103–18.
Curran, Andrew S. (2011), *The Anatomy of Blackness. Science and Slavery in the Age of the Enlightenment*, Johns Hopkins University Press.
D'Holbach, Baron (1820), *La morale universelle, ou les devoirs de l'homme, fondés sur la nature*, Tome II, Paris: Masson.
D'Holbach, Baron (1822), *Système social ou principes naturels de la morale et de la politique*, Tome I, Paris: Niogret.
Dallas, M. G. (2011), *1815: The Roads to Waterloo*, New York, Random House.
Davenant, Charles (1701), *Essays upon 1. The Ballance of Power. II. The Right of Making War, Peace, and Alliance, III. Universal Monarchy*, London: James Knapton.
Davenant, Charles ([1701] 1771), *An Essay upon the Balance of Power* in *The Political and Commercial Works of Charles Davenant LL.D.*, ed. Charles Whitworth, 5 vols, vol. III, 299–430, London: R. Horsfield.
"The Declaration of Pillnitz" (27 August 1791): https://en.wikisource.org/wiki/Declaration_of_Pillnitz.
Defoe, Daniel (1712), *A Weekly Review of the Affairs of France: Purg'd from the Errors and Partiality of News-Writers and Petty-Statesmen, of All Sides*, 3: 204 (July 12).
Dehio, Ludwig (1962), *The Precarious Balance: Four Centuries of the European Power Struggle*, New York: Alfred A Knopf.
Devji, Faisal (2013), *Muslim Zion: Pakistan as a Political Idea*. Cambridge: Harvard University Press.
Dhondt, Frederik (2015), *Balance of Power and Norm Hierarchy: Franco-British Diplomacy After the Peace of Utrecht*, Leiden: Brill.
Dickson, P. G. M. (1967), *The Financial Revolution in England: A Study in the Development of Public Credit, 1688–1756*, London: Macmillan.
Diderot, Denis (1994), *Histoire des Deux Indes*, in Œuvres III, ed. Laurent Versini, Paris: Robert Laffont.
Dodge, David Low ([1812] 1905), *War Inconsistent with the Religion of Jesus Christ*. Boston: Ginn & Company.
Donovan, Fiona (2004), *Rubens and England*, New Haven, CT: Yale University Press.
Doyle, Michael W. (1983), "Kant, Liberal Legacies and Foreign Affairs", *Philosophy and Public Affairs* 12, 205–353.
Dubos, Jean Baptiste (1719), *Réflexions critiques sur la poésie et sur la peinture*, 2 vols., Paris, n.p. .
Dupont, John ([1757]), *National Corruption and Depravity the Principal Cause of National Disappointments: In a Sermon Preach'd at Aysgarth, on Friday, the 11th of February, 1757, being the Day Appointed by Proclamation for a General Fast*, London:
Easley, Eric. S. (2004), *The War over Perpetual Peace: An Exploration into the History of a Foundation International Relations Text*, London: Palgrave Macmillan.
Edelstein, Dan (2011), *The Enlightenment: A Genealogy*, University of Chicago Press.

Eden, William and Gerard de Rayneval (1786), *Treaty of Navigation and Commerce between His Britannick Majesty and the Most Christian King. Signed at Versailles, the 26th of September, 1786*, London: T. Harrison and S. Brooke.

Erasmus, Desiderius ([1517] 1917), *The Complaint of Peace*. Translated from the *Querela pacis* (A. D. 1521[sic]) of Erasmus, Chicago and London: The Open Court Publishing Company.

Even, Pascal, and Isabelle Nathan, eds. (2015), *Le congrès de Vienne, l'invention d'une Europe nouvelle*, Versailles: Art Lys.

Fénelon, François de Salignac de la Mothe (1720), *Two Essays on the Ballance of Europe. The First written in French by the Late Archbishop of Cambray and translated into English. The Second by the Translator of the First Essay*, London: John Darby.

Fénelon, François de Salignac de la Mothe (1734), *Éducation royale ou Examen de conscience pour un grand prince*, Amsterdam: M. Magerus.

Fénelon, François de Salignac de la Mothe (1747), *Proper Heads of Self-Examination for a King*, Dublin: George Faulkner.

Fénelon, François de Salignac de la Mothe (1994), *Telemachus, Son of Ulysses*, ed. Patrick Riley, Cambridge: Cambridge University Press.

Fénelon, François de Salignac de la Mothe (1997), "Plans de gouvernement dits Tables de Chaulnes (Nov. 1711)," in *Oeuvres*, Tom. II, ed. Jacques Le Brun, Paris: Gallimard.

Ferguson, Adam ([1767] 1966), *An Essay on the History of Civil Society*, ed. Duncan Forbes, Edinburgh: Edinburgh University Press.

Ferguson, Adam (1995), *An Essay on the History of Civil Society*, ed. Fania Oz-Salzberger, Cambridge: Cambridge University Press.

Ferretti, Paola (1998), *A Russian Advocate of Peace: Vasilii Malinovskii (1765–1814)*. Dordrecht: Kluwer Academic Publishers.

Fisch, Jörg (1986), *Die europäische Expansion und das Völkerrecht*, Stuttgart: Steiner.

Fontana, Biancamaria (2016), *Germaine de Stael: A Political Portrait*, Princeton, NJ: Princeton University Press.

Forbes, Duncan (1966), "Introduction", in *Adam Ferguson, An Essay on the History of Civil Society 1767*, xiii–xli, Edinburgh, Edinburgh University Press.

Foucault, Michel ([1997] 2003), *"Society Must Be Defended." Lectures at the Collège de France, 1975–76*. New York: Picador.

Fox, George (1660), *A declaration from the harmless and innocent people of God, called Quakers, against all plotters and fighters in the world for the removing of the ground of jealousie and suspition from both magistrates and people in the kingdome concerning wars and fightings* . . . London: Robert Wilson.

Frederick II the Great, King of Prussia (1789), "The History of My Own Times," in *Posthumous Works of Frederick II. King of Prussia*, trans. Thomas Holcroft, Vol. 1, London: G. G. J. and J. Robinson.

Fuchs, Ingrid (2002), "The Glorious Moment: Beethoven and the Congress of Vienna," in *Denmark and the Dancing Congress of Vienna: Playing for Denmark's Future*, ed. Ole Villumsen Krog and Preben Ulstrup, 182–96, Copenhagen: Christiansborg Slot.

Fukuyama, Francis (1992), *The End of History and the Last Man*, New York: Free Press.

Gedo, John E. (2002), "Pompeo Batoni's Allegory of Peace and War," *The Burlington Magazine*, 144, 1195: 601–05.

Gee, Austin (2003), *The British Volunteer Movement, 1794–1814*, Oxford: Clarendon Press

Gee, Joshua (1738), *Trade and Navigation of Great-Britain Considered*, 4th edn, London: A. Bettesworth.

Gentz, Friedrich von ([1818] 1876), "Considérations sur le système politique actuellement établi en Europe", in *Dépêches inédites du chevalier de Gentz aux hospodars de Valachie*, ed. Anton Prokesch von Osten, 3 vols, vol. I, 354–79, Paris: Plon.

Gentz, Friedrich von (1802), *On the State of Europe before and after the French Revolution*, London: J. Hatchard.

Gert, Bernard (2010), *Hobbes: Prince of Peace*. Cambridge: Polity.

Ghervas, Stella (2008), *Rénventer la tradition: Alexandre Stourdza et l'Europe de la Sainte-Alliance*, Paris: Honoré Champion.

Ghervas, Stella (2014a), "La paix par le droit, ciment de la civilisation en Europe? La perspective du siècle des Lumières," in *Penser l'Europe au XVIIIe siècle: Commerce, Civilisation, Empire*, ed. Antoine Lilti and Céline Spector, 47–70, Oxford: Voltaire Foundation.

Ghervas, Stella (2014b), "Ten Lessons for Peace in Europe: From the Congress of Vienna and WWI, to the Failure of the G8," in *Multilateral Security Governance*, ed. Felix Dane and Gregory John Ryan, 212–27, Rio de Janeiro: Konrad-Adenauer-Stiftung.

Ghervas, Stella (2015), "The Long Shadow of the Congress of Vienna: From International Peace to Domestic Disorders," *Journal of Modern European History*, 15, 4: 458–64.

Ghervas, Stella (2017), "Balance of Power vs. Perpetual Peace: Paradigms of European Order from Utrecht to Vienna, 1713–1815," *The International History Review*, 39, 3: 404–25.

Ghervas, Stella (2019), "From the Balance of Power to a Balance of Diplomacy? Peace and Security in the Vienna Settlement", in *Securing Europe after Napoleon: 1815 and the New European Security Culture*, ed. Beatrice de Graaf, Ido de Haan and Brian Vick, 95–113, Cambridge: Cambridge University Press.

Ghervas, Stella (2020a), *Conquering Peace: From the Enlightenment to the European Union*. Cambridge, MA: Harvard University Press.

Ghervas, Stella (2020b), "Definitions of Peace 1815–1914," in *A Cultural History of Peace in the Age of Empire 1815–1914*, ed. Ingrid Sharp, 23–41, London: Bloomsbury.

Gibbon, Edward (1994), "General Observation on the Fall of the Roman Empire in the West," in *Decline and Fall of the Roman Empire*, Vol. 4, New York: Alfred A Knopf.

Gibbs, C. G. (1969), "The Revolution in Foreign Policy," in *Britain after the Glorious Revolution*, ed. Geoffrey Holmes, London: Macmillan.

Gimblett, Jennifer Leigh. (2011), "Painting and Propaganda: Napoleon and His Artists," PhD diss., University of Arizona, Tucson.

Godechot, Jacques (1983), *La Grande Nation. L'expansion révolutionnaire de la France dans le monde du 1789 à 1799*, 2nd edn., Paris: Aubier.

Goldstein, Joshua S. (2001), *War and Gender*, Cambridge: Cambridge University Press.

Grainger, John D. (2004), *The Amiens Truce: Britain and Bonaparte, 1801–1803*, Woodbridge: Boydell & Brewer.

Green, Karen (2014), *A History of Women's Political Thought in Europe, 1700–1800*, Cambridge: Cambridge University Press.

Gross, Louis (1948), "The Peace of Westphalia, 1648–1948," *American Journal of International Law*, 42, 1: 20–41.

Grotius, Hugo ([1603] 2006), *Commentary on the Law of Prize and Booty*, ed. M. J. v. Ittersum, Indianapolis: Liberty Fund.

Grotius, Hugo ([1625] 2005), *The Rights of War and Peace*, ed. Richard Tuck, 3 vols., Indianapolis: Liberty Fund.

Gruner, W. D. (2014), *Der Wiener Kongress 1814/15*, Stuttgart: Reclam.

Gudlaugsson, Sturla. (1959–60), *Geraert ter Borch*, 2 vols., The Hague: Martinus Nijhoff.

Gundling, Nicolaus Hieronymus (1734), *Ausführlicher Discours über die Natur- und Völcker-Recht*, 2nd edn., Frankfurt & Leipzig.

Gundling, Nicolaus Hieronymus (1757), *Erörterung der Frage: ob wegen der anwächsenden Macht der Nachbarn man Degen entblösössen könne?*, Frankfurt & Leipzig.

Hafez, Kai (2010), *Radicalism and Political Reform in the Islamic and Western Worlds*. Cambridge: Cambridge University Press.

Hare, Francis (1711a), *The Management of a War in a Letter to a Tory Member*, London: A. Baldwin.

Hare, Francis (1711b), *The Negociations for a Treaty of Peace, in 1709*, London: A. Baldwin.

Haslam, Jonathan (2002), *No Virtue like Necessity: Realist Thought in International Relations since Machiavelli*, New Haven, CT: Yale University Press.

Hassall, Arthur (1896), *The Balance of Power, 1715–1789*, New York: Macmillan.

Hassner, Pierre (1961), "Les concepts de guerre et de paix chez Kant," *Revue française de science politique* 11, 642–70.

Hazard, Paul (1963), *La Pensée européene du XVIIIe siècle*, Paris: Libraire Arthème Fayard.

Hébié, Mamadou (2015), *Souveraineté territoriale par traité. Une étude des accords entre puissances colonials et entités politiques locales*, Paris: PUF.

Heilbron, John (1995), *The Rise of Social Theory*, Cambridge: Polity.

Hinsley, F. H. (1967), *Power and the Pursuit of Peace: Theory and Practice in the History of Relations between States*, Cambridge: Cambridge University Press.

Hobbes, Thomas ([1640] 1969), *The Elements of Law Natural and Politic*, ed. Ferdinand Tönnies, London: Frank Cass.

Hobbes, Thomas ([1642] 1998), *On the Citizen*, eds. Richard Tuck and Michael Silverthorne, Cambridge University Press.

Hobbes, Thomas ([1651] 1991), *Leviathan*, ed. Richard Tuck, Cambridge University Press.

Hobbes, Thomas ([1651] 1994), *Leviathan with selected variants from the Latin edition of 1668*, ed. Edwin Curley, Indianapolis, IN: Hackett Publishing.

Hobbes, Thomas ([1651] 1996), *Leviathan*, intr. and ed. by J. C. A. Gaskin, Oxford University Press.

Hobbes, Thomas ([1651] 2012), *Leviathan*, ed. Noel Malcolm, Oxford: Clarendon Press, 3 vols.

Hobson, J. M. (2009), "Provincializing Westphalia: The Eastern Origins of Sovereignty", *International Politics*, 46, 6: 671–90.

Höffe, Otfried (2006), *Kant's Cosmopolitan Theory of Law and Peace*, trans. Alexandra Newton, Cambridge: Cambridge University Press.

Holbraad, Carsten (1970), *The Concert of Europe: A study in German and British international theory 1815–1914*, London: Longman.

Holmes, Stephen (1984), *Benjamin Constant and the Making of Modern Liberalism*, New Haven, CT: Yale University Press.

Hont, Istvan (2005) *Jealousy of Trade. International Competition and the Nation-State in Historical Perspective*, Cambridge, MA: Harvard University Press

Hont, Istvan (2005a), "Jealousy of Trade: An Introduction," in Istvan Hont, *Jealousy of Trade: International Competition and the Nation-State in Historical Perspective*, Cambridge, MA: The Belknap Press of Harvard University Press.

Hont, Istvan (2005b), "The 'Rich Country-Poor Country' Debate in Scottish Political Economy," in Istvan Hont, *Jealousy of Trade: International Competition and the Nation-State in Historical Perspective*, Cambridge, MA: The Belknap Press of Harvard University Press.

Hont, Istvan (2006), "The Early Enlightenment Debate on Commerce and Luxury," in *The Cambridge History of Eighteenth-Century Political Thought*, ed. Mark Goldie and Robert Wokler, Cambridge: Cambridge University Press.

Hont, Istvan (2007), "The Rich Country-Poor Country Debate Revisited: The Irish Origins and French Reception of the Hume Paradox," in *Hume's Political Economy*, ed. Margaret Schabas and Carl Wennerlind, London: Routledge.

Hoogensen, Gunhild (2005), *International Relations, Security and Jeremy Bentham*, Abingdon: Routledge.

Howard, Michael (2000), *The Invention of Peace: Reflections on War and International Order*, London: Profile Books.

Howard, Michael (2008), *War and the Liberal Conscience*, London: Hurst & Company.

Hughes, Edward (1956), ed., *Letters of Spencer Cowper, Dean of Durham, 1746–74*, Durham: Surtees Society, vol. CLXV.

Hume, David ([1752] 1994), "Of the Jealousy of Trade," in *Political Essays*, ed. Haakonssen Knud, Cambrifge: Cambridge University Press.

Hume, David ([1778] 1983) *The History of England from the Invasion of Julius Caesar to the Revolution in 1688*, 6 vols., Indianapolis, IN: Liberty Fund.

Hume, David (1985), *Essays Moral Political and Literary*, Eugene F. Miller ed. Indianapolis, IN: Liberty Classics.

Hume, David (1994a), "Of Public Credit," in *Political Essays*, ed. Knud Haakonssen, Cambridge: Cambridge University Press.

Hume, David (1994b), "Of the Balance of Power," in *Political Essays*, ed. Knud Haakonssen, Cambridge: Cambridge University Press.

Hume, David (1994c), "Of the Balance of Trade," in *Political Essays*, ed. Knud Haakonssen, Cambridge: Cambridge University Press.

Hume, David (1994d), "Of the Rise and Progress of the Arts and Sciences," in *Political Essays*, ed. Knud Haakonssen, Cambridge: Cambridge University Press.

Hume, David (1994e), "Of the Jealousy of Trade," in *Political Essays*, ed. Knud Haakonssen, Cambridge: Cambridge University Press.

Hurrell, Andrew (1990) "Kant and the Kantian paradigm in international relations", *Review of International Studies*, 16: 183–20.

Idris, Murad (2014), "Alternative Political Theologies: Erasmus on Peace, Speech, and Necessity," *Theory & Event*, 17, 4.

Idris, Murad (2019), *War for Peace: Genealogies of a Violent Ideal in Western and Islamic Thought*. Oxford: Oxford University Press.

Ingle, H. Larry (1994), *First among Friends: George Fox and the Creation of Quakerism*, New York: Oxford University Press.

Iovleva, Lidiya, ed. (1997), *Ekaterina Velikaya i Moskva: k 850-letiyu Moskvy posvyashaetsya*, Moscow: Tretyakovskaya galereya.

Jackson, Roy (2011), *Mawlana Mawdudi and Political Islam: Authority and the Islamic State*. New York: Routledge.

Janis, Mark Weston (2010), *America and the Law of Nations 1776–1939*. Oxford: Oxford University Press.

Jarrett, Mark (2013), *The Congress of Vienna and Its Legacy: War and Great Power Diplomacy After Napoleon*, London: I.B. Tauris.

Jennings, Judi (2006), *Gender, Religion, and Radicalism in the Long Eighteenth Century: The "Ingenious Quaker" and Her Connections*. Hampshire: Ashgate.

Jimack, Peter (2015), "Coconuts, Spice and Sugar: Indolence, Energy and Social Interaction in l'*Histoire des deux Indes*," in *Raynal's Histoire des Deux Indes, Colonialism, Networks and Global Exchange*, ed. Cecil Courtney and Jenny Mander, Oxford: Voltaire Foundation.

Johnson, Dorothy (1993), *Jacques-Louis David. Art in Metamorphosis*, Princeton, NJ: Princeton University Press.

Jones, D. W. (1988), *War and Economy in the Age of William III and Marlborough*, London: Basil Blackwell.
K'ang Youwei (1958), *Ta T'ung Shu: The One-World Philosophy of K'ang Yu-wei*, trans. Laurence G. Thompson. London: George Allen.
Kames, Henry Home, Lord (1774), *Sketches of the History of Man*, 2 vols., Edinburgh: W. Creech.
Kant, Immanuel ([1784] 1970), *Political Writings*, ed. H. S. Reiss, Cambridge: Cambridge University Press.
Kant, Immanuel ([1784] 2006), "An Answer to the Question: What Is Enlightenment?", in *Toward Perpetual Peace and Other Writings on Politics, Peace, and History*, ed. Pauline Kleingeld, 17–23, New Haven, CT: Yale University Press.
Kant, Immanuel ([1790] 1991) *The Critique of Judgement*, trans. James Creed Meredith, Oxford: The Clarendon Press.
Kant, Immanuel ([1795] 1970), *Political Writings*, ed. H. S. Reiss, Cambridge: Cambridge University Press.
Kant, Immanuel ([1795] 1983), *Perpetual Peace and Other Essays*, ed. Ted Humphrey Indianapolis: Hackett.
Kant, Immanuel ([1795] 1991), "Perpetual Peace. A Philosophical Sketch", in *Kants Political Writings*, H. S. Reiss, 2nd enlarged edn. Cambridge: Cambridge University Press.
Kant, Immanuel ([1795] 2006), "Toward Perpetual Peace: A Philosophical Sketch", in *Toward Perpetual Peace and Other Writings on Politics, Peace, and History*, ed. Pauline Kleingeld, 67–109, New Haven, CT: Yale University Press.
Kant, Immanuel ([1798] 1992) *The Conflict of the Faculties*, trans. Mary J. Gregor Lincoln: University of Nebraska Press.
Kant, Immanuel (1902–19) *Kant's gesammelte Schriften, Herausgegeben von der königlich preussischen Akademie der Wissenschaften*, Berlin: Walter de Gruyter.
Kant, Immanuel (1991a), "Idea for a Universal History with a Cosmopolitan Purpose," in *Kant's Political Writings*, ed. H. S. Reiss, 2nd enlarged edn., Cambridge: Cambridge University Press.
Kant, Immanuel (1991b), "On the Common Saying: 'This may be True in Theory, but It does not apply in Practice'," in *Kant's Political Writings*, ed. H. S. Reiss, 2nd enlarged edn., Cambridge: Cambridge University Press.
Kant, Immanuel (1991c), "Perpetual Peace: A Philosophical Sketch," in *Kant's Political Writings*, ed. H. S. Reiss, 2nd enlarged edn., Cambridge: Cambridge University Press.
Kant, Immanuel (1996a) *Religion and Rational Theology*, trans. and ed. Allen W. Wood and George di Giovanni, Cambridge: Cambridge University Press.
Kant, Immanuel (1996b), *Practical Philosophy*, ed. Mary J. Gregor, Cambridge: Cambridge University Press.
Kant, Immanuel (1997), *Lectures on Ethics*, eds. Peter Heath and J. B. Schneewind Cambridge: Cambridge University Press.
Kant, Immanuel (2007), *Anthropology, History and Education*, ed. Günter Zöller and Robert B. Louden, Cambridge: Cambridge University Press.
Kapossy, Béla, Isaac Nakhimovsky, and Richard Whatmore, eds. (2017), *Commerce and Peace in the Enlightenment*, Cambridge: Cambridge University Press.
Kayaoglu, Turan (2010), *Legal Imperialism: Sovereignty and Extraterritoriality in Japan, the Ottoman Empire, and China*, Cambridge: Cambridge University Press.
Kettering, Alison McNeil (1998), "Gerard ter Borch's Swearing of the Oath of Ratification of the Treaty of Münster as Historical Representation," in Klaus Schilling and Heinz Bussmann, eds., *1648: War and Peace in Europe*, Münster: Westfälisches Landesmuseum.

Khan, Aga (1918), *India in Transition: A Study in Political Evolution*, London: Philip Lee Warner.
Kippis, Andrew (1783), *Considerations upon the Provisional Peace Treaty with America and the Preliminary Articles of Peace with France and Spain*, 2nd edn., London: T. Cadell.
Kolla, Edward James (2017), *Sovereignty, International Law and the French Revolution*, Cambridge: Cambridge University Press.
Koskenniemi, Martti (2001), *The Gentle Civilizer of Nations: the Rise and Fall of International law 1870–1960*, Cambridge: Cambridge University Press.
Koskenniemi, Martti (2005), *From Apology to Utopia: The Structure of International Legal Argument*, Cambridge: Cambridge University Press.
Koskenniemi, Martti (2008), "Into Positivism: Georg Friedrich von Martens (1756–1821) and Modern International Law," *Constellations*, 15: 189–207.
Krook, Dorothea (1959), *Three Traditions of Moral Thought*. Cambridge: Cambridge University Press.
Langford, Paul (1989), *A Polite and Commercial People: England, 1727–1783*, Oxford:
Leibniz, G. W. (1988), *Political Writings*, ed. Patrick Riley, Cambridge: Cambridge University Press.
Leibniz, Gottfried Wilhelm (1988a), "Mars Christianissimus", in *Political Writings* ed. Patrick Riley, 119–45, Cambridge: Cambridge University Press.
Lesaffer, Randall (2002), "The Grotian Tradition Revisited: Change and Continuity in the History of International Law," *British Yearbook of International Law*, 73: 103–39.
Lloyd, Henry (1771), *An Essay on the Theory of Money*, London: J. Almon.
Locke, John ([1664] 1997), "Essays on the Law of Nature", in *John Locke, Political Essays*, ed. Mark Goldie, Cambridge: Cambridge University Press.
Locke, John ([1690] 1984), *Two Treatises of Government*, ed. Mark Goldie, London: Everyman's.
London Peace Society (1823), *Annual Report of the Committee of the Society for the Promotion of Permanent and Universal Peace for 1823*, London: London Peace Society.
London Peace Society (1824), *Annual Report of the Committee of the Society for the Promotion of Permanent and Universal Peace for 1824*, London: London Peace Society.
London Peace Society (1825), *Annual Report of the Committee of the Society for the Promotion of Permanent and Universal Peace for 1825*, London: London Peace Society.
Luard, Evan (1992), *The Balance of Power: The System of International Relations, 1648–1815*, New York: St. Martin's Press.
Lyttelton, George (1739), *Farther Considerations on the Present State of Affairs, at Home and Abroad*, London: T. Cooper.
MacGilvray, Eric (2011), *The Invention of Market Freedom*, Cambridge: Cambridge University Press.
Macintosh, Sir James (1828), *A Discourse on the Study of the Law of Nature and Nations*, 2nd edn, London: Goode.
MacLachlan, A. D. (1969), "The Road to Peace, 1710–1713," in *Britain after the Glorious Revolution*, ed. Geoffrey Holmes, London: Macmillan.
Macleod, Emma Vincent (1998), *A War of Ideas: British Attitudes to the Wars against to the Wars Against Revolutionary France, 1792–1802*, Aldershot: Ashgate, 1998.
Macmillan, Ken (2006), *Sovereignty and Possession in the English New World. The Legal Foundations of Empire 1576–1640*, Cambridge: Cambridge University Press.
Macpherson, C. B. ([1962] 2011), *The Political Theory of Possessive Individualism. Hobbes to Locke*, New edn, Oxford: Oxford University Press.
Maine, Henry Sumner (1888), *International Law*, London: John Murray.

Malettke, Klaus (2001), "Les traités de paix de Westphalie et l'organisation politique du Saint Empire romain germanique," *Dix-huitième siècle*, 210, 1: 113–44.

Malynes, Gerard (1629), *Consuetudo vel lex mercatoria, or The Antient Law-Merchant*, London.

Mandeville, Bernard ([1729] 1924), *The Fable of the Bees: Or, Private Vices, Publick Benefits*, ed. F. B. Kaye, Oxford: Oxford University Press.

Marin, Louis (1988), *Portrait of the King*, trans. Martha Houle, Minneapolis, MN: University of Minnesota Press.

Martin, Gregory (2011), *Rubens in London: Art and Diplomacy*, London: Harvey Miller Publishers.

Martens, Georg Friedrich de (1820), *Nouveau recueil des traités. . .tome IV (1808–1819)*, Göttingen: Dieterich.

Martens, George Frédéric de (1821), *Précis du droit des gens moderne de l'Europe*, 3ème édition, Göttingen: Dieterich.

Martens, Georg Friedrich von (1796), *Einleitung in das positive europäische Völkerrecht auf Verträge und Herkommen gegründet*, Göttingen: Dieterich.

Maurseth, Per (1964), "Balance of Power Thinking from the Renaissance to the French Revolution," *Journal of Peace Research*, 1: 120–36.

May, Larry (2013), *Limiting Leviathan: Hobbes on Law and International Affairs*. Oxford: Oxford University Press.

Mazower, Mark (2009), *No Enchanted Palace. The End of Empire and the Ideological Origins of the United Nations*, Princeton, NJ: Princeton University Press.

McBride, Ian (1998), *Scripture Politics: Ulster Presbyterianism and Irish Radicalism in the Late-Eighteenth Century*, Oxford: Clarendon Press.

McKanan, Dan (2002), *Identifying the Image of God: Radical Christians and Nonviolent Power in the Antebellum United States*, Oxford: Oxford University Press.

Melon, Jean-François (1738), *A Political Essay upon Commerce*, trans. David Bindon, Dublin: Philip Crampton.

Mikkeli, Heikki (1998), *Europe as an Idea and an Identity*, London: MacMillan Press.

Millar, John ([1771] 2006), *The Origins of the Distinction of Ranks: Or, An Inquiry into the Circumstances Which Give Rise to Influence and Authority in the Different Members of Society*, ed. Aaron Garrett, Indianapolis: Liberty Fund.

Millen, Ronald Forsyth and Robert Erich Wolf. (1989), *Heroic Deeds and Mystic Figures. A New Reading of Rubens' Life of Maria de' Medici*, Princeton, NJ: Princeton University Press.

Mirabeau, Victor Riquetti, marquis de (1756), *L'ami des homes, ou traité de la population*, Avignon: s. n.

Mirkine-Guetzévitch, Boris (1928), "L'influence de la révolution française sur le développement du droit international dans l'Europe orientale," *Receuil des cours de l'Académie de la Haye*, 22: 295–458.

Mitchell, Leslie (1992), *Charles James Fox*, Oxford: Clarendon Press

Mitzen, Jennifer (2013), *Power in Concert: The Nineteenth-Century Origins of Global Governance*, Chicago: The University of Chicago Press.

Molloy, Charles ([1676] 1722), *De jure maritimo et navali: or a Treatise of Affairs Maritime and of Commerce in Three Books*, London: T. Waller.

Montesquieu, Charles-Louis de Secondat ([1748] 1949), *The Spirit of the Laws*, trans. Thomas Nugent, New York: Hafner.

Montesquieu, Charles-Louis de Secondat (1989), *The Spirit of the Laws*, trans. and ed. Anne M. Cohler, Basia C. Miller, and Harold S. Stone, Cambridge: Cambridge University Press.

Montesquieu, Charles-Louis de Secondat (1999), *Considerations on the Causes of the Greatness of the Romans and Their Decline*, trans. David Lowenthal, Indianapolis, IN: Hackett.
Morgenthau, Hans J. (1961), *Politics among Nations: The Struggle for Power and Peace*, New York: Alfred A. Knopf.
Mori, Jenifer (2000), *Britain in the Age of the French Revolution*, London: Pearson
Mori, Massimo (2004), *La pace e la ragione Kant e le relazioni internazionali: diritto, politica, storia*, Bologna: Il Mulino.
Morris, Matthew Robinson (1777), *Peace the Best Policy*, 2nd edn., London: J. Almon.
Murphy, Andrew (2016), *Liberty, Conscience, and Toleration: The Political Thought of William Penn*. Oxford: Oxford University Press.
Muthu, Sankar (2012), "Conquest, Commerce, and Cosmopolitanism in Enlightenment Political Thought," in *Empire and Modern Political Thought*, ed. Sankar Muthu, Cambridge: Cambridge University Press.
Nakhimovsky, Isaac (2011), "The 'Ignominious Fall of the European Commonwealth': Gentz, Hauterive, and the Debate of 1800", *Collegium: Studies Across Discipline in the Humanities and Social Sciences*, 10: 212–28.
Nakhimovsky, Isaac (2017), "The Enlightened Prince and the Future of Europe: Voltaire and Frederick the Great's Anti-Machiavel of 1740," in *Commerce and Peace in the Enlightenment*, ed. Béla Kapossy, Isaac Nakhimovsky, and Richard Whatmore, Cambridge: Cambridge University Press.
Nussbaum, Felicity A. (1984), *The Brink of All We Hate: English Satires on Women, 1660–1750*, Lexington: The University Press of Kentucky.
O'Brien, David. (2006), *After the Revolution: Antoine-Jean Gros, Painting and Propaganda Under Napoleon*, University Park: Pennsylvania State University Press.
Onnekink, David (2016), "Pride and Prejudice: Universal Monarchy Discourse and the Peace Negotiations of 1709–1710," in *Performances of Peace: Utrecht 1713*, ed. Renger E. de Bruin, Cornelis van Haven, Lotte Jensen, and David Onnekink, Amsterdam: Brill.
Osiander, Andreas (2001), "Sovereignty, International Relations, and the Westphalian Myth," *International Organization*, 55, 2: 251-87.
Pagden, Anthony (1995), *Lords of All the World: Ideologies of Empire in Spain, Britain, and France, c. 1500 – c. 1800*, New Haven, CT: Yale University Press.
Paine, Tom (1791), *Rights of Man: Being an Answer to Mr. Burke's Attack on the French Revolution*, London: J. Parsons.
Paine, Tom (1792), *Rights of Man. Part the Second. Combining Principle and Practice*, London: J. S. Jordan.
Parliamentary Debates (1742), *The History and Proceedings of the House of Commons from the Restoration to the Present Time*, Vol. 9, London: Richard Chandler.
Parson, Kenneth A.C. (1984), ed., *The Church Book of the Independent Church . . . Isleham, 1693–1805*, Cambridge: Cambridgeshire Antiquarian Records Society, vol. VI.
"Peace and Friendship Treaty of Utrecht between Spain and Great Britain" (Treaty of Utrecht) (1713), Art. II: https://en.wikisource.org/wiki/Peace_and_Friendship_Treaty_of_Utrecht_between_Spain_and_Great_Britain.
"Peace Treaty between the Holy Roman Emperor and the King of France and their respective Allies" (Treaty of Westphalia) (1648): http://avalon.law.yale.edu/17th_century/westphal.asp.
Penn, William (1693), *An Essay towards the Present and Future Peace of Europe, by the Establishment of an European Dyet, Parliament, or Estates*, London: Randal Taylor.

Piirimäe, Partel (2010), "The Westphalian Myth and the Idea of External Sovereignty," in *Sovereignty in Fragments: The Past, Present and Future of a Contested Concept*, ed. Hent Kalmo and Quentin Skinner, 64–80, Cambridge: Cambridge University Press.

Pinker, Steven (2011), *The Better Angels of Our Nature: Why Violence Has Declined*, New York: Viking.

Pocock, J. G. A. (1975), *The Machiavellian Moment: Florentine Political Thought and the Atlantic Republican Tradition*, Princeton, NJ: Princeton University Press.

Pocock, J. G. A. (1997), "What Do We Mean by Europe?" *The Wilson Quarterly*, 21: 12–29.

Pocock, J. G. A. (1999a), *Barbarism and Religion*, vol. 1: *The Enlightenments of Edward Gibbon, 1737–1764*, Cambridge: Cambridge University Press.

Pocock, J.G.A. (1999b), *Barbarism and Religion*, vol. II: *Narratives of Civil Government*, Cambridge: Cambridge University Press.

Polišensky, Josef V. (1970), "Comenius, the Angel of Peace, and the Netherlands in 1667," *Acta Comeniana*, 1: 59–66.

Polišensky, Josef V. (1979), "The Social and Political Premises of the Work of J.A. Comenius," *Acta Comeniana*, 4: 5–26.

Porteus, Beilby (1779), *A Sermon Preached before the Lords Spiritual and Temporal, . . . February 10, 1779*, London: T. Payne.

Poulain de la Barre, François ([1673] 1990), *The Equality of the Sexes*, trans. with an introduction and notes Desmond M. Clarke, Manchester: Manchester University Press.

Pownall, Thomas (1774), *The Administration of the British Colonies*, 2 vols, London: J. Walter.

Price, Jacob M. (1996), "English Merchants and War at Sea, 1689–1783," in Price, *Overseas Trade and Traders: Essays on Some Commercial, Financial, and Political Challenges Facing British Atlantic Merchants, 1660–1775*, Aldershot: Ashgate.

Price, Richard (1780), *An Essay on the Population of England, from the Revolution to the Present Time*, 2nd edn., London: T. Cadell.

Pufendorf, Samuel ([1667] 2007), *The Present State of Germany*, ed. Michael J. Seidler, trans. Edmund Bohun, Indianapolis: Liberty Fund.

Pufendorf, Samuel ([1674] 1994), "On the Law of Nature and of Nations," in *The Political Writings of Samuel Pufendorf*, ed. and trans. Craig L. Carr and Michael J. Seidler, Oxford University Press.

Pufendorf, Samuel ([1678] 1990]), *De Statu Hominum Naturali: The 1678 Latin Edition and English Translation*, ed. Michael Seidler, Lewiston/Queenston/Lampeter: E. Mellen Press.

Pufendorf, Samuel ([1688] 1934), *De Jure Naturae et Gentium Libri Octo*, ed., James Brown Scott, trans. Charles Henry Godfather, Washington, DC: Carnegie Endowment for International Peace.

Pufendorf, Samuel (2013), *An Introduction to the History of the Principal Kingdoms and States of Europe*, trans. Jodocus Crull, Indianapolis: Liberty Fund.

Reddie, James (1851), *Inquiries in International Law Public and Private*, 2nd edn., Edinburgh: Blackwood.

Riley, James (2014), *The Seven Years' War and the Old Regime in France: The Economic and Financial Toll*, Princeton: Princeton University Press.

Riley, Patrick (1974), "The Abbé de St. Pierre and Voltaire on Perpetual Peace in Europe," *World Affairs*, 137, 3: 186–94.

Riley, Patrick (1994), "Introduction," in François de Salignac de la Mothe Fénelon, *Telemachus, Son of Ulysses*, ed. Riley, Cambridge: Cambridge University Press.

Robertson, William (1769), *The History of the Reign of the Emperor Charles V*, 3 vols, London: William Strahan and Thomas Cadell.

[Roscoe, William] (1808), *Considerations on the Causes, Objects, and Consequences of the Present War, and on the Expediency or the Danger of Peace with France*, London: J. M'Creery.

Rose, J. H. (1909), "Great Britain and the Dutch Question in 1787–1788," *The American Historical Review*, 14, 2: 262–83.

Rosecrance, Richard N. (1963), *Action and Reaction in World Politics: International Systems in Perspective*, Boston: Little, Brown & Company.

Rosenblatt, Helena (2003), "Commerce et religion dans le libéralisme de Benjamin Constant," *Commentaire*, 26: 415–26

Rosenthal, Lisa. (2005), *Gender, Politics, and Allegory in the Art of Rubens*, New York: Cambridge University Press.

Rothkrug, Lionel (1965), *Opposition to Louis XIV: The Political and Social Origins of the French Enlightenment*, Princeton, NJ: Princeton University Press.

Rousseau, Jean-Jacques ([1755] 1984), *A Discourse on Inequality*, trans. Maurice Cranston, Harmondsworth: Penguin.

Rousseau, Jean-Jacques ([1762] 1958), *The Social Contract*, trans. Maurice Cranston, Harmondsworth: Penguin.

Rousseau, Jean-Jacques ([1781] 1986), *On the Origin of Language*, trans. John H. Moran and Alexander Gode, Chicago, IL: University of Chicago Press.

Rousseau, Jean-Jacques (1915), *The Political Writings of Jean Jacques Rousseau*, ed. C. E. Vaughn, 2 vols., Cambridge University Press.

Rousseau, Jean Jacques (1964), *Œuvres Complètes III, Du contrat social, Écrits politiques*, ed. Bernard Gagnebin and Marcel Raymond, Paris: Bibliothèque de la Pléiade.

Rousseau, Jean-Jacques (1985), *The Government of Poland*, trans. Willmoore Kendall, Indianapolis: Hackett.

Rousseau, Jean-Jacques (1991), "Abstract and Judgement of Saint-Pierre's Project for Perpetual Peace," in *Rousseau on International Relations*, ed. Stanley Hoffman and David P. Fidler, Oxford: Clarendon Press.

Rousseau, Jean Jacques (1997a), *The Discourses and Other Early Political Writings*, ed. Victor Gourevitch, Cambridge University Press.

Rousseau, Jean-Jacques (1997b), *The "Social Contract" and Other Later Political Writings*, ed. Victor Gourevitch, Cambridge: Cambridge University Press.

Rousseau, Jean-Jacques (2008a), "Extrait de paix perpétuelle", in Rousseau, *Ecrits sur la paix perpetuelle*, ed. Blaise Bachofen and Céline Spector, Paris: Vrin.

Rousseau, Jean-Jacques (2008b), "Jugement sur la paix perpétuelle," in Rousseau, *Ecrits sur la paix perpetuelle*, ed. Blaise Bachofen and Céline Spector, Paris: Vrin.

Rousseau, Jean-Jacques (2008c), "Principes du droit de la guerre," in *Ecrits sur la paix perpetuelle*, ed. Blaise Bachofen and Céline Spector, Paris: Vrin.

Russett, Bruce (1993), *Grasping the Democratic Peace: Principles for a Post-Cold War World*. Princeton, NJ: Princeton University Press.

Saint-Pierre, Charles Castel ([1712] 1717), Mémoire du projet pour rendre la paix perpetuelle (pour le ministre M. de Torcy, 1 septembre, 1712), *Projet pour rendre la paix perpetuelle entre les Souverains Chretiens*, Utrecht: Schouten.

Saint-Pierre, Charles Irénée Castel, Abbé de ([1713] 1986), *Project pour rendre la paix perpétuelle en Europe*, Paris: Fayard

Saint-Pierre, Charles-Irénée, Abbé de (1714), *A Project for settling an Everlasting Peace in Europe*, London: J. Watts.

Saint-Pierre, Charles-Irénée, Abbé de (1719), *Discours sur la polysynodie*, Amsterdam: Du Villard et Changuin.

Saint-Pierre, Abbé de (1729), *Abregé du projet de paix perpetuelle*, Rotterdam: Beman.
Saint-Simon, comte de ([1814] 1925), *De la Réorganisation de la société européenne* ed. Alfred Pereire, Paris: Les Presses universitaires françaises.
Saward, Susan. (1982), *The Golden Age of Marie de' Medici*, Studies in Baroque Art History, 2, Ann Arbor, Michigan: UMI Research Press.
Schiffer, Walter (1954), *The Legal Community of Mankind*, New York: Columbia University Press.
Schmitt-Maaß, Christoph, Stefanie Stockhorst, and Doohwan Ahn, ed. (2014), *Fénelon in the Enlightenment: Traditions, Adaptations, and Variations*, Amsterdam: Rodopi.
Schneewind, J. B. (2009), "Good out of Evil: Kant and the Idea of Unsocial Sociability," in *Kant's Idea for a Universal History with a Cosmopolitan Aim: A Critical Guide*, ed. Amelie Oksenberg Rorty and James Schmidt, Cambridge: Cambridge University Press.
Schofield, Philip (2009), *Utility & Democracy: The Political Thought of Jeremy Bentham*, Oxford University Press.
Schröder, Meinhard (1999), *350 Jahre Westfälischer Friede. Verfassungsgeschichte, Staatskirchenrecht, Völkerrechtsgeschichte*, Berlin: Duncker & Humblot.
Schröder, Peter (2017), *Trust in Early Modern International Thought, 1598–1713*, Cambridge: Cambridge University Press.
Schroeder, Paul W. (1994), *The Transformation of European Politics, 1763–1848*, Oxford: Clarendon Press.
Schuurman, Paul (2012), "Fénelon on Luxury, War and Trade in the Telemachus," *History of European Ideas* 38, 2: 179–99.
Schwoerer, Lois G. (1974), *"No Standing Armies!": The Antiarmy Ideology in Seventeenth-Century England*, Baltimore, MD: The Johns Hopkins University Press.
Scott, Hamish (2001), *The Emergence of the Eastern Powers, 1756–75*, Cambridge: Cambridge University Press.
Sheehan, Michael (1996), *The Balance of Power: History and Theory*, London: Routledge.
Shelburne, 2nd Earl of, William Petty, 1st Marquis of Lansdowne (1783), *The Speech of the Right Honourable the Earl of Shelburne, in the House of Lords, on Monday, February 13, 1783, on the Articles of Peace*, Ipswich: Charles Punchard.
Shelburne, 2nd Earl of, William Petty, 1st Marquis of Lansdowne (1790), *The Substance of the Speech of the Marquis of Lansdowne, in the House of Lords, on the 14th of December, 1790; On the Subject of the Convention with Spain, which was Signed on the 28th of October, 1790*, London: J. Debrett.
Sheridan, Eugene R., ed. (1993), *The Papers of Lewis Morris*, vol. 3, 1738–1746, Newark, NJ: New Jersey Historical Society, vol. 26.
Sheriff, Mary D. (1996), *The Exceptional Woman. Elisabeth Vigée-Lebrun and the Cultural Politics of Art*, Chicago and London: The University of Chicago Press.
Smith, Adam ([1759] 1976), *The Theory of Moral Sentiments*, ed. D. D. Raphael and A. L. Macfie, Oxford: Clarendon Press.
Smith, Adam ([1776] 1999), *The Wealth of Nations*, ed. Andrew Skinner, Harmondsworth: Penguin.
Somerville, Thomas (1996), *My Own Life and Times, 1741–1814*, ed. Richard B. Sher, Bristol: Thoemmes Press.
Spector, Céline (2008), "Le Projet de paix perpétuelle: de Saint-Pierre à Rousseau,", in Jean-Jacques Rousseau, *Principes du droit de la guerre: écrits sur la paix perpétuelle*, ed. Blaise Bachofen, Céline Spector et al., 229–94, Paris: Vrin.
Spinoza, Baruch ([1677] 2000), *Political Treatise [Tractatus Politicus]*, trans. Samuel Shirley, Indianapolis, IN: Hackett.

St. John, Henry, Viscount Bolingbroke (1932), *Bolingbroke's Defence of the Treaty of Utrecht, being Letters VI-VIII of the Study and Use of History*, ed. G. M. Trevelyan, Cambridge: Cambridge University Press.

Stauber, Reinhard (2014), *Der Wiener Kongress*, Vienna: Böhlau.

Steuart, Sir James (1767), *An Inquiry into the Principles of Political Oeconomy*, 2 vols, London: A. Millar and T. Cadell.

Stollberg-Rilinger, Barbara (1986) *Der Staat als Machine. Zur politischen Metaphorik des absolutischen Fürstenstaats*, Berlin: Duncker & Humblot.

Stollberg-Rilinger, Barbara (2013), *Das Heilige Römische Reich Deutscher Nation: Vom Ende des Mittelalters bis 1806*, Munich: C. H. Beck.

Stråth, Bo (2016), *Europe's Utopias of Peace: 1815, 1919, 1951*, London: Bloomsbury.

Swift, Jonathan (1712), *The Examiner*, 16 January.

Swift, Jonathan (1916), *The Conduct of the Allies*, ed. C. B. Wheeler, Oxford: The Clarendon Press.

Synod of Ulster (1890–98), *Records of the General Synod of Ulster, from 1691 to 1820*, 3 vols., Belfast: Archer and Sons.

Te Brake, Wayne P. (2017), *The Religious War and Religious Peace in Early Modern Europe*, Cambridge: Cambridge University Press.

Teschke, Benno (2003), *The Myth of 1648: Class, Geopolitics, and the Making of Modern International Relations*, London: Verso.

Terjanian, Anoush Fraser (2013), *Commerce and Its Discontents in Eighteenth-Century French Political Thought*, Cambridge: Cambridge University Press.

Theibault, John (1994), "Jeremiah in the Village: Prophecy, Preaching, Pamphlets, and Penance in the Thirty Years' War," *Central European History*, 27, 4: 441–60.

Thompson, Andrew C. (2011), "Balancing Europe: Ideas and Interests in British Foreign Policy," in *Ideology and Foreign Policy in Early Modern Europe*, ed. David Onnekink and Gijs Rommelse, Farnham: Ashgate.

Thoyras, Rapin de (1744), *The History of England*, trans. Nicholas Tindal, London: John & Paul Knapton.

Tibbutt, H. G. (1976), ed., *The Minutes of the First Independent Church (Now Bunyan Meeting) at Bedford, 1656–1766*, Bedford: Bedfordshire Historical Record Society, vol. 55.

Todorov, Tzvetan (1984), *The Conquest of America. The Question of the Other*, trans. Richard Howard, New York: Harper & Row.

Tomaselli, Sylvana (2001), "The Most Public Sphere of All: The Family", in *Women and the Public Sphere: Writing and Representation, 1700–1830*, ed. Elizabeth Eger, Charlotte Grant, Cliona O. Gallchoir and Penny Warburton, Cambridge: Cambridge University Press.

Tomaselli, Sylvana (2006), "The Spirit of Nations", in *The Cambridge History of Eighteenth-Century Political Thought*, ed. Mark Goldie and Robert Wokler, Cambridge: Cambridge University Press.

Tomaselli, Sylvana (2012), "Mary Wollstonecraft: The Reunification of Domestic and Political Spheres", in *Geschlechterordnung und Staat. Legitimationsfiguren der politischen Philosophie (1600–1850)*, ed. Marion Heinz and Sabine Doyé, Berlin: Akademie Verlag.

Tomaselli, Sylvana (2015), "On Labelling Raynal's *Histoire*: Reflections on its Genre and Subject", in *Raynal's Histoire des Deux Indes, Colonialism, Networks and Global Exchange*, ed. Cecil Courtney and Jenny Mander, 73–87, Oxford: Voltaire Foundation.

Tomaselli, Sylvana (2016), "Reflections on Inequality, Respect and Love in the Political Writings of Mary Wollstonecraft", in *The Moral and Political Thought of Mary Wollstonecraft*, ed. Alan Coffee and Sandrine Berge, 14–33, Oxford: Oxford University Press.

Toulmin, Joshua (1776), *The American War Lamented*, London: J. Johnson.

Tourme-Jouannet, Emmanuelle ([2013] 2014), "Des origins coloniales du droit international: A propos du droit des gens moderne au 18ème siècle," in *The Roots of International law. Liber amicorum Peter Haggenmacher*, ed. Pierre-Marie Dupuy and Vincent Chetail, 649–72, Leiden: Nijhoff.

Trenchard, John and Thomas Gordon (1995), *Cato's Letters: Or, Essays on Liberty, Civil and Religion, and Other Important Subjects*, ed. Ronald Hamowy, Vol. 2, Indianapolis: Liberty Fund.

Tuck, Richard (1993), *Philosophy and Government, 1572–1651*, Cambridge: Cambridge University Press.

Tuck, Richard (1999), *The Rights of War and Peace: Political Thought and the International Order from Grotius to Kant*, Oxford: Clarendon Press.

Van der Linden, W.H. (1987), *The International Peace Movement, 1815–1874*, Amsterdam: Tilleul Publications.

Vattel, Emer de ([1760] 2008), *Mélanges de Littérature, de Morale et de Politique*, eds., Béla Kapossy and Richard Whatmore, *History of European Ideas* 34:1.

Vattel, Emer de (2008), *The Law of Nations, Or, Principles of the Law of Nature, Applied to the Conduct and Affairs of Nations and Sovereigns, with Three Early Essays on the Origin and Nature of Natural Law and on Luxury*, ed. Béla Kapossy and Richard Whatmore, Indianapolis: Liberty Fund.

Vick, Brian E. (2014), *The Congress of Vienna: Power and Politics after Napoleon*, Cambridge, MA: Harvard University Press.

Vidal, Mary (2000), "David's *Telemachus and Eucharis*: Reflections on Love, Learning, and History," *The Art Bulletin*, 82 (4): 702–29.

Vitoria, Francisco de (1991), "Relection on the American Indians, 1539," in *Vitoria, Political Writings*, ed. Anthony Pagden Anthony and Jeremy Lawrence, Cambridge University Press.

Voltaire (François-Marie Arouet) (1770) "De la paix perpétuelle par le docteur Goodheart," in *L'Evangile du Jour*, London [i. e., Amsterdam]: Marc-Michel Rey.

Voltaire (François-Marie Arouet) ([1761] 2005), *Rescript of the Emperor of China on the Occasion of the Plan for Perpetual Peace*, in Rousseau. *The Plan for Perpetual Peace, On the Government of Poland, and Other Writings on History and Politics*, trans. Christopher Kelley and Judith Bush. Hanover, NH: Dartmouth College Press.

Voltaire (François-Marie Arouet) (1827), *Œuvres complètes de Voltaire avec des remarques et des notes historiques, scientifiques et littéraires*, Vol. II: *Annales de l'empire*, Paris: Delangle Frères.

Ward, Robert (1795), *An Enquiry into the Foundation and History of the Law of Nations from the Time of the Greeks and the Romans to the Age of Grotius*, 2 vols., London: Butterworth.

Warner, Marina (1983), *Joan of Arc: The Image of Female Heroism*, Harmondsworth: Penguin.

Watanabe-O'Kelly, Helen (2010), *Beauty Or Beast?: The Woman Warrior in the German Imagination from the Renaissance to the Present Day*, Oxford: Oxford University Press.

Weddle, Meredith Baldwin (2001), *Walking in the Way of Peace: Quaker Pacifism in the Seventeenth Century*. Oxford: Oxford University Press.

Weinbrot, Howard D. (1988) "The Rape of the Lock and the Contexts of Warfare", in *The Enduring Legacy: Alexander Pope Tercentenary Essays*, ed. G.S. Rousseau and Pat Rogers, 21–48, Cambridge: Cambridge University Press.

Welch, David (2005), "Painting, Propaganda and Patriotism" in *History Today*, 55, 7: 42–50.

Wesley, Charles H. (1917), "The Struggle for the Recognition of Haiti and Liberia as Independent Republics," *Journal of Negro History*, 2: 369–83.

Whatmore, Richard (2012), *Against War and Empire: Geneva, Britain, and France in the Eighteenth Century*, New Haven, CT: Yale University Press.

White, R. S. (2008), *Pacifism and English Literature: Minstrels of Peace*. London: Routledge MacMillan.

Wilson, Arthur McCandless (1936), *French Foreign Policy during the Administration of Cardinal Fleury, 1726–1743: A Study in Diplomacy and Commercial Development*, Cambridge, Massachusetts: Harvard University Press.

Wilson, Jasper (1793), *Letter, Commercial and Political; Addressed to the Rt. Hon. William Pitt in which the Real Interests of Britain, in the Present Crisis, are Considered, and Some Observations are Offered on the General State of Europe*, London: G. G. J. and J. Robinson.

Wilson, Kathleen (1995), *The Sense of the People: Politics, Culture, and Imperialism in England, 1715–1785*, Cambridge: Cambridge University Press

Winch, Donald (1996), *Riches and Poverty. An Intellectual History of Political Economy in Britain, 1750–1834*, Cambridge University Press.

Winchester, Angus L. (1994), ed., *The Diary of Isaac Fletcher*, Kendal: Cumberland and Westmorland Antiquaries and Archaeological Society, extra series, vol. XXVII

Wolf, John B. (1970), *Toward a European Balance of Power, 1620–1750*, Chicago: Rand McNally.

Wolff, Christian ([1749] 1934), *Jus gentium methodo scienitifica pertractatum*, trans. J. H. Drake, Oxford: Clarendon Press.

Wollstonecraft, Mary ([1790; 1792] 1995) *A Vindication of the Rights of Woman*, in *A Vindication of the Rights of Men and A Vindication of the Rights of Woman and Hints*, ed. Sylvana Tomaselli, Cambridge: Cambridge University Press.

Wollstonecraft, Mary ([1794] 1989), *An Historical and Moral View of the Origin and Progress of the French Revolution*, in *The Works of Mary Wollstonecraft*, ed. Janet Todd and Marilyn Butler, 7 Vols. Vol 6, London: William Pickering.

Wollstonecraft, Mary ([1798] 1989), "Introductory To A Series of Letters on the Present Character of the French Nation," in *The Works of Mary Wollstonecraft*, ed. Janet Todd and Marilyn Butler, 7 Vols., Vol 6, London: William Pickering.

Worcester, Noah [Philo Pacificus] ([1814] 1816). *A Solemn Review of the Custom of War; Showing That War is the Effect of Popular Delusion and Proposing a Remedy*. Cambridge, MA: Hilliard and Metcalf.

Worcester, Noah [Philo Pacificus] (1817), *The Friend of Peace*. Greenfield, MA: Ansel Phelps.

Wyvill, Christopher (1774–1802), *Political Papers*, 6 vols., York: W. Blanchard.

Yoder, John Howard (2009), *Christian Attitudes to War, Peace, and Revolution*. Grand Rapids: Brazos Press.

Yonan, Michael (2011), *Empress Maria Theresa and the Politics of Habsburg Imperial Art*, University Park, PA: The University of Pennsylvania Press.

Yovel, Yirmiahu (1980), *Kant and the Philosophy of History*. Princeton, NJ: Princeton University Press.

Ypi, Lea (2014) "Commerce and Colonialism in Kant's Philosophy of History," in Katrin Flikschuh and Lea Ypi, eds., *Kant and Colonialism. Historical and Critical Perspectives*, 99–126, Oxford: Oxford University Press.

Ziegler, Karl-Heinz ([2004] 2008), "The Peace Treaties of the Ottoman Empire with European Christian Powers," in Ziegler, *Fata Iuris Gentium. Kleine Schriften zur Geschichte des europäischen Völkerrechts*. Baden-Baden: Nomos.

Ziegler, Valarie H. (2001), *The Advocates of Peace in Antebellum America*. Macon, GA: Mercer University Press.

Zielonka, Jan (2007), *Europe as Empire: The Nature of the Enlarged European Union* Oxford: Oxford University Press.

Zielonka, Jan (2014), *Is the EU Doomed?* Cambridge: Polity Press.

CONTRIBUTORS

Doohwan Ahn is Associate Professor of International History at Seoul National University. He was a Radcliffe-Yenching Joint Fellow at Harvard University in 2017–18. He is the co-editor of *Fénelon in the Enlightenment: Traditions, Adaptations, and Variations* (2014). He is currently working on the political economy of post-1688 Britain.

David Armitage is the Lloyd C. Blankfein Professor of History at Harvard University. Among his publications are *The Ideological Origins of the British Empire* (2000), *The Declaration of Independence: A Global History* (2007), *Foundations of Modern International Thought* (2013) and *Civil Wars: A History in Ideas* (2017).

Theodore Christov is Associate Professor of History and International Affairs at George Washington University. He is the author of *Before Anarchy: Hobbes and his Critics in Modern International Thought* (2015). He is currently working on a study of the intellectual history of self-determination since the Enlightenment.

Stephen Conway is a Professor of History at University College London. Among his publications are *The British Isles and the War of American Independence* (2000), *War, State, and Society in Mid-Eighteenth-Century Britain and Ireland* (2006), *Britain, Ireland, and Continental Europe in the Eighteenth Century: Similarities, Connections, Identities* (2011) and *Britannia's Auxiliaries: Continental Europeans and the British Empire, 1740-1800* (2017).

Stella Ghervas is Professor of Russian History at Newcastle University and an Associate of the Department of History at Harvard University. Among her publications are *Réinventer la Tradition: Alexandre Stourdza et l'Europe de la Sainte-Alliance* (2008), *Lieux d'Europe: Mythes et limites* (co-ed., 2008), and *Conquering Peace: From the Enlightenment to the European Union* (2020). She is currently working on a new history of the Black Sea from the Russian expansion to the present day.

Murad Idris is Assistant Professor of Political Theory at the University of Virginia. He is the author of *War for Peace: Genealogies of a Violent Ideal in Western and Islamic Thought* (2018) and co-editor of *The Oxford Handbook of Comparative Political Theory* (forthcoming).

Martti Koskenniemi is Professor of International Law at the University of Helsinki. Among his publications are *From Apology to Utopia. The Structure of International Legal Argument* (1989/2005) and *The Gentle Civilizer of Nations. The Rise and Fall of International law 1870-1960* (2001). He is now working on a history of the legal imagination as applied to international power.

Jennifer Milam is Professor of Art History at the University of Melbourne. Her books include *Women, Art and the Politics of Identity in Eighteenth-Century Europe* (2003),

Fragonard's Playful Paintings (2007), *Historical Dictionary of Rococo Art* (2011), and *Beyond Chinoiserie* (2018). Her next book addresses cosmopolitan ideals in garden spaces.

Anthony Pagden is Distinguished Professor of Political Science and History at the University of California, Los Angeles. His most recent publications are *The Enlightenment and Why It Still Matters* (2012) and *The Burdens of Empire* (2015). He is completing a study of the idea of a unified Europe from 1815 until the present.

Sylvana Tomaselli is the Sir Harry Hinsley Lecturer in History at St John's College, Cambridge. Among her publications are *Rape* (co-ed., 1986), *The Dialectics of Friendship* (co-ed., 1989) and Mary Wollstonecraft, *A Vindication of the Rights of Men, and A Vindication of the Rights of Woman* (ed., 1995).

Richard Whatmore is Professor of Modern History and director of the Institute of Intellectual History at the University of St Andrews. He is the author of *Republicanism and the French Revolution: An Intellectual History of Jean-Baptiste Say's Political Economy* (2000), *Against War and Empire: Geneva, Britain, and France in the Eighteenth Century* (2012) and *What is Intellectual History?* (2015).

INDEX

absolute sovereignty 6, 135
Achenwall, Gottfried 145–6
Achilles in Vietnam ix
Aga Khan 82
agency
   human 50, 83–4
   moral 36
   political 41
Ahmadiyya movement, South Asia 85
Ahn, Doohwan 175 (*see also* chapter 7)
Aix-la-Chapelle, Treaty of (1748) 121, 128, 147
Alecto 92
Alexander I of Russia 18
Alexander the Great and Thalestris, Queen of the Amazons (painting) 55
allegory
   art and 88–9
   Baroque 89–92
Allegory on the Victory of Catherine the Great over Turks and Tatars (painting) 96, 97
Amazons 54–6
American Independence, War of (1774–83) 106, 109–11, 116
American Revolution (1765–1783) 82–3
   peace societies 82–3, 84, 105
Amiens, treaty of (1802) 16, 114
Angel of Peace 76
Anglo–French Alliance (1716–31) 127
Anjou, Philippe Duc d' 118
Anna Ivanovna of Russia 15, 127
Anne of Austria 119
Anne of England 15, 127
antagonism 81
anti-war movements xi
anti-war sentiments 105, 110
Antin, Marquis d' 126
arbitration 105, 138
Armitage, David 175 (*see also* Introduction)
art
   allegory and 88–9
   diplomacy and 92, 151n.6
   peace and portraiture 99–101
   the politics of peace and 89–92

l'art de la paix (the Art of Peace) 2
arts and sciences, diminishing levels of violence and 65, 67
Augsburg, League of (1689) 112, 118, 121
Augustus 8
Austria
   War of Austrian Succession (1740–48) 13, 15, 99, 106, 107, 112, 125, 127
   Habsburg dynasty 7, 11, 12, 16, 21, 93, 99–100
authority, sovereign 43
autonomy 35, 36
Les aventures de Télémaque, fils d'Ulysse 124
Aztec empire 146

Bacchus 92
Baden, Treaty of (1714) 125
balance of powers 10–12, 18, 21, 25, 31, 118–27, 129, 134, 135, 136, 147
   "Of the Balance of Power" 128
Barclay, Robert 76
Batoni, Pompeo 87–8, 102
Becker, Johann Gottlieb 3
Bellers, John 106, 124
beneficence 26
benevolence 46
Bentham, Jeremy 53, 111, 143–4
Besse, Joseph 106
The Better Angels of Our Nature: Why Violence Has Declined ix
Black, William 112
Blois, Countess of 54
Blood, Fanny 63
Blumenbach, Johann Friedrich 146
Bodin, Jean 8
Bolingbroke, Viscount *see* St. John, Henry 122–3, 125
Bolotov, A.T. 97
Bonaparte, Napoleon 16, 34, 103–4, 137
Borch, Gerard ter 6, 89, 90, 91
Bourbon dynasty 11, 12
Bourgogne, Duc de 117, 124, 125

Bradley, James 110
Brède, Baron de la. *See* Montesquieu
Britain
   Anglo–French Alliance (1716–31) 127
   ascendancy of 128–9, 140
   the balance of power and 120, 121–3
   colonialism and 11
   commerce and integration 140–4
   conditions of peace in 141
   the cost of wars 122
   financial crisis (1797) 113
   Glorious Revolution (1688–89) 11, 112
   London Peace Society 105, 111, 115–16
   Netherlands and 11
   pacifism in 105–6
Burke, Edmund 112, 130–1
Burke, William 111

Callières, François de 125, 134
Campbell, John 127
Carlos II of Spain 120
Carthage 28
Cartwright, John 109
Castel, Charles-Irénée. *See* Saint-Pierre, Abbé de
Catherine I of Russia 15
Catherine II of Russia (the Great) 15, 87, 95–8
Catherine the Great in the Guise of Minerva, Patroness of Art (painting) 95–6
Cato's Letters 127
Cavendish, Margaret 54, 57–62
Ceadel, Martin 110
Ceres 92
Chapelain, John 54
Charlemagne 8
Charles I of England 91, 92
Charles I of Spain 93
Charles II of England 11, 121, 122
Charles II of Spain 11
Charles V, Holy Roman Emperor 8, 10
"A Child-bed Womans Funeral Oration" 61
childbirth 61, 63
China 78
chivalry 54
Christianity
   converting pagans of the New World 144
   Hobbes and 73–4
   humanity and xii
   integration and 147
   Latin 3, 8, 9, 12

   pacifism and 72
   peace and 84
   rational Christians 113
   wars and 106
Christov, Theodore 175 (*see also* chapter 2)
Cicero 1, 23
citizen soldiers 109
La Citta delle dame (Book of the City of Ladies) 56
De Cive 37, 39–41, 42
civil society 145
civil wars 61
civilization, violence and 68–9
civilizing process 125
civilizing rhetoric 145
civitas maxima 23–4
Clausewitz, Carl von 34
Codex Iuris Gentium Diplomaticus 42
Coke, Roger 38
colonialism 11, 71, 133, 145, 146 (*see also* imperialism)
Comenius, John Amos 76, 79
commerce (*see also* trade)
   the balance of power and 127
   the "Continental system" 1806–07 114
   diminishing levels of violence and 67
   dire consequences of 129
   doux commerce 14, 140
   globalization and 29
   integration and 140–4
   with native communities 144–5
   politics and 126
   power and 127, 142
   violence and 67
   war, peace and 14, 26–30, 44, 50, 111, 113, 126, 130, 139, 142
common law 141
commonwealths 35, 41, 44, 45, 46, 47, 142
Concert of Europe 119
Concordia 57
Congress System (1815–1823) 18
"Conjectural Beginning of Human History" 81
conscience, pacifism and 85
conscientious objection 72, 82, 86
Considérations sur les causes de la grandeur des Romains et de leur décadence 121
Constant, Benjamin 27–9, 149n.8
Continental System (1806–07) 114
Du contrat social; ou Principes du droit politique 129

INDEX

Conway, Stephen 175 (*see also* chapter 6)
Conybear, John 107
Cookson, J.E. 113, 114
Cornbury, Viscount, Henry Hyde 122
cosmopolitan law 137
Cowper, William 84
Crimean War 105
criminality of war 85
Critique of Pure Reason 136
Cromwell, Oliver 121–3
culture peace and 4

Dahomey, Kingdom of 54
Dastarnamah 85
Davenant, Charles 12, 121–2
David, Jacques-Louis 102–3
deaths, caused by wars 20
debt, wars and 122, 128, 129
Déclaration du droit des gens 140
Declaration from the Harmless and Innocent People of God, called Quakers, against all Plotters and Fighters in the World 76
"The Declaration of Pillnitz" (1791) 16
Declaration of the rights of nations 137
Defoe, Daniel 123
degeneracy 69
Delian League 32
democratic peace theory 32
deterrence policies xii, 129
Diderot, Denis 29
difference, the management of 82
diplomacy
    integration and 147
    Peace of Westphalia and 21
    Rubens and 92, 151n.6
    war and peace as 48
    warlike of the 18c. 136
Discours Physique et Moral de l'Egalité des deux Sexes, ou l'on voit l'Importance de se défaire des Préjugez 62
Dissertation on War and Peace 81
Dodge, David Low 82–3, 84–5
dominium, right of 37
doux commerce 14, 140
Dover, Secret Treaty of (1670) 121
Le droit des gens; ou Principes de la loi naturelle 53, 128, 136
Dubos, Abbé 94, 95
Dutch Republic. *See* Netherlands
Dutch Wars (1672–78) 11
On Duties 1

economic naturalism 139
economic prosperity, peace and 77, 78 (*see also* commerce; trade)
economics, natural law of 143
economy(ies)
    economic warfare 114
    monetary 142
    political economy 108
Eden, William 130
education
    pacifism and 76, 79
    of women 66
effeminacy 53, 63, 64–5, 68, 69
Eighty Years' War (1568–1648) between Spain and the Dutch Republic 89
Eirene 19, *20*, 57
The Elements of Law 43
Elizabeth of Russia 15
emasculation, peace and 63, 70
Émile 42, 64
England. *See* Britain
enlightened absolutism 135
Enlightenment
    peace and the 1, 3–4, 12–16, 21
    Scottish 108
    Utrecht Enlightenment 12, 118
    wars and 118
    Westphalian Enlightenment 10
equality, principle of 45
Erasmus, Desiderius 22
De l'esprit des lois 67, 125, 139
Essai politique sur le commerce 126
An Essay on the History of Civil Society 68
Essay on the Origin of Language 49
An Essay Toward the Present and Future Peace of Europe 1, 14, 77
Essays upon I. The Ballance of Power. II. The Right of Making War, Peace, and Alliances. III. Universal Monarchy 121
ethnography 146
European league of states 26, 124
European Republic of States 12
European unification 14
European Union 33, 119, 138, 140
Extract of the Plan for Perpetual Peace 138

families, natural sovereignty of 47
al-Fatawa al-Hindiyya (Indian Legal Opinions) 85
fear
    among nations 139
    the establishment of states and 47

Felipe IV of Spain 120
Felipe V of Spain 118
Fénelon, François 117–18, 124–5, 127
Ferguson, Adam 68–9, 108, 129
financial crisis
   Britain 113
   France 150n.16
Fleury, André-Hercule de 125
food crises, war and 114
foreign policy 48
Fox, Charles James 112
Fox, George 76, 77
France (*see also* names of monarchs)
   Anglo–French Alliance (1716–31) 127
   anti-Habsburg foreign policy of 93
   the ascendancy of 119–20, 122–3
   becoming a "civilised monarchy" 125
   emasculation and effeminacy in 63
   financial crisis 150n.16
   French Revolution (1789–99) 16–17, 33–4, 66, 112
   French Revolutionary Wars (1792–1802) 1, 14, 111–15, 116
   Germany and 120
   Netherlands and 120
   Salic law 92
   Sweden and 119–20
   from universal monarchy to European nation 137–40
Franklin, Benjamin 145
Frederick II of Prussia (the Great) 87, 96, 99, 127–8, 129
Friedrich Wilhelm I of Prussia 127–8
The Friend of Peace (periodical) 84
Friends of Peace 115

Gee, Joshua 126
gender
   conventions and female sovereigns 99
   peace, war and xi
   and the representation of peace 87–8, 95, 101
   virtues and 64, 67
Gentz, Friedrich von 21, 147
geometric method 135
George I of Great Britain 127
Germany
   France and 120
   peace under the law of nature and of nations 135–7
   Third Reich 6
   wars of religion 9

Ghervas, Stella 175 (*see also* Introduction)
Gibbon, Edward 131
globalization, commerce and 29
Glorious Revolution (1688–89), Britain 11, 121
Glover, Jonathan ix
Godwin, Mary (Shelley) 63, 74
Goldsmith, Oliver 129
Gordimer, Nadine viii
Gordon, Thomas 127
Gouges, Olympe de 63, 67
government
   human 133
   systems of 31, 32
Grand Design 25, 31
Graneri, Pietro 88
"Great Discoveries" 8
Great Northern War (1700–21) 127
Great Powers 5, 32, 34, 133, 145
Grégoire, Abbé 137, 140
Gros, Antoine-Jean 103, 104
Grotius, Hugo 8, 9, 36, 37, 133
la guerre en dentelles 14
Gulliver's Travels 74
Gundling, Hieronymus 136
Guyon, Abbé 54

Habsburg dynasty 7, 11, 12, 16, 21, 93, 99–100
Handel, G. F. 3
Hardouin-Mansart, Jules 93
Harley, Robert 121
Hartley, David 111
Henri IV of France 25, 92 (*see also* Sully, duc de)
Hercules unter denen Amazonen (Hercules Amongst the Amazons) 56
Histoire de mon temps 128
Histoire des Amazonnes Anciennes et Modernes 54
Histoire des deux Indes (History of the Two Indies) 29, 64, 145
History of England 54, 121
History of the Rise and Fall of the Roman Empire 131
Hobbes, Thomas 8, 22–3, 28, 35, 37–41, 42–3, 44–5, 48–9, 72–4, 134
Holbach, Paul-Henri d' 140
Holy Roman Empire 5, 8, 10, 16, 89, 99–100, 135
human agency 50, 83–4
human nature 28
humanism 84

humanity xii, 22–3, 144
Humanity: A Moral History of the Twentieth Century ix
Hume, David 29, 54, 125, 126, 128, 129, 142
Hyde, Henry. *See* Cornbury, Viscount

Idea for a Universal History with a Cosmopolitan Aim 51, 79, 80–1
idleness 65
Idris, Murad 175 (*see also* chapter 4)
Illustrious Women 56
imbecility 46
Imlay, Fanny 63
imperialism, violence and 72 (*see also* colonialism)
India in Transition 82
India, Sunni Islam 85
De Indis 36, 37
industry, safety of states and 138 (*see also* commerce; trade)
inequality 49
Innocent X, Pope 10
integration 133, 134, 138, 140–4, 145, 147–8
inter-state relations 21, 134
International Arbitration League 105
international law 21, 137, 143–4
international relations 42, 43, 50, 129, 135–6
international systems, types of 117–18
International Workman's Peace Association 105
internationalism 77
interpersonal relations 41
Intervention of the Sabine Women (painting) 103
An Introduction to the History of the Principal Kingdoms and States of Europe 119
Irish volunteers 109
De iure belli ac pacis 36, 133

Jacobite rebellion (1745–46) 108
Jacobites 106
James II of England 11, 121, 122
James, William viii
jealousy, among nations 139
Joan of Arc 54
Johnson, Dorothy 103
Johnson, Samuel 54
Joseph I, Holy Roman Emperor 123
Joseph II, Holy Roman Emperor 99, 130
Jubilate 3
Judgment on Perpetual Peace 138
De jure maritimo et navali 141

jurisprudence, natural 36
jus gentium 43, 45
justice 1

Kames, Lord 108
K'ang Youwei 81, 85
Kant, Immanuel 2, 3, 13, 14, 30–4, 50–1, 53, 79–80, 119, 136–7, 150n.13
Karl VI, Holy Roman Emperor 123, 127
Khwushhal Khan 85
The King Governs by Himself, 1661 (painting) 94, 95
Knowles, Mary 82
Koskenniemi, Martti 175 (*see also* chapter 8)

La Beaumelle, Laurent Angliviel de 128–9
Lafitau, Joseph-François 69
land-grabs, by Europeans 145
language (*see also* linguistic difference)
language, humans and 49
The Law of Nations or Principles of the Law of Nature, applied to the Conduct and Affairs of Nations and Sovereigns 24–5
law(s)
  common law 141
  cosmopolitan law 137
  inter-state relations and 134–5
  international law 21, 137, 143–4
  law of continuity (*lex continuo*) 33
  law of Europe 140
  law of nations 12, 13, 22, 30–1, 43, 44, 45, 83, 135–7, 141, 147
  natural law 49–50, 73–4, 106, 133, 135–7, 141–2, 143, 144, 145
  natural-law theory 22, 23, 24, 41, 43–4, 46
  prize law 145
  Salic law 92, 99
  Treasonable Practices Act and the Seditious Meetings Act 113
Le Brun, Charles 93, 95
Leibniz, Gottfried Wilhelm 19, 25, 26, 42
Lenape people 101
Leo III, Pope 8
Leopold I, Holy Roman Emperor 121
The Letters of Valens 111
Letters on the Study and Use of History 122
Leviathan 38, 43, 55, 72–4
liberal democracies 32
Liberal Party 105
liberty, war and 109

linguistic difference, war and 81 (*see also* language)
Liverpool, Lord 115
Locke, John 141–2
The London Journal 127
London Peace Society 105, 111, 115–16
Louis XIII of France 93
Louis XIV of France 10–11, 12, 93, 94, 99, 112, 118, 119, 120, 121, 122, 124, 126, 152n.6
Louis XVI of France 16, 150n.16
love, war and 54, 56
Lubki 98
luxury 69, 139
Lyttelton, George 126

Machiavellianism 134
Mackintosh, James 143
The Maid of Orléans (Schiller) 54
Maine, Henry Sumner 19, 34
Malinovsky, Vasily 81
Malynes, Gerard 140–1
Mandeville, Bernard 29, 47
De la manière de négociér avec les Souverains 125
Marat, Jean-Paul 16
Maria Theresa of Austria 15, 87, 93, 99–101
Mariana of Austria 120
maritime capture 143
Maron, Anton von 100
Mars 87, 92, 94, 95, 98
Martens, Georg Friedrich von 137, 140, 147
Mary II of England 15
masculinity 68
Massachusetts Peace Society 82, 84, 105
Mazarin, Jules 119
The Mediator's Kingdom Not of this World, but Spiritual, Heavenly, and Divine 83
Medici cycle 93, 95
Medici, Marie de' 92–3, 94
Melon, Jean-François 126
Mémoire pour rendre la paix perpetuelle en Europe 138
Mémoires Secrets 89
Mennonites 105
Mercury 92
Metaphysics of Morals 31
Metternich, Klemens von 18
Mignard, Pierre 55
Milam, Jennifer 175–6 (*see also* chapter 5)
militarism 74
military, effeminacy of the 64–5

military service 108, 109
Millar, John 56, 68, 69
Milton, John 74
Minerva 57, 92, 94, 95, 97
Minerva Protects Pax from Mars (painting) 89, 90, 92
Mirabeau, Victor Riquetti, Marquis de 26
misogyny 55
modernity, global 139
Moeurs des Sauvages Amériquains 69
Molloy, Charles 141
monarchy *see also* names of individual monarchs
    monarchic states 133–4
    universal 117, 131, 134, 137–40
Montague, Mary Wortley 69
Montesquieu, Charles de Secondat de 14, 27, 63–4, 67, 121, 125–6, 139, 146
Montfort, Countess of 54
moral agency 36
moral community 140
moral corruption, peace and 53
moral regeneration, through military service 109
morality, politics and 137
Morris, Matthew Robinson 111
multi-polarity, international system of 118
Münster, Treaty of (1648) 6, 7, 10, 71, 91, 135

Napoleon on the Battlefield of Eylau (painting) 103–4
Napoleonic Empire, fall of 18 (*see also* Bonaparte, Napoleon)
nation-states 71
native peoples 144–6
natural law 49–50, 73–4, 106, 133, 135–7, 141–2, 143, 144, 145
natural-law theory 22, 23, 24, 41, 43–4, 46
natural man 48–9, 50
natural rights 36, 44
natural science 133
nature, state of 36, 39, 42–3, 73, 74, 142
naval captures 145
Netherlands
    Dutch dominance in overseas trade 121
    Dutch realism 89–92
    Dutch revolt against Spain 37
    Dutch Wars (1672–78) 11
    England and 11
    France and 120
    United Netherlands 21, 37

INDEX

new order 147
New Testament, Matthew 5:9 1
New York Peace Society 82, 105
Nine Years' War (1688–97) 121

old regime 137, 140
Oman 71
One-World Philosophy 81
Orange, house of 11
"Oration against War" 60
"An Oration for Peace" 60
"An Oration for War" 59–60
Orations of Divers Sorts, Accommodated to Divers Places 57
Origins of the Distinction of Ranks 69
Osnabrück, Treaty of (1648) 7, 71
Ottoman Empire 78, 97, 133, 144, 153n.20

pacific league (*foedus pacificum*) 32
pacificist 106
pacifism
    beyond state boundaries 75–82
    in Britain 105–6
    Christianity and 72
    conscience and 85
    different strands of 72, 86
    differing understandings of xi
    education and 76, 79
    pacifist movements 14
    Quakers and 76–9, 82, 106–7
    religion and 75–6, 82–5
Pagden, Anthony 176 (*see also* chapter 1)
Paine, Thomas 130
Papacy, role in the Holy Roman Empire 10 (*see also* names of individual Popes)
Paradise Lost 74
Paris, Treaty of (1783) 130
passions 38
Pax 19, 57, 87
Pax deorum 19
Pax Napoleonica 16
Pax perpetua 25
Pax romana 19
peace
    the collapse of shared beliefs on 16–17
    as a cultural value 1
    negative views of 58, 108
    outside Europe 135, 144–6
    peace history viii
    peace movements xi, 82 (*see also* chapter 6)
    peace societies 82–3 (*see also* names of individual societies)

peace treaties 7, 21, 31 (*see also* names of individual treaties)
perpetual peace 20–2, 24, 25–6, 30, 31, 32
    representations of xi, 87–8, 89, 93–4, 95, 101, 104
    theologies of 82–5
    through war 58
Peace Bringing Back Abundance (painting) 60–1, 88, 89
Peace of Westphalia. *See* Westphalia, Peace of (1648)
Penn, William 1, 14, 77–9, 81, 101, 106, 124, 145
Pennsylvania 107
Permanent society 26
Perpetual Peace: a Philosophical Sketch 53, 136
Persian Letters 146
persons, natural and artificial 35, 36, 44
Peter I of Russia (the Great) 14, 97
Peter III of Russia 129
Petty, William 130
Philip IV of Spain. *See* Felipe IV of Spain 92, 93
Philip of Anjou 11
Philippa of Hainault 54
Philippe II, Duc d'Orléans 125
Physiocratic movement 139–40
Pinker, Steven ix, 5
Pitt, William (the Younger) 111, 112, 113, 114, 130
Pizan, Christine de 56
"A Plan for an Universal and Perpetual Peace" 53, 143
Pocock, J.G.A. 12, 54, 118
Poland
    First Partition of 87
    Second Partition of (1793) 119
    War of Polish Succession (1733–38) 13
policy-science 136
Polish–Lithuanian Commonwealth 131
politics
    commerce and 126
    modern 41
    morality and 137
    of peace 89–92
    political agency 41
    political economy 108
    political sovereignty 144
    political union 34
    states and 136
    women and 15
Pope, Alexander 56

Pope, the figure of 8 (*see also* names of individual popes)
Porteus, Beilby 109
Portrait of Empress Maria Theresa as a Widow 100
Portrait of Louis XIV 99
Poulain de la Barre, François 62
power
    balance of 10–12, 18, 21, 25, 31, 118–27, 129, 134, 135, 136, 147
    commerce and 127, 142
    English turn to the balance of 10–12
    of the Papacy 10
    right to assert power over one's enemy 37
Pownall, Thomas 142
Pragmatic Sanction 99, 127
Précis du droit des gens moderne de l'Europe fondé sur les traités et l'usage 137
The Present State of Europe 127
Price, Jacob 107
prize law 145
Projet pour rendre la paix perpétuelle en Europe ("Plan for making peace perpetual in Europe") 14, 25–6, 53, 138
property rights 37, 141, 142, 144
Protestant Reformation 8
Protestant religious groups 105
Protestantism 8, 107, 130
Prussia, rise of 15 (*see also* names of individual monarchs)
Public Celebration that was Held on the Khodynka Field on 19 July 1775 (print) 98
"Of Public Credit" 128
public life, women in 15–16
La Pucelle 54
La Pucelle d'Orléans (*The Maid of Orléans*) (Voltaire) 54
Pufendorf, Samuel von 22, 23, 44, 45–6, 47–8, 119–21, 135–6
punishment, right of 37
Puritans of New England 107
Pyrenees, Treaty of the (1659) 122

Quadruple Alliance 125
Quakers 14, 72, 76–9, 82–3, 101, 106–8, 109
Qutb, Sayyid 82, 85

racialism, European 146
Ramsay, Allan 15
The Rape of the Lock 56
The Ratification of the Treaty of Münster (painting) 6, 89, 90, 91
Raynal, Guillaume-Thomas-François 29, 64, 145
Rayneval, Gerard de 130
realism, Dutch 89–92
reason 138
Reddie, James 143
Reflections on the Revolution in France 112
Réflexions critiques sur la poésie et sur la peinture 94
relationships
    inter-state relations 21, 134
    international relations 42, 43, 50, 129, 135–6
    interpersonal relations 41
    between nations 23
    social relations 49
religion
    Mennonites 105
    non-Christian 78, 81
    non-European 85–6
    pacifism and 75–6, 82–5
    peace and 71
    Protestant religious groups 105
    Protestantism 8, 107, 130
    Quakers 14, 72, 76–9, 82–3, 101, 106–8, 109
    reconciliation between the Catholic and Protestant factions 14
    religious liberty 77
    religious strife 135
    sovereignty and 73
    Sunni Islam 85
    Unity of the Brethren 76
    war and 10, 21, 72, 73, 74, 81, 106
    Wars of Religion 8–9, 20
Religious Society of Friends. *See* Quakers
representation, war and 34
republics 32, 136–7, 150n.13
De rerum humanarum emendatione consultatio catholica (General Consultation on the Reform of Human Affairs) 76
Rescript of the Emperor of China on the Occasion of the Plan for Perpetual Peace 78
resistance, conscientious objection as 86 (*see also* conscientious objection)
Richard, Henry 105
Rigaud, Hyacinthe 99

rights
    individual 36, 37
    of man 32
    of native peoples 145
    natural 36, 44
    negative rights 10
    of persons to govern themselves 35
    property rights 37, 141, 142, 144
    right of conquest 144
    three fundamental 37
    of women 66
Riquetti, Victor. *See* Mirabeau, Victor Riquetti, Marquis de 26
"Of the Rise and Progress of the Arts and Sciences" 125
Robertson, William 108
Robespierre, Maximilien de 16
Rockingham Whigs 112–13
Roman Empire 8, 19, 28
Roscoe, William 114
Rousseau, Jean-Jacques 14, *15*, 22, 26, 29, 38, 42, 48–9, 50, 64, 128, 129, 131, 138–9, 146
Rubens, Peter Paul 89, 90, 91–2, 93, 151n.6
Russia (*see also* names of monarchs)
    entry into the European political arena 14
    inclusion of in peace plans 78
    Russian Empire 129
    Westernization reforms 97
Ryswick, Treaty of (1697) 117

Saint Domingue 148
Saint Petersburg, Treaty of (1762) 129
Saint-Pierre, Abbé de 14, 16, 25–6, 53, 119, 124, 125, 137–8, 139
Saint-Simon, Henri de 26
Salic law 92, 99
Schiller, Friedrich 54
Schuppen, Pieter Louis van 57
science, natural 133
Scudéry, Madeleine de 56
Second Discourse 49
Second Treatise of Government 141
secularism 8, 12
security dilemma xii, 124
self-determination 81, 140
self-interest 47
self-love 46, 47, 50
self-preservation, principle of 36, 41, 44, 45, 46, 47–8, 50
self-protection 135
Senate system 138

Sermon on the Mount 1
Seven Years' War (1756–63) 15, 99, 107, 109, 128, 129, 142, 145
sex, war and 54, 56
Shay, Jonathan ix
Shelburne, 2nd Earl of 130
Shelley, Mary 63, 74
Skeptics 36
slavery
    condemnation of 69
    foreign trade and 146
    Seven Years' War and 109
    the slave trade 67
    women as slaves 63, 67, 70
sluggishness 59, 63, 65, 70
Smith, Adam 68, 142–3
sociability 22, 23, 38–9, 46, 47, 49–50, 51, 133, 134
    unsocial sociability 50, 131
social contract 39
social relations 49
socialitas 47
societies
    the formation of 23–5
    Permanent society 26
Society for the Promotion of Permanent and Universal Peace 105
A Solemn Review of the Custom of War 83, 84
solitude 38
South Asia, Ahmadiyya movement 85
Southey, Robert 54
sovereignty
    absolute 6, 135
    concept of 134
    of families 47
    peace and 92–8
    political 144
    religion and 73
    state 35, 37, 134
    war and 43
    Westphalia and 5
Spain
    Dutch revolt against 37
    France and 120
    Wars of Spanish Succession (1701–14) 12, 112, 117, 122, 123–4, 145
Spice Islands 144
The Spirit of the Laws 146
St. John, Henry 122, 123
Staël, Germaine de 64
state of nature 36, 39, 42–3, 73, 74, 142

"The State of War" 48
states
    domestic theory of the state 41
    early modern theories of 35
    establishment of 47, 135
    European league of states 26, 124
    European Republic of States 12
    federation of free states 137
    inter-state relations 21, 134
    monarchic 133–4
    nation-states 71
    peace and 147
    peace/pacifism beyond state boundaries 75–82
    political system of 136
    the safety of 138
    sovereignty of 35, 37, 134
    sovereign nation-states 71
    violence and 73
status quo ante 12
Steuart, James 108, 110
Strutt, William 115
Stuart dynasty 107, 108
suffering 61
Sufism 85
Sully, duc de 25, 31, 78, 152n.6
Sunni Islam, India 85
Sweden, France and 119–20
Swift, Jonathan 74, 75, 123
Swiss Confederation 21

Taj al-'Arus 85
The Tale of a Tub 75
Talestri regina delle Amazzoni (Talestri, Queen of the Amazons) 56
taxation 111, 113, 114, 122
Te Deum 3
teleology, hazards of 5
theologies, of peace 82–5
Thirty Years' War (1618–48) 1, 9, 20, 89, 135
Thoyras, Rapin de 121
throne and altar, alliance of 7, 8
Thulden, Theodor van 4
Tilsit, treaty of (1807) 16
Tomaselli, Sylvana 176 (*see also* chapter 3)
Torelli, Stefano 95–6
Toulmin, Joshua 110, 111
Toward perpetual peace, a philosophical project 14, 30, 79, 81
trade
    balance of power and 126–7, 129
    Dutch dominance in overseas 121
    economic warfare and 114
    era of Protestantism in trade 130
    free trade 126, 139, 142
    peace and 139, 140, 141
    safety of states and 138
    slavery and 67, 146
    wars and 14, 27, 29, 113
Trade and Navigation of Great-Britain considered 126
Trafalgar, battle of 114
Treasonable Practices Act and the Seditious Meetings Act 113
Trenchard, John 127
Triple Alliance 121
Turkey 138

uni-polarity, international system of 117
United States. *See* American Independence, War of; American Revolution
Unity of the Brethren 76
universal monarchy 117, 131, 134, 137–40
unsociability 49
unsocial sociability 50, 131
utilitarianism 143
utility 136
"Utrecht Enlightenment" 12, 118
Utrecht, Treaty of (1713) 3, 12, *13*, 16, 25, 118, 121, 122, 125, 126, 134, 137–8

Vattel, Emer de 12, 21, 22–3, 24, 29–30, 31, 43, 45, 49–50, 53, 128, 136, 145
Vedomosty newspaper 98
Versailles 93–4
Vienna, Congress of (1814–15) 1, *17*, 71, 119, 134
Vigée-Lebrun, Elisabeth 60–1, 88–9, 102
A Vindication of the Rights of Woman 64, 65, 66
violence
    arts and sciences and 65, 67
    civilization and 68–9
    commerce and 67
    imperialism and 72
    Quakers and 76
    states and 73
virtues
    the commercial spirit and 139
    gender and 64, 67
    peace and 70
Volney, Constantin 140
Voltaire 7, 20, 25, 54, 78, 138

Wagner, Richard 56
Walpurgis, Maria Antonia 56
War and Peace (painting) 87–8
War Inconsistent with the Religion of Jesus Christ 83
"War" (poem) 74
Ward, Robert Plumer 143
war(s)
   Anglo–Dutch naval wars 120
   the case for 70
   civil wars 61
   colonialism and 11, 71
   commerce and 14, 26–30, 111, 113, 126, 130, 139, 142
   Crimean War 105
   criminality of 85
   debt and 122, 128, 129
   defensive 45
   as a divine punishment for national sins 109
   Dutch Wars (1672–78) 11
   economic warfare 114
   Eighty Years' War (1568–1648) between Spain and the Dutch Republic 89
   financial cost of 113–14, 122
   French Revolutionary Wars 1, 14, 111–15, 116
   Great Northern War (1700–21) 127
   hidden 70
   in history 20
   humanity and 22–3
   justifiable 64, 144
   Napoleonic Wars (1803–15) 34
   as a natural condition 42
   Nine Years' War (1688–97) 121
   numbers of casualties of 20
   peace and 81
   positive conceptions of 53, 60, 61, 108
   religion and 10, 21, 72, 73, 74, 81, 106
   Religious Wars 8–9, 20
   right of conquest 37
   role of 30
   Seven Years' War (1756–63) 15, 99, 107, 109, 128, 129, 142, 145
   sex and 54, 56
   the state of war 39
   Thirty Years' War (1618–48) 1, 9, 20, 89, 135
   total war 16
   trade and. *See* trade
   War of American Independence (1775–83) 106, 109–11, 116
   War of Austrian Succession (1740–48) 13, 15, 99, 106, 107, 112, 125, 127
   War of Devolution 121
   War of Jenkins' Ear (1739) 126, 127
   War of Polish Succession (1733–38) 13
   War of the League of Augsburg 112
   Wars of Spanish Succession (1701–14) 12, 112, 117, 122, 123–4, 145
wealth, the accumulation of 69
West, Benjamin 79, 101, 102
Westphalia, Peace of (1648) 1, 3, 5, 7–10, 16, 20–1, 71, 89, 133, 135
Whatmore, Richard 176 (*see also* chapter 7)
Whelpley, Samuel 83
Whigs 112–13, 123
William III of England (William of Orange) 118, 121
William Penn's Treaty with the Indians (painting) 79, 101–2
Wolff, Christian 22, 23–4, 45, 136
Wollstonecraft, Mary 15, 54, 62–7, 68
women
   Amazons 54–6
   childbirth 61, 63
   education of 66
   enslavement of 63, 67, 70
   the establishment of civilization and 103
   female rulers 15–16
   female soldiers and fighters 54, 56
   peace and 63
   politics and 15
   in public life 15–16
   rights of 66
   the suffering of 61–2
   war, peace and 53–7, 64
Worcester, Noah 82, 83–4, 85

al-Zabidi, Murtada 85
"Zelo Domus Dei" 10
Zouche, Richard 43